Practical Applications of Transforming the Attachment Relationship to God

Practical Applications of Transforming the Attachment Relationship to God discusses four distinct attachment relationships to the God of personal spiritual experience and considers how each of these relationships has implications for working with clients in psychotherapy.

Geoff Goodman uses Attachment-Informed Psychotherapy (AIP) to explore the connection between a relationship to God and a relationship to caregivers during childhood. By analyzing the attachment relationships evident in the lives of four public figures—human rights activist Coretta Scott King, Jewish Holocaust victim Anne Frank, Alcoholics Anonymous co-founder Bill W., and founder of psychoanalysis Sigmund Freud—this book demonstrates how their attachment relationships with their caregivers during childhood helped to determine the quality of their attachment relationship (or nonrelationship) to God in later life. Goodman demonstrates how to use AIP to work with these attachment relationships, formulating a psychotherapeutic treatment plan for each one with the goal of restoring wholeness and unity.

This book will be a valuable resource for psychoanalysts, psychotherapists, and marriage and family therapists in practice and in training.

Geoff Goodman is Professor of Psychiatry and Behavioral Sciences in the Emory University School of Medicine and Associate Professor of Psychology and Spiritual Care in the Emory University Candler School of Theology in Atlanta, Georgia, USA. He holds board certifications in clinical psychology and psychoanalysis from the American Board of Professional Psychology.

Practical Applications of Transforming the Attachment Relationship to God

Using Attachment-Informed Psychotherapy

Geoff Goodman

Routledge
Taylor & Francis Group
LONDON AND NEW YORK

Designed cover image: Kauernde Frau mit Kind in Schob, 1916, in Käthe Kollwitz and Fritz Boettger, *Handzeichnungen in originalgetreuen Wiedergaben*. Dresden: E. Richter, 1920. F. 741.943 K83H, Architecture and Art Library, University of Illinois at Urbana-Champaign

First published 2025
by Routledge
4 Park Square, Milton Park, Abingdon, Oxon OX14 4RN

and by Routledge
605 Third Avenue, New York, NY 10158

Routledge is an imprint of the Taylor & Francis Group, an informa business

© 2025 Geoff Goodman

The right of Geoff Goodman to be identified as author of this work has been asserted in accordance with sections 77 and 78 of the Copyright, Designs and Patents Act 1988.

All rights reserved. No part of this book may be reprinted or reproduced or utilised in any form or by any electronic, mechanical, or other means, now known or hereafter invented, including photocopying and recording, or in any information storage or retrieval system, without permission in writing from the publishers.

Trademark notice: Product or corporate names may be trademarks or registered trademarks, and are used only for identification and explanation without intent to infringe.

British Library Cataloguing-in-Publication Data
A catalogue record for this book is available from the British Library

ISBN: 9781032944104 (hbk)
ISBN: 9781032944098 (pbk)
ISBN: 9781003570578 (ebk)

DOI: 10.4324/9781003570578

Typeset in Times New Roman
by Newgen Publishing UK

To Carlyn Chantal Dent Goodman
Once riding on Daddy's shoulders
Now climbing up the canyon boulders
Fly away, my butterfly
Fly to the tip-top of the sky

Contents

Acknowledgments	ix
Note on the Text	xi
1 Introduction	1

PART I
Using Autobiographies to Illustrate Attachment to God: Three Attachment Relationship Patterns — **19**

2 Coretta Scott King: Secure Attachment to the Living God	21
3 Anne Frank: Anxious-Resistant Attachment—Higher Power as Compensation	47
4 Bill W.: Anxious-Avoidant Attachment—Higher Power as Compensation	92
5 Sigmund Freud: Anxious-Avoidant Attachment—in Denial About the Possibility of a Higher Power	127

PART II
A Clinical Application of Attachment-Informed Psychotherapy — **175**

6 A Yogi in Attachment-Informed Psychotherapy: A Spiritually Informed Case Conceptualization	177

| 7 | What I Have Personally Learned from Writing this Book | 196 |

Author Index *202*
Subject Index *205*

Acknowledgments

I have often read the conventional wisdom, "Don't make your hobby your job." By writing this book, I openly defied this advice. I have always been passionate about the integration of psychology and spirituality. My first journal article, written in graduate school, explored the meaning of empathy for Carl Rogers, Heinz Kohut, and Jesus. As a graduate student, I took as many courses related to psychology and spirituality as I could fit into my schedule. Yet I never pursued this interdisciplinary area as one of my research interests, perhaps due to my own ambivalence about the existence of a Higher Power (see Chapter 1). Now, having written this book, I can now claim that making my hobby my job has only inspired me to write more about the integration of psychology and spirituality. It has helped that my relationship with my Higher Power is now on firmer ground.

I want to thank my wife, Valeda Dent, who was present during this book's inception and who provided me with library books, journal articles, and her incisive editing skill. Her cheerleading was necessary for the writing process. Uli Guthrie edited the entire book and made me sound almost like a professional writer. Susannah Frearson and Saloni Singhania and Susan Dunsmore at Routledge took a chance on me and on this unusual subject matter, and I am grateful to them for valuing this work. My former student and now trusted colleague, Taylor Perlman, also provided a PowerPoint reproduction of Figure 1.1. My student, Chenyu Li, assisted me with sorting out some of the references.

I would like to express gratitude to the patient who agreed to share his story and the content of his sessions for Chapter 6. I would also like to thank Hannah Mate for conducting the two interviews and Gabriela Bronfman and Lindsey Myers for coding these interviews for Chapter 6. Emory University librarian Kim Collins and John Morgenstern assisted me with obtaining the rights to use the powerful book cover by Käthe Kollwitz.

Dean Jan Love at the Candler School of Theology at Emory University took a chance on hiring someone with no formal theology degree. I feel so grateful that she did, and I hope she feels the same way. My mentor at the Candler School of Theology, Ian McFarland, provided me with the encouragement I needed to complete this book. I also want to thank my Emory colleagues John Snarey, Wendy Jacobson, and Andy Miller for believing in me and listening to me pitch some of my ideas. First Presbyterian Church of Atlanta, including pastors Tony and Katie Sundermeier, Rob Sparks, and Barry Gaeddert, have provided me every week with spiritual resources and support.

I also want to thank the people whose work inspired the ideas contained in this book. As a graduate student at Columbia University in the fall of 1985, Larry Aber introduced me to attachment theory and research, which resulted in a lifelong love affair with studying the development of relationships of all kinds. The following semester, in Ann Belford Ulanov's Union Theological Seminary course, Religion and the Unconscious, I read the classic *Birth of the Living God* by Ana-Maria Rizzuto, which blew my mind. Rizzuto's book is where my psychological understanding of human relationships to God began. My book is merely an extension and application of her work. Pehr Granqvist, especially through his *Attachment in Religion and Spirituality*, has mentored me in applying attachment theory to the development of human relationships to God. I have appreciated our e-mail correspondence over the past couple of years. I also want to acknowledge Russell Siler Jones and Wayne Gustafson for their supervision in spiritually integrated psychotherapy, and James Griffith and Kenneth Pargament for their practical insights in using spiritual and religious patient material in psychotherapy sessions. I appreciate their distinctive approaches to working with patients who discuss spiritual issues, either explicitly or implicitly. I would be remiss if I neglected to acknowledge the significant influence of my instructors and supervisors during psychoanalytic training, as well as my personal psychoanalyst, all of whom helped me to become the certified psychoanalyst that I am today.

I am most grateful for the support that my institution has shown me since joining the Emory University faculty two years ago. The Candler School of Theology awarded me a research grant to conduct the interview assessments discussed in Chapter 6. The Emory University Center for Faculty Development and Excellence sent me on a writing retreat to complete this book.

I also want to express gratitude to Marvin Markowitz, Andy Phillips, and Juarlyn Gaiter for their personal support of me during the writing process. All my patients have taught me how to be a more effective therapist and a better version of myself.

Finally, I want to thank my 11-year-old daughter, Carlyn, to whom this book is dedicated, for making me stay forever young.

Note on the Text

I wrote this book, *Practical Applications of Transforming the Attachment Relationship to God: Using Attachment-Informed Psychotherapy*, while I was writing my other book, *Using Psychoanalytic Techniques to Transform the Attachment Relationship to God: Our Refuge and Strength*. Both books address humans' attachment relationships to God and their transformation by using Attachment-Informed Psychotherapy (AIP). While this book is more practically oriented, the first book is more theoretically oriented. I strongly recommend that the reader read both books to optimize their learning experience. Because theory and practice go hand in hand, these two books complement each other.

Chapter 1

Introduction

Attachment Relationships to God and to My Parents from the Perspective of a Middle-Aged White Man

In this autobiographical narrative, I will focus almost exclusively on my relationships with my mother, father, and God as well as inanimate substitutes for these relationships. I could focus on many other facets of my life, but the intricacies of these relationships, followed over time, will form the evidence in support of my thesis that: (1) these relationships are interconnected, and (2) transforming one relationship has the potential to transform the other.

I came into the world in a small town in rural northern central Pennsylvania as the first-born child into a white, evangelical Christian, lower-middle-class family that included my mother, father, and maternal grandmother. My mother was the first person in her family to graduate from college with a teaching certificate; my father attended college but never graduated (I was the first from his line to graduate from college). My earliest childhood memory is of sitting in a car outside a hospital with my maternal grandmother while my mother was giving birth to my younger sister. I was 2½ years old. I presume that my father was with my mother. Thus, my earliest memory has to do with separation from my parents.

Another early childhood memory, this time from when I was age 5, also had to do with separation. My parents took me to an airplane show at our local airport: all types of airplanes were on display. The event was crowded, and somehow I lost my grip on my mother's hand and got separated from her. I started crying, and a stranger took me to the flight control tower, where someone made a public announcement, and my father came to the tower. I hugged him for a long time. I remember feeling comforted by his presence. During these early years, I would describe both my parents as loving, devoted, and exciting to be around. I felt a secure attachment to my parents (for an explanation of "secure attachment," see Chapter 2).

By late childhood, I began to distinguish myself academically. Both my parents valorized achievement: my father extolled the virtues of academic excellence, while my mother displayed a strong interest in my success in Cub Scouts, Webelos, and later, Boy Scouts, helping me meet the requirements for earning various merit badges. Although not consciously aware of it at the time, upon reflection, I probably started making connections between achievement and love, especially in my relationship to my father. If I were academically successful, I would earn my father's love, I reasoned. During these years, I developed a few close friends at school and attended weekly Bible Club meetings held after school on Wednesdays in a nearby church. I became increasingly interested in God, and particularly, Jesus. I remember that at age 9, I asked Jesus into my heart at the invitation of my Bible Club teacher. I did not know exactly what that meant, but in my 9-year-old mind, I probably understood it as inviting Jesus to live inside me. If He lived inside me, I would never be separated from Him. At Bible Club, I also became skilled at memory verse contests and "sword drills"—looking up specific Bible verses more quickly than anyone else (the secret to winning this contest was memorizing the 66 books of the Bible in order).

Just before I hit puberty, the Bible Club teacher permitted me to give a "sermon" to the other children—my only experience with preaching. I was in sixth grade and would be graduating to junior high school, which was far away from Bible Club. At around this time, I also started having conflicts with my father. These conflicts often resulted in harsh corporal punishment as well as emotional abuse such as silent treatments that sometimes lasted months (which I would learn to use against each parent later in life). In retrospect, I suppose that he was struggling with my prepubertal need for autonomy. These conflicts coincided with the onset of an addiction that I would struggle with for the next 38 years (I will not identify the specific addiction here).

By middle adolescence, the conflicts with my father escalated. I ran away from home for five-and-a-half weeks after he had humiliated me in front of my brother. I lived with one of my best friends in his basement until his mother found out and forced me to go home. The frequency of my addictive behavior likewise increased. I was only nominally involved in my church, attending on Sunday mornings with my family and singing in the choir but otherwise showing little interest. By contrast, my sister was involved in the Baptist Youth Fellowship (BYF) and, I believe, held a leadership position in this group.

During the later years of adolescence, my father and I learned to tolerate each other. My mother seemed preoccupied with her own thoughts and rarely challenged my father's parenting decisions. My maternal grandmother was the only person who I felt actually *saw* me. She would comfort me after one of my father's draconian punishments. During my high school years, perhaps sensing that I would be going away to college soon, my father did try, in his own way, to re-establish a connection with me. He would come into my brother's and my bedroom early on Saturday mornings and announce that he was going to Elby's, the local diner. My brother, six years younger than I, would bound down the bunk bed ladder to join my father, while I would roll over with my face to the wall and continue sleeping. Thus, feeling rejected, I likewise rejected my father's breakfast invitations. I never did go to breakfast with my father and brother. Instead, I became obsessed with academic success, which pleased my father. Thus, in spite of my animosity toward my father, I still strived to please him in ways that I knew mattered to him.

In the meantime, I began making unsuccessful attempts to curb my addictive behavior or stop it altogether. Even though this behavior was not interfering with my grades, I nevertheless became alarmed. I would be leaving for college soon; I did not want to bring this addiction with me. I kept this behavior a secret from my parents. I felt that they would punish me for it rather than help me to overcome it.

I moved to Cambridge, Massachusetts, for college. Unexpectedly, now that I was out of the house and living on my own, my relationship to my father improved. We experienced a rapprochement, which felt good to both of us. My father had access to an 800 number at his job, and this access allowed us to connect without having to pay long-distance telephone bills. I also tried to get to know my mother better—someone who felt mysterious to me—but these attempts went nowhere. We maintained a weekly letter correspondence, which continued for 35 years, but her letters were disappointingly superficial. I always knew she loved me, but who was she? I did not know.

In the context of escalating addictive behavior, I became actively involved in a Christian group on campus. I prayed to God about my behavior, which would help for a while, but then I would resume old habits. For the first time, I spoke to someone about my addiction—the young adult minister of my church. Surprisingly, he responded with a variation on Nancy Reagan's slogan, "Just Say No." I did not feel judged by him, but neither did I feel supported.

After struggling to find a major, I settled on psychology and writing and was accepted into a Christian clinical psychology doctoral program near Los Angeles, California. Soon after moving to the West Coast, my maternal grandmother died. Around this time, I started questioning the Bible's infallibility, which prompted me to question my enrollment at a conservative evangelical Christian university. I decided to drop out of my doctoral program and work full-time in a psychiatric hospital inpatient unit in California. In southern California, one must rely on a car to get around, so I asked my father for money. He refused, however, informing me that I would have bought "a lemon"—and in so doing be wasting his money. Incensed by this response, I stopped communicating with my family for a year. I worked and lived completely on my own for the first time, which felt good. I decided that the Bible was indeed fallible and that evangelical Christianity, the tradition in which I was raised, treated the Bible like a "paper pope"—unable to acknowledge its obvious contradictions and scientific inaccuracies. Around this time, I entertained the possibility that God does not exist or no longer exists. I maintained my faith but felt the responsibility of figuring out what I believed rather than what I thought the Bible (or my childhood faith community) told me to believe. My addictive behavior continued to develop on its own trajectory, seemingly propelled by forces beyond me. Working full-time also afforded me the financial independence to pursue this passion, which only hastened its trajectory.

After that year of independence, I returned to the East Coast and enrolled in a master's degree program in developmental psychology in New York City.

Although we never processed what had happened between us, I again experienced a rapprochement in my relationship with my father and to the rest of my family. My father recommended a church in New York City that he knew about from a Christian magazine to which he subscribed. I started going to that church, which turned out to be much more liberal than my father would have liked, had he known. The pastor's sermons were filled with psychological as well as spiritual wisdom, which would obviously appeal to someone like me who was hungering for an integration of these two worlds. Just as I had done as an undergraduate, I became actively involved in a campus Christian group and enjoyed learning about and relating to God with my peers; however, I did not tell them that I did not believe in the Bible's infallibility. Perhaps I feared that the group would reject me, just as I feared that my father would reject me if I informed him that his son now believed that the Bible contains all sorts of errors. During my master's degree, I also took a graduate course at the liberal theological seminary affiliated with my university. While I did not agree with every theological point it brought to my attention, I was at least considering alternative points of view to my own. My addiction stabilized during this time, but on the day of my graduation, I went on an all-night bender that shocked me. No one knew. In retrospect, this extreme behavior might have reflected my worry about moving on to the next stage in my life: a clinical psychology doctoral program in Chicago, Illinois.

Within the first year of my doctoral program, my father and I had a relationship-ending fight over my use of his health insurance benefits (I was still on his plan) to help pay for psychotherapy, which, ironically, I wanted to access to work through my issues with him. He refused to allow me to access his benefits, explaining that he did not want his boss to find out that his son was in psychotherapy. He never explained how his boss would find out. I realized that we were both experiencing profound feelings of shame: whereas I was ashamed of my addiction, my father was ashamed of his own son's desire for psychotherapy, perhaps because it signified to him that he was a flawed father whose son needed such help. I thus stopped all communication with him for the rest of his life, which lasted only four more years. He died of a sudden heart attack, four months before I graduated with my doctorate.

Within the same few months of severing all ties to my father, I became an agnostic. Reading biblical passages that seemed to condone slavery and the treatment of women as men's property, I reasoned I could no longer trust the Bible to tell me anything truthful about anything, including Jesus. Renouncing my faith also enabled me to engage in my addiction more freely with less guilt over my behavior. I finally stopped listening to any still, small voice that signified a Power greater than myself abiding in me.

Despite this formal break from Christianity and theism, I cross-registered in four theology courses at a nearby university's liberal divinity school, which counted as electives toward my doctorate. I maintained an interest in learning more about God and the intersection of religion and psychology, even though I was no longer sure whether God existed. During these years in my doctoral program, I continued to invest significant time in my addiction, although it never seemed to affect the quality of my work. I do believe, however, that the addiction made me emotionally distant from others and from myself. Notably, circumventing my father's health insurance and his disapproval by finding low-cost treatment, I did open up about my addictive behavior with my therapist, but surprisingly, it continued unabated.

After graduation, I moved back to New York City, where I completed an internship program and two two-year postdoctoral fellowships and later applied for academic positions. After completing the second of these fellowships, I joined the full-time clinical faculty at Cornell University Medical College, working on the children's psychiatric inpatient unit. Having become interested in psychoanalytic training during graduate school, I entered formal psychoanalysis four times per week at a psychoanalytic candidate's fee, which I could afford. I spent most of these sessions talking about my father, my mother, and my addiction. To my surprise, disappointment, and worry, this most intensive form of psychotherapy was not helping me overcome my addiction. Despite this lackluster outcome, I continued in psychoanalysis for the next 16 years. Although I found that this method of treatment helped me work through my feelings about my father's treatment of me, his death, and his lingering power over me, it did not help me with my addiction. In fact, I witnessed a steady increase in frequency and risk associated with this behavior during these 16 years.

During those years of psychoanalysis, I became a professor in a clinical psychology doctoral program and a certified psychoanalyst, but not even this most intensive treatment was working. Despite my outward success, I felt like a personal failure—weak, unworthy of love, secretive, ashamed. Over eight years into my personal psychoanalysis, I consulted with two world-renowned psychoanalysts in New York City about my addiction. The first analyst suggested that I had experienced an early trauma, which he said is difficult to treat. The second analyst suggested that I needed to switch analysts because the current one was not helping me. No one asked about my relationship to God. Neither my analyst, nor these two consultants, nor I mentioned anything about God. Like Lord Voldemort in *Harry Potter*, God was He Who must not be named.

After moving back to New York City, I did return to the church my father had recommended to me six years earlier, attending perhaps several times a year. I always enjoyed the pastor's sermons. He was adept at weaving together spirituality and psychology in a way that always made me feel good when I left the sanctuary. Outside these occasional Sunday morning excursions, however, I had no discernible relationship to God. Returning to Pennsylvania to visit my mother and less often, my siblings, I would pretend I was still a believer, attending my mother's church and even singing in that church. As the church organist, my mother would always ask me to sing on the Sunday after Christmas, which I enjoyed doing. I still experienced a sense of awe in the emotional power of Christian hymns—sometimes becoming tearful even though I was an agnostic. If I did not know whether a Higher Power existed, then what was I crying about?

Fifteen years after my father died, a series of events changed the trajectory of my life. By this time, I had earned tenure at my university, opened a thriving part-time private practice in child, adolescent, and adult psychotherapy, and was busily working on completing my psychoanalytic training. I was still attending on-the-couch classical psychoanalysis four times per week (a training requirement at my psychoanalytic institute). Gradually, I began to feel more emotionally available, especially in romantic relationships. I began dating a wonderful person who became my wife two years later. Simultaneously and despite (or perhaps because of) the positive changes going on in my life, my addictive behaviors continued an ever-upward trajectory. Early on in my relationship with Valeda, I told her about my addiction. Not only did I not want to keep secrets from her, but I also needed to know whether she was going to accept me for who I was at that time—all of me. By the time we got married, I secretly hoped that our marriage would be the catalyst to stop the addiction in its tracks. That did not happen, and by the time I realized that not even marriage to the woman of my dreams could stop me, I scrambled to find another source of help other than my psychoanalyst.

During this first year of marriage, I also learned some shocking information about my mother. Here is how it happened: Valeda, my mother, and I were visiting my maternal great-aunt, who lived in a town close to that of my mother. This aunt mentioned that my grandparents "loved my mother just the same," which seemed to imply that my mother had been adopted by them. At the time, my great-aunt was in her nineties, so I initially attributed her comment to misremembering. Nevertheless, when we got into my car to leave, I asked my mother about this curious statement. What did Aunt Rhoda mean? Then my mother dropped the bomb: my grandparents had adopted her at birth. Immediately, I realized that my maternal grandmother—a member of my nuclear family and the woman who helped raise me—was not biologically related to me. The obvious question was, "Why didn't you tell me?" I received the supremely disappointing reply: "I didn't think it was that big a deal." Not a big deal? It took a long time to metabolize that information into my mind and my life. It also prompted a long search for my biological maternal grandparents, which ended just two years ago, when I finally learned who my biological grandfather was. During this search, my mother provided only very modest assistance, informing my sister and me that whatever this search yielded did not interest her.

Around this time, I began to realize that my mother was suffering from her own addictive behavior (different from my own). Several years earlier, my sister had read in one of my mother's diaries about this addiction and told me about it. When we asked our mother about some of these diary entries, she readily acknowledged her addictive behavior but declared that she had stopped cold turkey when we were young children. Now aware of this history, I became more observant and soon realized that her addictive behavior was in fact still active. I do not doubt that my mother had stopped cold turkey, but upon reflection, I pieced together a narrative for myself in which my mother had reactivated her addiction sometime shortly after my father died. Living alone for the first time in her life and grieving the loss of her life partner were stresses that overwhelmed her. Interestingly, she never disclosed to us children that she was struggling. She did not cry at my father's funeral or at any time before or after. I remember standing in the kitchen around the time of the funeral, watching her unceremoniously scooping up my father's insulin bottles from the refrigerator shelf and dumping them in the trash without a word. I thought, "She's not a normal person." Everyone processes grief in their own way, but something about my mother's emotions seemed off.

In retrospect, learning about my mother's adoption and addiction clarified a lot of issues for me. She was a master at keeping secrets—something to which I could relate—and she must have experienced shame as a constant companion throughout her life—something to which I could likewise relate. At the same time, however, I felt angry that she had kept me in the dark all those years about her adoption, and her addiction, both of which she vehemently denied. I wanted my mother to be a whole person—even if I could not be.

All these events—my wedding, my knowledge of my mother's adoption and current addictive behavior, my self-realization that marriage was not going to stop my own addictive behavior—provided the context for the next step in my life: I turned to a 12-step program as a last resort. That meant having to return to God and leaving my agnosticism behind, which caused an intellectual and emotional conflict for me. I enjoyed the ambiguity of not knowing whether a Higher Power exists. I certainly did not owe a Supreme Being anything if this Supreme Being did not exist. I could live my own life in any way I pleased. But this stubborn addiction would not go away, no matter how much attention I paid to it in my psychoanalysis or at all the other times in my life when I reflected on the potential damage to my marriage, my career, and my friendships. My addiction did not care about these things. It had a mind of its own.

I had dabbled in 12-step recovery eight years earlier, having attended four meetings. At the time, I felt that "the rooms" just were just not for me. I rationalized that most of the participants were older, married, and suffering from multiple addictions. I could not locate myself among them in the rooms. In addition, my psychoanalyst thought that I was diluting our work together by seeking outside help through a 12-step program. I could understand that reasoning, but psychoanalysis was not working. After all, it had been 14 years since I began this long, strange trip with him. Certainly, a lot of good things had come out of my relationship with him—except that the addiction had only escalated. I was ready to try something else.

I turned to 12-step literature, meetings, a sponsor, prayer, meditation, and fellowship members for help. I also prioritized self-care. In my reading, I encountered a quotation from the French philosopher Voltaire that helped me to surrender to a Higher Power: "If God did not exist, it would be necessary to invent Him" (Voltaire, 1919, p. 231). I interpreted this aphorism to mean that it does not matter whether a Higher Power exists or does not exist; the fact remains that I need a Benevolent Being stronger and wiser than I am to break free of this prison of addiction—a Higher Power Who cares about me and wants to protect me from destroying myself. In short, I needed a Higher Power in my life to begin and to continue the process of recovery.

I then asked myself what this Higher Power would consist of. The 12-step literature emphasizes the "decision to turn our will and our lives over to the care of God *as we understood Him*" (Alcoholics Anonymous World Services, Inc., 2012, p. 5; italics added). How did I understand God now, after almost 23 years of agnosticism? I considered exploring Unitarianism/Universalism—a broad, accepting, progressive view of God. Ultimately, however, I returned to Christianity because its primary message of hope—the promise of forgiveness of my rebellion against God and subsequent reconciliation with God through a radical act of grace, not through my own effort—still resonated with me powerfully. Christianity was also familiar to me, and I craved familiarity amid all the frightening changes I was making in my life. This Christianity would be progressive, however, not conservative evangelical Christianity. Over the next five years, my church was my weekly 12-step meeting—a group of men and women sharing from the depths of their vulnerability their struggles with addiction and with their Higher Power as well as their progress over our common disease and their growing trust in a Higher Power of their own understanding. After having tried everything else (including many so-called "solutions" not mentioned in this narrative), I gradually began to trust in the care of my Higher Power. Then a strange thing happened. I started to experience relief from my addiction. It was still there (and is still there), but by taking steps along this path of recovery, I learned that I could live without my addiction and even thrive without it. I had replaced a "false god" (Pargament, 2011, p. 137) with a "living God" (Rizzuto, 1979, p. 87) Who was concerned about me and actively involved in my life. Some persons can live secure, well-adjusted lives without trust in a Higher Power. That has not been my personal experience. I need God in my life to live a secure, well-adjusted life. I wrote this book for spiritually curious psychotherapists like me who want to help spiritually curious patients like me to live secure, well-adjusted lives.

There is an addendum to this story. I want to share how I responded to my mother's addiction in the ensuing years and how it affected me. Two or three years after I began my recovery process, I began to talk to my mother about her addiction—without mentioning anything to her or to my family about my own. Unfortunately, she had developed a troubling delusion of microscopic worms traveling underneath the skin on her arm, which made her scratch them until they bled. Inexplicably, when she went to the doctor with her complaint, they diagnosed her with scabies. They observed a rash—caused by her scratching—and just assumed that is what it was. When the doctor prescribed a cream for her, and her symptoms did not subside, the doctor finally examined her more carefully and determined that she did not, in fact, have scabies. My mother had also developed a severe paranoia that the pastor of her church was talking badly about her behind her back and trying to get rid of her as the church organist. Of course, none of this was true. In fact, the church had just held a celebration of her 25 years of service to this church. Finally, she was having dizzy spells, which, one year later, resulted in a fall in which she hit the side of her head on her coffee table and landed in the intensive care unit for a couple of days. She turned out to be fine, but the prospect of a stroke or brain damage occupied my mind.

Talking to my mother about her addiction did not go anywhere. She claimed that she suffered from abdominal pain, and that her addictive behavior was the only method that alleviated this pain. Of course, many doctors over the years had examined her abdomen, but no one ever found anything to account for her pain. I felt betrayed, frustrated, sad, and helpless. I decided to file a complaint with the state medical board against her primary care physician, which alienated my siblings as well as my mother, who stopped talking to me. Months later, my mother reversed course, but it was too late. She (as well as my siblings) refused to cooperate with the state medical examiner, and so my complaint was discarded in the circular file. At that point, I had had enough. I completely withdrew from her. Within months of my decision to withdraw from her, I began to attend church on a weekly basis, becoming actively involved in the children's ministry. Years later, I became a Stephen Minister in my church and still later, a Stephen Leader. I remain committed to my new 12-step fellowship group and new church here in Atlanta, where my family moved last year. I am continuing my Stephen Ministry work as well as my private practice and professorship with a dual appointment at the Emory University School of Medicine and the Candler School of Theology.

My preparation for writing this book drew me closer to my Higher Power, and as a possible by-product, I repaired the insecure and broken relationship with my mother, who is in an assisted-living community overseen by a nursing staff. Unfortunately, she never did confront her addiction, but she is receiving ongoing medical monitoring. I am taking a gentler stance toward my mother after years of feeling guilty for the role I played in our lack of communication. I did not want to relive the anguish of my relationship to my father, who died before I had a chance to reconcile with him. My life is not perfect, but it is better knowing that a Higher Power is watching over me, protecting me, and loving me. I can now declare that God is my refuge (see Psalm 46:1; NIV, 1978).

Reflections on My Autobiographical Narrative

I want to reflect on certain aspects of this autobiographical narrative that illustrate my thesis, namely, that: (1) relationships to parents and relationship to God are interconnected, and (2) transforming one relationship has the potential to transform the other. At this point, I want to introduce two hypotheses that will feature prominently in this book: the correspondence hypothesis and the compensation hypothesis. These twin hypotheses will help us to make sense of my autobiographical narrative as well as the analysis of the autobiographical narratives I present in Chapters 2–5 and the case illustration in Chapter 6. As originally formulated by Kirkpatrick and Shaver (1990) and elaborated by others (e.g., Granqvist, 2020; Granqvist & Kirkpatrick, 2018; for an in-depth exploration, see also Goodman, 2025, Chapter 3), the correspondence hypothesis refers to the strong positive correlation found between the quality of the attachment relationship between a person's parents and the quality of the attachment relationship to their Higher Power (I use the terms "Higher Power" and "God" interchangeably in this book). This observed correspondence seems to be most evident among those persons who are securely attached to their parents (see Chapter 2 for an overview of attachment theory). With roots in the writings of James (1902), the compensation hypothesis, on the other hand, refers to the strong negative correlation found between the quality of attachment relationship to a person's parents and the quality of attachment relationship to their Higher Power, which is most evident among those persons who are insecurely attached to their parents. In other words, the correspondence hypothesis applies mostly to securely attached persons, while the compensation hypothesis applies mostly to insecurely attached persons. The compensation hypothesis, however, has received only mixed support in the research literature (see also Goodman, 2025, Chapter 3).

Both hypotheses—the correspondence hypothesis and the compensation hypothesis—propose that relationships to parents and relationship to God are interconnected, only in opposite directions. British philosopher Popper (1959) argued that a hypothesis is scientific if it is falsifiable (or refutable), that is to say, if an empirical test can logically contradict it. These twin hypotheses of correspondence and compensation, however, seem to be unfalsifiable: every person's relationships to parents and to God would seem to fall under one of these two hypotheses. I explore this issue more extensively in Chapter 3. Adding nuance (and falsifiability) to the compensation hypothesis, Granqvist and Kirkpatrick (2018) suggested that persons insecurely attached to their parents from childhood *compensate* for these insecure relationships when they "cannot bear the high levels of suffering experienced sufficiently well by employing his or her usual [insecure] strategy for managing stress" (p. 934). In bearable situations of stress, however, insecurely attached persons' relationship (or nonrelationship) to God *corresponds* to these insecure parental relationships. In other words, compensation is activated *only when* an insecure attachment relationship to parents from childhood *and* high levels of stress co-occur.

This qualification provided by Granqvist and Kirkpatrick (2018) circumvents the falsifiability problem inherent in the compensation hypothesis. Unfortunately, however, it does not solve the problem of determining the stress threshold when compensation is hypothesized to be activated, which no doubt depends on many factors (e.g., stress intensity, frequency, and duration; developmental phase; personality organization; defensive structure; type of insecure attachment subcategory; nature of the relationship to the significant other with whom the stress is occurring; and genetic predisposition).

We can use these two hypotheses descriptively to characterize a process that seems to be going on between attachment relationships to parents and to God. In addition to high stress levels moderating the relationship between insecure attachment relationships to caregivers from childhood and a secure attachment relationship to God, I want to propose that the specific caregiver attachment relationship might also act as a moderator. In my relationship to my father and maternal grandmother, the correspondence hypothesis seems to be evident, while in my relationship to my mother, the compensation hypothesis seems to be evident. In other words, when I was not getting along with my father, and when my grandmother died, my relationship to God suffered; there is a correspondence between these two sets of relationships. When I was not getting along with my mother, however, my relationship to God improved; one relationship compensated for the deficiencies in the other. Although by adulthood, mental representations of early caregivers typically form a more global attachment organization (Main et al., 1985), infants' attachment relationships are person-specific: an infant can form a secure attachment with one parent and an insecure attachment with the other parent (see also Goodman, 2025, Chapter 2). Some attachment researchers have speculated that adults also maintain aspects of person-specific attachment relationships (e.g., Daniel, 2015). The patterns I have identified between my relationships to each parent and my relationship to God could indicate differences in the quality of my attachment relationship to each parent.

What are the data for my observations? First, in considering my relationship to my father, my adolescent conflicts with him (which included running away from home) corresponded with a drifting apart from God. The rapprochement with my father in college corresponded with a re-invigoration of my spirituality. While living in Los Angeles, my father's lack of confidence in my ability to purchase a used car coincided with my belief that the Bible was merely a "paper pope," which naturally stimulated questioning about God's existence. Finally, my decision to discontinue my relationship with my father during graduate school in Chicago coincided almost exactly with my adoption of agnosticism (see the timeline in Figure 1.1). When my maternal grandmother died, I started questioning the Bible's infallibility.

Second, in considering my relationship to my mother, our relationship was considerably more stable. My marriage, coupled with my accidental discovery of my mother's adoption secret, placed a strain on our relationship. Within that same year, I entered recovery and renewed my spiritual belief and desire, which, I would suggest, compensated for the lost closeness to my mother. Several years later, as my attempts at helping my mother to enter her own recovery failed, I discontinued my relationship with her. Within that same year, I recommitted to regular church attendance and active church involvement, thus compensating for the loss of our relationship. Just this year, as I was drawing closer to my Higher Power in preparation for writing this book, I rekindled my relationship to my mother, thus reversing the compensation hypothesis. Now, my relationship to my mother and my relationship to my Higher Power correspond. Did this turn of events mark a new spiritual and relational harmony within me? Perhaps my spiritual growth enabled me to change the valence of my attachment relationship to my mother from anxious-avoidant to secure, thus restoring a correspondence

12 Practical Applications: Transform Attachment Relationship to God

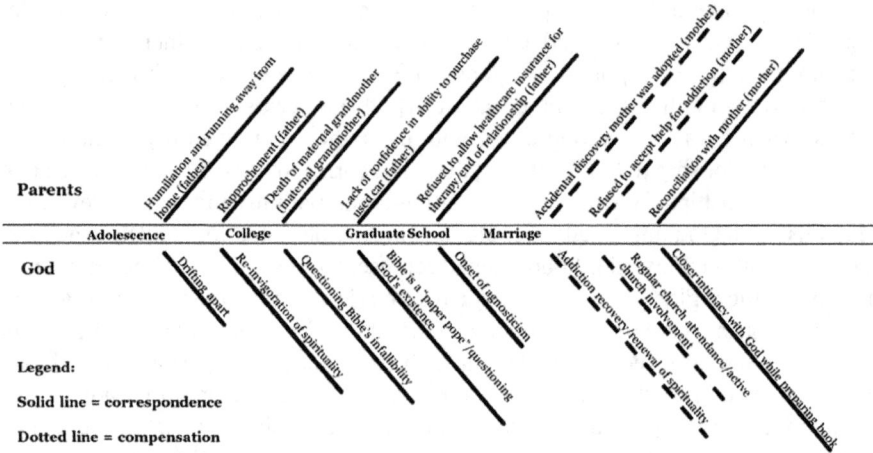

Figure 1.1 Timeline of events related to my attachment relationships to my parents and to God: correspondence and compensation.

between the two relationships (for more discussion about these ideas, see also Goodman, 2025, Chapter 3).

I seem to be suggesting unidirectional causality: ruptures and repairs occurred in my parental relationships, which consequently influenced my relationship with God. I wonder, however, whether causality might have occurred in the opposite direction: ruptures and repairs occurred in my relationship to God, which consequently influenced my parental relationships. More likely, these two sets of relationships are mutually influencing each other all the time in a synchronous dance. In support of my spiritual desire influencing my human relationships, my commitment to my 12-step fellowship at the birth of my recovery inspired a profound change in my human relationships, later including my relationship to my mother. That act of faith—entering recovery—is perhaps the greatest influence on me because it saved my life. This book is not about abstractions. It is about the concrete realities that make our lives worth living. Thus, at least in my life, I have tried to demonstrate the second part of my thesis: that transforming my relationship to my Higher Power through my 12-step fellowship hs transformed my human relationships. I suspect that my relationship to my therapist and to my 12-step sponsor also transformed my relationship to my Higher Power. These two resources—spiritual and human—can potentiate each other in an upward or downward trajectory.

Numerous other factors might be operating in my story. For example, I made a connection between the collapse of my relationship to my mother and my regular attendance and active involvement in my church. Also occurring during this time, however, was the birth of our daughter. I wanted to provide her with a consistent church experience. Thus, human motivation is always more complicated than a brief autobiographical narrative can convey.

The Problem of False Gods and Small Gods

A person often enters psychotherapy to address problems that Pargament (2011) refers to as "problems of spiritual destinations" (p. 136)—two of which he identifies as "false gods" and "small gods" (p. 137). The theologian Tillich (1957) argued that faith is "the state of being ultimately concerned" (p. 1), which consists of whatever a person regards as ultimately important in their life. This ultimate concern demands the allegiance of the total self—emotionally, volitionally, and intellectually. Despite his stature as an eminent theologian, Tillich likely suffered from sex addiction (May, 1973). He was alleged to have had numerous affairs and an extensive pornography collection. In spite of Tillich's belief in God, one could interpret his addiction as his ultimate concern. Pargament (2011) would characterize Tillich's relationship to sex addiction as a false god because it "fail[s] to contain the range of human needs and potentials [and] leaves people with a spiritual vacuum at their core" (p. 139). Recalling my own addiction, I experienced first-hand this spiritual vacuum and the empty disconnection from a Higher Power prior to my entry into recovery. Addiction is a popular false god, a modern-day form of idolatry. It replaces the true source of love and security with a cheap imitation.

Turning to a false god such as addiction suggests dissatisfaction with the true God. Perhaps the person assumes that God has been inconsistently present in their life, especially when God has been most needed. Or the person assumes that God has outright rejected them. Both these scenarios indicate an insecure attachment relationship to God (see also Goodman, 2025, Chapter 3), which could lead to turning away from God and turning instead to a false god, such as addiction. The literature suggests that the quality of early parental attachment relationships determines the assumptions people make about God; however, circumstances outside these relationships might also influence these assumptions, circumstances such as personal failures. Turning away from God and turning to addiction can also influence the quality of parental relationships, even distorting the memories of early parental relationships. In my autobiographical narrative, turning away from God in graduate school coincided with turning away from my father. The literature does offer the possibility that I viewed God as having failed to help me with my addiction and then misattributed that dissatisfaction to my father. Regardless of the direction of causality, I turned away from God, which then gave me *de facto* permission to explore my false god—addiction—with greater abandon.

Having a small god presents a similar problem. According to Pargament (2011), small gods "represent a problem because they fail to shed light on the profound dilemmas of life" (p. 138). In my experience, I worship a small god when I indulge my perfectionistic tendencies. If I am not perfect, then God will be displeased with me. This belief suggests that God's love is not unconditional; I must earn it. In this scenario, my God is a small god because this god is not large enough to forgive me for my insufficiencies. In Christianity, the apostle Paul wrote that "all have sinned and fall short of the glory of God" (Romans 3:23, NIV, 1978, p. 1270), but despite this imperfect state of being, all "are justified freely by His grace through the redemption that came by Christ Jesus" (Romans 3:24, NIV, 1978, p. 1270). Paul wrote that the God of Christianity is not a small god; He forgives imperfection. Thus, every time I strive for perfection, I am unconsciously putting my faith in a small god who could not forgive me for my shortcomings. The belief in a god who loves conditionally suggests an insecure attachment relationship to God because I am assuming that this god's care and protection will be forthcoming only if I behave perfectly. If I fail, then this small god will withhold care and protection. Thus, the twin problems of believing in false gods and believing in small gods are fundamentally insecurities in a person's attachment relationship to God, which is the topic of this book (see also Goodman, 2025, Chapter 3).

I hope that this background material has aroused your interest in understanding the relationship to God as an attachment relationship that has specific properties that resemble the properties of attachment relationships to parents and emotionally significant others. Further, interventions, such as Attachment-Informed Psychotherapy (AIP) and 12-step programs, can transform the attachment relationship to God from insecure to secure, enabling the living God to be worshiped in all God's infinitude. The ultimate purpose of this transformation is to rely on the care and protection of a Higher Power so that a person can actualize their spiritual purpose in life, whatever that spiritual purpose might be. As we shall see, therapeutic work on a person's attachment relationship to God can improve human attachment relationships, while at other times, therapeutic work on a person's human attachment relationships can improve the attachment relationship to God. By the end of treatment, the person will be able to rely on God as their refuge.

The Structure of the Book

Part I Using Autobiographies to Illustrate Attachment to God: Three Attachment Relationship Patterns

Chapter 2 Coretta Scott King: Secure Attachment to the Living God

I explore the autobiography of human rights activist Coretta Scott King (King, 2017), who writes about her relationships with her parents growing up in Perry County, Alabama. How might these parental attachment relationships have influenced her attachment relationship to God? I argue that Scott King developed a secure attachment to her parents and correspondingly developed a secure attachment to God. I use the nine interpersonal markers of attachment quality of Sarah Daniel (2015) to characterize both King's attachment relationship to her parents and her attachment relationship to God. These nine interpersonal markers are: (1) proximity/distance, (2) trust/expectations of others, (3) attitude to seeking and receiving help, (4) expression and regulation of emotions, (5) self-image/self-esteem, (6) openness and self-disclosure, (7) dependence/independence, (8) conflict management, and (9) empathy. I show a correspondence between Scott King's attachment relationships to her parents and her attachment relationship to God that endured throughout her life. I end the chapter by formulating a brief treatment plan for King, as if she had been referred to me for treatment.

Chapter 3 Anne Frank: Anxious-Resistant Attachment—Higher Power as Compensation

I explore the autobiography of Jewish Holocaust victim Frank (1993), who writes about her relationships to her parents while in hiding from the Nazis in Amsterdam. Frank idealizes her father and expresses severe conflict with her mother, which I argue suggests an anxious-resistant attachment pattern. Do we observe the same ambivalence in her relationship to God? I use the same interpersonal markers introduced in Chapter 2 to explore the correspondence between Frank's attachment relationships to her parents and her attachment relationship to God. I end the chapter by formulating a brief treatment plan for Frank, as if she had been referred to me for treatment.

Chapter 4 Bill W.: Anxious-Avoidant Attachment—Higher Power as Compensation

I discuss the posthumous autobiography of Alcoholics Anonymous co-founder Bill W. (Anonymous, 2000), a man from rural Vermont who wrote about his relationships to his parents, who divorced when he was 11 years old. I argue that Bill W. wrote about both his parents in a schematic, emotionally absent fashion that suggests an anxious-avoidant attachment pattern. I also argue that when he established a relationship with a Higher Power at age 39, Bill W. compensated for these emotionally unfulfilling parental attachment relationships with a secure attachment relationship to God. I use James (1902) to discuss Bill W.'s conversion process and follow Kirkpatrick (2005) to suggest that sudden conversions are more likely to occur in persons with anxious-avoidant attachment patterns whose parents are not religious. I end the chapter by formulating a brief treatment plan for Bill W. as if he had been referred to me for treatment.

Chapter 5 Sigmund Freud: Anxious-Avoidant Attachment—in Denial About the Possibility of a Higher Power

Finally, I explore the autobiography of psychoanalysis founder Sigmund Freud (Freud, 1925, along with several other of his writings), who idealized his mother and denigrated or otherwise ignored his relationship to his father while growing up in Victorian Vienna. His writings suggest a dismissing attachment pattern, which I interrogate with the nine interpersonal markers of Daniel (2015). What is fascinating about Freud's autobiography is his staunch denial of a Higher Power, interpreting belief in God as a childish fantasy. Whereas one might predict a conversion experience like Bill W.'s to compensate for unsatisfying parental relationships, instead, we find a repudiation of his father's Judaism and a denial of his "relationship" to God. I end the chapter by formulating a brief treatment plan for Freud, as if he had been referred to me for treatment.

Part II A Clinical Application of Attachment-Informed Psychotherapy

Chapter 6 A Yogi in Attachment-Informed Psychotherapy: A Spiritually Informed Case Conceptualization

I discuss a psychotherapy treatment from my own practice of a 41-year-old Caucasian man who grew up in the Presbyterian Church but abandoned the church by the time he reached adulthood (he has provided written consent to the publication of his narrative). He entered treatment for a somatic symptom that he characterized as an "energy" migrating upward from his groin to his upper chest, neck, and jaw that formulates the words, "I'm gay." This patient has been exploring Eastern spirituality, including Hinduism, yogic philosophies, and psychedelic trips, which have helped him to gain insight into his relationships to members of his family of origin as well as clarify a sense that someone—perhaps a priest—sexually abused him at the age of 8 or 9. I discuss the similarities and differences between this patient's attachment relationships to his parents and to God. I then use the Adult Attachment Interview (AAI) to assess the quality of his attachment relationships to his parents, and use my own modified version of this interview—the Adult Attachment to God Interview (AAGI)—to assess the quality of his attachment relationship to his conceptualization of a Higher Power. I also discuss the attachment-informed interventions I used in Attachment-Informed Psychotherapy (AIP) that have propelled the treatment forward, and I end the chapter by posing spiritual and emotional questions that linger in my ongoing treatment of this man.

Chapter 7 What I Have Personally Learned from Writing this Book

Finally, I discuss what I have personally learned from writing this book. I have gained four insights while writing this book. First, based on my own narrative in this chapter and Anne Frank's narrative (see Chapter 3), I learned that the correspondence and compensation pathways can be caregiver-specific. Internal working models of attachment relationships are not always integrated into a unitary mental structure but instead can exist in multiple forms, depending on the attachment quality of each attachment relationship. Second, based on Bill W.'s narrative (see Chapter 4), I learned that both external and internal forces predispose a person to turn to God as a surrogate attachment figure to compensate for insecure attachment relationships to the caregivers during childhood. Third, I learned that regardless of religious or spiritual belief or nonbelief, every person has a spiritual essence, of which the therapist must maintain an acute awareness. Finally, during the process of writing this book, I wondered whether I had mislabeled humans' primary attachment relationship. Throughout this book, I have assumed that the attachment relationships to the caregivers during childhood are primary, while the attachment relationship to a Higher Power is secondary. Is this assumption valid?

References

Alcoholics Anonymous World Services. (2012). *Twelve steps and twelve traditions*. Alcoholics Anonymous World Services, Inc.
Anonymous. (2000). *Bill W. my first 40 years: An autobiography of the cofounder of Alcoholics Anonymous* (2nd ed.). Hazelden Publishing.
Daniel, S. I. F. (2015). *Adult attachment patterns in a treatment context: Relationship and narrative*. Routledge.
Frank, A. (1993). *Anne Frank: The diary of a young girl* (B. M. Mooyaart, Trans.). Bantam Books.
Freud, S. (1925). An autobiographical study. In J. Strachey (Ed. and Trans.), *The standard edition of the complete psychological works of Sigmund Freud* (Vol. 20, pp. 1–74). Hogarth Press.
Goodman, G. (2025). *Using psychoanalytic techniques to transform the attachment relationship to God: Our refuge and strength*. Routledge.
Granqvist, P. (2020). *Attachment in religion and spirituality: A wider view*. Guilford Press.
Granqvist, P., & Kirkpatrick, L. A. (2018). Attachment and religious representations and behavior. In J. Cassidy & P. R. Shaver (Eds.), *Handbook of attachment: Theory, research, and clinical applications* (pp. 917–940). Guilford Press.
James, W. (1902). *The varieties of religious experience: A study in human nature*. Longmans, Green, and Co.
Kirkpatrick, L. A. (2005). *Attachment, evolution, and the psychology of religion*. Guilford Press.
Kirkpatrick, L. A., & Shaver, P. R. (1990). Attachment theory and religion: Childhood attachments, religious beliefs, and conversion. *Journal for the Scientific Study of Religion*, 29, 315–334.
Main, M., Kaplan, N., & Cassidy, J. (1985). Security in infancy, childhood, and adulthood: A move to the level of representation. *Monographs of the Society for Research in Child Development*, 50(1–2, Serial No. 209), 66–104..
May, R. (1973). *Paulus: Reminiscences of a friendship*. Harper & Row.
NIV (New International Version). (1978). *The holy Bible*. Zondervan.
Pargament, K. I. (2011). *Spiritually integrated psychotherapy: Understanding and addressing the sacred*. Guilford Press.
Popper, K. (1959). *The logic of scientific discovery*. Routledge.
Rizzuto, A.-M. (1979). *The birth of the living God: A psychoanalytic study*. University of Chicago Press.
Scheib, K. D. (2016). *Pastoral care: Telling the stories of our lives*. Abingdon Press.
Scott King, C. (2017). *My life, my love, my legacy*. Henry Holt and Company.
Tillich, P. (1957). *Dynamics of faith*. Harper & Bros.
Voltaire. (1919). *Voltaire in his letters: Being a selection from his correspondence* (S. G. Tallentyre, Trans.). Putnam. (Original work published in 1769).

Part I

Using Autobiographies to Illustrate Attachment to God

Three Attachment Relationship Patterns

Chapter 2

Coretta Scott King

Secure Attachment to the Living God

It is daunting to write about a revered character in the history of the United States, particularly an icon of the civil rights era, such as Coretta Scott King. Analyzing her personal history might seem sacrilegious. I choose to explore her life and specifically, her attachment to the living God through her autobiography, *My Life, My Love, My Legacy* (Scott King, 2017), to find out for myself what gave this civil rights icon her strength during one of the darkest times in our nation's history. What aspects of her faith enabled her to survive and indeed thrive during the turbulence of racial violence of the 1950s and 1960s? What faith did she need to have to survive as well as thrive after the murders of her husband (1968), mother-in-law (1974), her closest friend, Indira Gandhi (1984), and perhaps her brother-in-law (1969)? How did the great-grand-daughter of former slave Delia Scott come to occupy such a revered position in our national psyche?

Through studying her life in her own words, I concluded that Scott King had developed a secure attachment relationship to her parents and to God. The secure attachment relationships to her parents lasted long after their deaths (her mother in 1996 and her father in 1998). Because of these secure attachment relationships, as well as her exposure to Christianity through her parents and other family members, she naturally developed a secure attachment relationship to God. Her life's words illustrate the correspondence hypothesis in the religion-as-attachment model (see, e.g., Granqvist & Kirkpatrick, 2018) because the quality of her attachment relationships to her parents *corresponds* to the quality of her attachment relationship to her Higher Power.

In this chapter, I identify the interpersonal indicators of these secure attachment relationships to her parents and explore their catalyzing effects on her achievements. Finally, flirting with hubris—but only taking her as an example of someone who might have come to me for therapy—I formulate a brief treatment plan for Scott King—or securely attached persons like her.

Scott King was born in rural Perry County, Alabama, in 1927, to Obadiah and Bernice Scott, well-established farmers in the area. Obadiah also owned a general store frequented by both blacks and whites in the area. Her childhood in this era was fraught with traumatic events. These included the lynching of her great-uncle, the burning down of her home by white racists when she was age 15, the burning down of her father's sawmill a few years later, and her ongoing experience of "islands of hostility" (Scott King, 2017, p. 19) embedded in the Jim Crow South, such as separate restrooms, separate restaurants, and cross burnings. At age 18, she escaped the particularly racist confines of Alabama to pursue higher education in the North at Antioch College, higher education not being available to blacks in Alabama at the time. Later, Scott King attended the New England Conservatory of Music, where she met and eventually married Martin Luther King Jr. As she describes in her autobiography, Scott King exerted a powerful influence on her husband's philosophy of nonviolence in the service of social justice, having been exposed to Quakerism and the teachings of Mohandas Gandhi at Antioch (p. 37). Among her many achievements, Scott King went on to found the King Center in Atlanta and orchestrated the Martin Luther King, Jr., National Holiday in the US, which not only commemorates King's birthday but is also an occasion for the nation to remember and grieve the past wrongs of slavery and, later, voter suppression and racial discrimination as well as celebrate the remarkable achievements of the Civil Rights Movement enshrined in the Civil Rights Act of 1964 and the Voting Rights Act of 1965 (later gutted by the conservative US Supreme Court in 2013, just seven years after Scott King's death (The Shelby County Decision; www.justice.gov/crt/shelby-county-decision).

Scott King's Attachment Relationships to Her Parents

Coretta discusses her relationships with her parents mostly in the first 22 pages of her autobiography (Scott King, 2017). She describes her mother as having "a sweet disposition, but [being] a no-nonsense kind of person" (pp. 11–12). This characterization suggests that Scott King's mother was loving but perhaps not as warm and fuzzy as daughter Coretta would have liked. Scott King continues: "She loved to help others and was very compassionate, but she needed to know people, and she didn't warm up to you until she knew you" (p. 12). In rural Alabama during this pre-civil rights era, one might expect such reticence to be an asset to one's survival. But how might that maternal reticence have affected Scott King? "I must admit, I'm a lot like her. I've never warmed up to people quickly. Once I feel comfortable, though, I'm very open" (p. 12).

This personality trait of reticence, which Scott King called "discernment" (p. 12), extended to her mother's career advice to Coretta: "If you get an education and try to be somebody, you won't have to depend on anyone—not even a man" (p. 13). The implication is that she valued independence and not being entirely dependent on others, specifically one's husband. As Scott King points out (p. 13), her mother's life's path was largely determined for her by age 17, when she married Scott King's father. Perhaps her mother had unfulfilled aspirations that she wanted to fulfill vicariously through her children—Edythe, Coretta, and Obie, and dependence on a husband, especially for a woman, might curtail her children's aspirations (perhaps sound advice to a daughter in this era). Nevertheless, I might consider Scott King's mother's devaluing of dependence as an indicator of a tendency toward an anxious-avoidant attachment pattern, even if this tendency exists within an overall secure attachment pattern (for a discussion of secondary attachment strategies, see Goodman, 2025, Chapters 2 and 6). Because of Scott King's mother's ongoing emotional availability and sensitivity to her daughter's needs, I am suggesting that Scott King formed a secure attachment relationship to her mother, with some provisional anxious-avoidant features. Scott King's own words confirm this conclusion: she describes her mother as "loving, nurturing, farsighted" (p. 9) and "the most important woman in my life" (p. 39).

Regarding her father, Scott King clearly loved and admired him as "hardworking, faithful, courageous" (p. 9). Of her father's appearance following the fire that consumed their home, she writes: "I did not see fear in my father's eyes. In fact, the very next day he exhibited nerves of steel … My father was one of the most fearless men I've ever met" (p. 9). Scott King internalized this personality trait, seeking to "obtain that same kind of internal fortitude that my dad exemplified" (p. 9). The use of the word "dad" instead of "father" suggests an emotional closeness and identification with him that would indicate a secure attachment relationship. She portrays him as a protector of the family, the key feature of the safe haven component of the prototypical secure attachment relationship. She also describes her father as "independent" (p. 9), which drew the attention and perhaps envy of the white people in town. He admonished his children to get up early "so you won't be lazy" (p. 10). Yet, in addition to his courage, independence, and industry, Scott King's father was also giving:

> Dad would lend folks money out of his pocket … The amount people owed him for groceries and loans over a span of forty years added up to hundreds of thousands of dollars. He never let the mounting debt worry him.
>
> (p. 11)

She also emphasizes that her father blamed environmental conditions rather than whites for the way blacks were treated. He did not hold grudges (p. 11).

Regarding her childhood as a whole and her relationships with both parents, Scott King remarks, "I was never alone" (p. 4), and "most of my childhood was happy. My parents provided a nurturing environment, and most of the people in our all-black community were kinfolk" (p. 14). Although this brief statement might be defensive—in other words, Scott King might be concealing from her audience as well as herself some darker reality about her childhood relationships to her parents—there is nothing in her narrative that definitively suggests this possibility. I noticed, however, that she does not write about any childhood memories of physical closeness to either parent. There is no mention of overt hugging, kissing, or comforting taking place between her parents and herself. This observation does not mean that she and her parents never engaged in this behavior, but it is conspicuously missing from her narrative. We might surmise that this lack of physical contact and comforting served a broader purpose: "We were self-reliant, as [self-] reliant as any black could be in the racist South" (p. 15). Because the cultural context of Jim Crow demanded it, black children were taught from an early age to rely on themselves because no one knew whether a parent would return home:

> Once, I overheard [my father] telling Mother, "I don't know if I'll get back tonight because they just might kill me." Every time we heard a car coming, and it wasn't my dad's, my sister and I would tremble. We thought it was somebody coming to tell us our dad had been killed.
>
> (p. 10)

This cultural context no doubt shaped the parenting strategies of many southern black households, including the Scott's. But this emphasis on self-reliance and a possible absence of physical contact suggest a secondary attachment strategy of anxious-avoidance in the context of an overall secure attachment relationship to both parents.

Scott King's Attachment Relationship to God

The evidence that the quality of Scott King's attachment relationship to God corresponds to the quality of her attachment relationships to her parents is overwhelming. In fact, Scott King's attachment relationship to God seems to have been more secure than her attachment relationships to her parents because the evidence for a secondary attachment strategy of anxious-avoidance seems to be lacking from her narrative related to her attachment relationship to God. From the beginning of her autobiography, Scott King notes her secure connection to her Higher Power: "To discover what you're called to do with your life, I believe you have to be connected to God, to that divine force in your life, and that you have to continue to pray for direction. I did that" (Scott King, 2017, pp. 2–3). She provides numerous examples of her secure attachment relationship to God. She believed that God had given her "a divine calling" (p. 3) that lasted her entire life. This strong sense of calling by her Higher Power even put her at odds with her husband:

> During one exchange, he told me, "You see, I am called [by God], and you aren't." I responded, "I have always felt that I have a call on my life, too. I've been called by God, too, to do something. You may not understand it, but I have a sense of a calling, too."
>
> (p. 97)

How secure must her connection to her Higher Power have been for her to affirm her divine calling by God, putting her husband, leader of the Civil Rights Movement, in his place?

This sense of God's presence in Scott King's life was deeply embedded in the fabric of her life, having originated in early childhood. She declared herself to be a deeply religious child, I placed my faith in God to provide answers and a path. I would ponder His awesome work; how He had put the universe, the planets, and the galaxies together; and yet, He hadn't forgotten about me down on the farm.

(p. 16)

She maintained this close connection to God throughout her life, even after her husband was assassinated. Despite her intense grief, Scott King drew parallels between her husband's life and "that of Jesus[, and these parallels] gave me some consolation, which I sorely needed" (p. 163). She also underscored the parallels between her own suffering and that of Jesus: "Christians are often called by God to participate not only in the victory of the risen Christ, but in His agony and His suffering" (p. 154). Even when tempted to turn her back on God, she never did. Her attachment relationship to her Higher Power remained secure, even to the end. Summing up her relationship to God across the years of her life, Scott King writes:

When I wasn't praying or in tune with God's will and purpose, I wasn't happy. In contrast, when I was in tune with the will and purpose of God, things may not have gone well, but I still felt good about what I was doing, and about myself. My story is one of divine preparation. I was prepared to lead. I was called, and I was chosen.

(p. 328)

In discussing her connection to God, she always placed her unshakable faith in a stronger, wiser Being in the foreground:

I was caught up by and thrust into a whirlwind, guided by a force beyond myself and shaped to a purpose I often did not understand until I had to fulfill it ... I prayed to God for guidance; I asked Him to give me the strength to accept His will in my life, even if it meant my death.

(p. 327)

Markers of a Secure Attachment Relationship

Daniel (2015) identifies two sets of markers that indicate a secure attachment relationship: interpersonal and narrative markers. I will consider only the first set of markers to provide further evidence for my thesis that Scott King's attachment relationships to her parents were secure and that these secure attachment relationships correspond to her secure attachment relationship to God. I will not consider the narrative markers here because her book manuscript (as well as the other autobiographies we will be analyzing in later chapters) no doubt was scrutinized and edited by numerous reviewers and editors rather than being a spontaneously generated text or speech from which we can seek reliable clues about her attachment relationships. The Adult Attachment Interview (AAI)—the gold standard assessment instrument for adult attachment (see Goodman, 2025, Chapter 2)—was designed to "surprise the unconscious" (George et al., 1985, p. 6); however, there is nothing surprising about a carefully manicured text. I consequently focus instead on the interpersonal markers, which I believe are more impervious than text to such sanitation.

Why are interpersonal characteristics important to identify in a person when considering how to treat them in psychotherapy? Daniel (2015) notes that these characteristics "are systematically and meaningfully connected in treatment providers' assessment of clients" (p. 113). Research conducted by Westen et al. (2006) strongly suggests that interpersonal markers can discriminate among the four attachment patterns—secure, anxious-resistant, anxious-avoidant, and disorganized/disoriented. Clients provide all sorts of clues about their underlying attachment patterns by how they interact with the therapist and how they talk about themselves and others, particularly significant others as well as significant losses or traumas. The therapist can then use this information to formulate a treatment plan that will aid in the conduct of the treatment and facilitate a successful treatment outcome.

Interpersonal Markers of Scott King's Secure Attachment Relationships to Her Parents and to God

Daniel (2015) identified nine interpersonal markers that discriminate among the four attachment patterns. These nine interpersonal markers are: (1) proximity/distance, (2) trust/expectations of others, (3) attitude to seeking and receiving help, (4) expression and regulation of emotions, (5) self-image/self-esteem, (6) openness and self-disclosure, (7) dependence/independence, (8) conflict management, and (9) empathy. In the second column of Table 2.1, I include a key phrase from Daniel (2015) that most closely represents the specific attachment pattern suggested by the quotation. In the third column, I include a key quotation from Scott King's autobiography (Scott King, 2017) that supports each of the nine interpersonal markers related to her attachment relationships to her parents. In the fourth column, I include a key phrase from Daniel (2015) that most closely represents the specific attachment pattern suggested by the quotation. Finally, in the fifth column, I include a key quotation that supports each of these markers related to her attachment relationship to God.

Proximity/Distance

This interpersonal marker of the attachment pattern is especially evident through visual observation. Thus, it is difficult to assess proximity/distance in a person's writing, and so my assessment is speculative. We might, however, be able to estimate Scott King's comfort level with proximity through her narrative. Based on my earlier analysis, we are looking for both secure and anxious-avoidant dimensions of her attachment relationships to her parents and to God. Regarding this marker, Daniel (2015) wrote that securely attached persons "value and are comfortable with proximity," whereas anxious-avoidant persons "prefer distance and

Table 2.1 Nine interpersonal markers of attachment for Coretta Scott King

Interpersonal markers	Primary marker with parents	Key quotation/parents	Primary marker with God	Key quotation/god
Proximity/distance	Values/is comfortable with proximity	"[I] sleep at this [nursing] facility with her ... I visited her practically every day"	Values/is comfortable with proximity	"I believe you have to be connected to God"
Trust/expectation of others	Trusting/positive expectations	"[I] had the trusted help of family and of other people who became like family"	Trusting/positive expectations	"I placed my faith in God"
Attitude to seeking and receiving help	Open to seeking help	"She was always there when you needed her"	Open to seeking help	"I relied on God, engaging in serious prayer"
Expression and regulation of emotions	Balanced expressions of positive and negative emotions	"[I] ma[de] sure I had my emotions in check"	Balanced expressions of positive and negative emotions	"When I rose to speak, I felt the most powerful sense of His presence"
Self-image/self-esteem	Nuanced self-image/ solid self-esteem	"Even though I have those problems, I love me"	Nuanced self-image/solid self-esteem	"Whenever my life was guided by prayer, I felt good about what I was doing"
Openness and self-disclosure	Reticent about sharing thoughts and feelings	"[I] agonized over asking my parents [for money], but decided against it"	Pleased to share thoughts and feelings, dosed according to situation	"My private thoughts ... were a soliloquy, spoken to no one but God"

(Continued)

Table 2.1 (Continued)

Interpersonal markers	Primary marker with parents	Key quotation/parents	Primary marker with God	Key quotation/god
Dependence/independence	Greatly values independence from others	"Coretta was never a dependent woman"	Feels comfortable in committed relationships, capable of autonomy	"[I] relied on my faith to show me the path forward"
Conflict management	Constructive strategies for handling conflicts	"The most violent of adversaries can be approached in a true spirit of reconciliation"	Constructive strategies for handling conflicts	"Pacifism felt right to me…love thy neighbor as thyself"
Empathy	Empathy with and care for others	"She would do anything in the world for you. I must admit, I'm a lot like her"	Empathy with and care for others	"We were coworkers with God in His creative activity"

Source: Modeled after Daniel (2015, p. 115).

are uncomfortable with proximity. [They c]onsider self 'different'" (p. 115). What follows are select key quotations that address the Proximity/Distance marker.

Although not specifically related to her attachment relationships to her parents, at boarding school, Scott King felt "nurtured and embraced" (Scott King, 2017, p. 19) by the families with whom she stayed. She also made a clear statement about her general attitude toward physical proximity when she discussed her meeting with Jacqueline Kennedy shortly after her husband Martin Luther King Jr.'s death: "I have a tendency to hug people, and I wanted to embrace her" (p. 169). On a trip to Spain in 1970, she also felt secure in the love she was receiving from the people she encountered through their physical proximity: "The people proved to be so loving and embracing. They were perpetually hugging and kissing me; it was just overwhelming" (p. 192). Her writing assistant, Barbara Reynolds, also indicated that "when she would go out, she would give everyone a hug" (p. 342). Near the end of her mother's life, as her mother's health declined, Scott King "would sometimes sleep at this [nursing] facility with her ... I visited her practically every day" (p. 322). On the other hand, Scott King sought distance from her family and hometown of Heiberger by age 13: "My mind left home before I packed my physical bags" (p. 2). Thus, although Scott King's need for physical proximity predominates in her narrative, she does not share memories of physical closeness or affection with either parent. Nevertheless, on this interpersonal marker of attachment, I would assess Scott King as securely attached to her parents.

Regarding Scott King's Proximity/Distance marker in her attachment relationship to God, she provides plenty of examples of proximity and emotional closeness to God. At the outset of her narrative, Scott King described her connection to God as influential in her life's calling: "To discover what you're called to do with your life, I believe you have to be connected to God, to that divine force in your life, and that you have to continue to pray for direction. I did that" (pp. 2–3). She listened for a response "until I got a strong signal from God" (p. 39). In recalling her experiences with Quakers in high school as well as college, Scott King wrote:

> I used to sit quietly in the chapel at Antioch and try to deepen my relationship with God in the Quaker way. The Quakers would sit and wait for hours for the Holy Spirit to move them. The process is like meditating and communing with the Spirit.
>
> (p. 29)

After her husband's assassination, she described wanting "to be useful and available to God, and I was praying to God for direction" (p. 167). Barbara Reynolds, who had been a close friend of Scott King for many years, commented that "prayer was central to everything she did" (p. 337). A final example among many demonstrates, in the classic attachment theory tradition, Scott King's proximity to and reliance on God as a divine secure base. She asked God "to continue His watch, to protect and guide us as we made our way forward" (p. 189). Thus, in these quotations referencing the interpersonal marker of Proximity/Distance, we observe a correspondence between Scott King's secure attachment relationships to her parents and her secure attachment relationship to God and note occasional anxious-avoidant markers.

Trust/Expectations of Others

This interpersonal marker of the attachment pattern is evident in Scott King's descriptions of her attachment relationships to her parents and to God. Based on my earlier analysis, we are looking for both secure and anxious-avoidant dimensions of her attachment relationships to her parents and to God. Concerning this marker, Daniel (2015) wrote that securely attached persons "are trusting and have positive expectations," whereas anxious-avoidant persons "fear rejection or ridicule, but try to ignore feelings of insecurity" (p. 115). I will now select key quotations that address the marker of Trust/Expectations of Others.

Regarding her attachment relationships to her parents, Scott King acknowledges that she "had the trusted help of family and of other people who became like family" (Scott King, 2017, p. 191). Just as her elementary school teachers and parents "loved us and expected us to excel" (p. 14), so too did Scott King have secure expectations of her parents: "I was shaped by my mother's discernment and my father's strength" (p. 9), remarking that she could rely on her mother's "sweet disposition" (p. 11) and her father's "nerves of steel" (p. 9). Although she does not explicitly mention trust or expectations of her parents, the preceding quotations strongly suggest parental trust and secure expectations that her parents would be there for her, especially during a crisis. Contrary evidence consists of one passage describing her mother's initial distrust of people, with which Scott King identifies:

> She didn't warm up to you until she knew you. She had to look you over and feel you out. Once she felt that you were okay, she would do anything in the world for you. I must admit, I'm a lot like her. I've never warmed up to people quickly. Once I feel comfortable, though, I'm very open.
>
> (p. 12)

Thus, we observe a vestige of an anxious-avoidant attachment in the context of underlying secure attachment relationships to her parents.

Regarding Scott King's marker of Trust/Expectations of Others in her attachment relationship to God, she provides numerous examples of her childlike faith in a Higher Power: "A deeply religious child, I placed my faith in God" (p. 16). In looking back on the course of her life, she sums up how she accomplished her "divine calling" (p. 3):

> All this kept me on my knees, calling on God. Over the years, as I prayed for strength, I felt a sense of relief. I was doing God's work, I knew, and He would take care of me and my family.
>
> (p. 3)

She expresses faith in her Higher Power, with the expectation that this Higher Power would take care of her and her family. Scott King also discusses what it took to make her dream of a Martin Luther King, Jr., national holiday a reality: "One person is particularly chosen to hear the charge, the divine calling, and to step out on faith" (p. 265).

Scott King even viewed tribulations through the lens of a loving God she trusted. In the wake of her Montgomery house being bombed, she writes:

> That night, fear mixed with the faith I had known since childhood. In Montgomery, when tragedy hit, when I was tested, I found that the fear had left. It had been overcome by faith ... Even in the midst of terror, there is always a way out. I had been taught, and have come to believe in, the words of the gospel song: "God will make a way out of no way."
>
> (pp. 51–52)

Even after her husband was stabbed in New York City in 1958, Scott King wonders what God is doing, but she never loses her faith:

> I tried to make sense of what had happened and to reflect on it with spiritual curiosity. Was this a trial, a test of some kind? ... Not only my husband was being tested, but his followers as well—including me.
>
> (p. 88)

Thus, even amid grave tragedy, Scott King maintains a childlike trust in God and expected God to take care of her and her family. In these quotations referencing the interpersonal marker of Trust/Expectations of Others, we again observe a correspondence between Scott King's secure attachment relationships to her parents and her secure attachment relationship to God, noting only one example of an interpersonal marker of anxious-avoidant attachment to her mother.

Attitude to Seeking and Receiving Help

This interpersonal marker of the attachment pattern is evident in Scott King's descriptions of her attachment relationships to her parents and to God. Based on my earlier analysis, we are looking for both secure and anxious-avoidant dimensions of her attachment relationships to her parents and to God. Regarding this marker, Daniel (2015) wrote that securely attached persons "are open to seeking help," whereas anxious-avoidant persons "prefer to handle things themselves" (p. 115). Which parts of Scott King's book address the Attitude to Seeking and Receiving Help marker?

Regarding her attachment relationships to her parents, she does not provide many concrete examples; however, she does demonstrate the capacity to seek help from parental figures. In describing her mother, Scott King remarks, "She was always there when you needed her" (Scott King, 2017, p. 12). At the New

England Conservatory of Music, she met Mrs. Bertha Wormley, someone who would become a maternal figure in Scott King's early life. Speaking to Wormley on the phone, Scott King recalls:

> I paused and cradled the phone, not wanting to lay myself bare and admit that I was broke. I was proud and embarrassed, but I could not hold back my feelings of desperation. I blurted out my troubles ... She [later] handed me a sealed envelope ... What joy! It contained fifteen dollars.
>
> (p. 32)

After her husband died, Scott King relied on others, both within and outside her family, for help: "My sister, Edythe, provided a lot of administrative support and helped with our initial cultural events. I also had trusted help from people who weren't family" (p. 191). She also received financial help from the likes of Harry Belafonte (p. 181) and Oprah Winfrey (p. 323) as well as other "friends" (p. 322). Interestingly, however, perhaps to spare them from worrying about her, there is no record that she ever sought financial or emotional help from her parents in college or after college. In fact, Scott King explicitly states that she "decided against" asking her parents for money because she "wanted them to enjoy the fruits of their labor instead of financing my dreams" (p. 31). Notably, in her narrative, she only occasionally mentions her parents after she left home for college. Thus, although it seems that Scott King was able to seek and receive help from others, she might have felt reluctant to seek and receive help from her parents. For this interpersonal marker, I observe a primary attachment strategy of security and a secondary attachment strategy of anxious-avoidance (see Goodman, 2025, Chapter 6) in her attachment relationships to her parents.

Regarding her Attitude to Seeking and Receiving Help marker in her attachment relationship to God, there are many more examples of this marker than there are for her parents. A couple will suffice. Recalling someone who helped her financially during college, Scott King remarks, "There is no situation in which we can find ourselves where God won't send help" (Scott King, 2017, p. 32). Similarly, she later writes, "I relied on God, engaging in serious prayer and meditation to help me settle a matter I felt strongly about in my heart. I couldn't involve my whole heart until I got a strong signal from God" (p. 39). We again observe a correspondence between Scott King's secure attachment relationships to others and her secure attachment relationship to God. It is possible, however, that Scott King used her attachment relationship to God in this area of help-seeking and help-receiving to compensate for her presumed inability to seek help from her parents.

Expression and Regulation of Emotions

This interpersonal marker of the attachment pattern is evident in Scott King's descriptions of her attachment relationships to her parents and to God. Based on my earlier analysis, we are looking for both secure and anxious-avoidant dimensions of her attachment relationships to her parents and to God. Regarding this marker, Daniel (2015) notes that securely attached persons demonstrate "balanced expressions of both positive and negative emotions," whereas anxious-avoidant persons demonstrate "limited expression of emotions; false positivity; suppression of negative emotions" (p. 115). What aspects of Scott King's autobiography address the Expression and Regulation of Emotions marker?

Regarding Scott King's attachment relationships to her parents, it is challenging to find illustrations of the expression and regulation of emotions in a narrative (Scott King, 2017). It is easier to observe emotions in person. Daniel (2015) recommends using these interpersonal markers to determine attachment quality in psychotherapy sessions. I am applying this marker in a slightly different context: as discussed earlier, presumably, the author and a variety of editors and reviewers revised and edited the text, with the likely result that the author's emotional expressions are no longer captured in spontaneous gestures but rather in calculated, sanitized words meant for public consumption. In the context of remembering dreams, Freud (1900) called this process "secondary revision"—an effort to create the appearance of narrative coherence and rationality. An autobiographer would typically want to engage in a similar process to make their irrational emotional expressions as rational and intelligible as possible. I find examples of balanced expressions of positive and negative emotions in her attachment relationships to her parents and to God, but whether these examples represent genuine, spontaneous emotional expressions or secondary revision is beyond my ken.

Scott King does not disclose directly how she felt about her parents. For example, she does not directly express that she loved them. She describes her mother as "loving, nurturing, farsighted" (Scott King, 2017, p. 9), but that does not capture her own emotional expression toward her mother or father. She does, however, directly express love to her own younger daughter: "I put my arms around her and said, 'Bunny, I love you'" (p. 171). She also includes examples of intense emotional expressions that she nonetheless exhibited the capacity to control. In her effort to continue emotionally responsive caregiving to her children in the aftermath of her husband's assassination, she describes how she managed her intense grief:

> Sometimes I just wanted to stay there under the covers. But I could not break down. I did not want my children to see me out of control, because then they might lose their way. So I had my cry before I came out of my room, and then I opened the door with a forceful determination I had never known before.
> (p. 173)

Elaborating on these efforts, she writes, "Sometimes I paused at the door, my hand on the knob, making sure I had my emotions in check. Then, with a prayer in my heart and a smile on my face, I could greet the morning" (p. 173). At other times, Scott King reports feeling overwhelmed by her emotions, especially at the peak of the Civil Rights Movement, when her husband was repeatedly jailed: "I felt so alone and vulnerable. I had tried to control my emotions and tie down my feelings, but I felt I could stomach no more. The feeling of losing my grip on life was not normal for me" (p. 89). Nevertheless, Scott King portrays herself as balanced in her emotional expressions, comparing herself with the demonstrative Baptists in her hometown: "As a good Methodist, my style of worship was much quieter than that of the more emotional 'shouting Baptists'" (p. 34). On this interpersonal marker of attachment, I would assess Scott King as securely attached.

Regarding Scott King's balanced expression of positive and negative emotions in her attachment relationship to God, her narrative articulates a wide range of emotions. Early in her life, Scott King shares feeling awe in relationship to God when she "ponder[s] His awesome work; how He had put the universe, the planets, and the galaxies together; and yet, He hadn't forgotten about me down on the farm" (p. 16). Juxtaposed with feelings of awe are also feelings of fear and judgment early in her life: "I was afraid of committing sins that would condemn me to burn in hell instead of joining God in that mysterious heaven hidden beyond the clouds" (p. 17). Later, when becoming a member of Mount Tabor AME Zion Church as an adolescent, Scott King describes her feelings toward God "bec[oming] so intense and emotional that I thought I felt something, and I stood up and joined the Church" (p. 18). Her emotional yet meditative connection to God is also suggested in how she "used to sit quietly in the chapel at Antioch and try to deepen my relationship with God in the Quaker way" (p. 29). Again, she "couldn't involve my whole heart until I got a strong signal from God" (p. 39). In speaking publicly for the first time at the 1958 Women's Day Address in Denver, Scott King articulates knowing that "God was with me, because when I rose to speak, I felt the most powerful sense of His presence" (p. 86). Thus, on this interpersonal marker, Scott King demonstrated a balanced expression of positive and negative emotions in her attachment relationship to God. Although she does not include in the narrative much emotional content regarding her attachment relationships to her parents, we observe that she expresses a variety of emotions in a variety of circumstances, and that these emotions are neither constricted nor expansive. We observe again a correspondence between her style of emotional expression in her interactions with others and in her interactions with her Higher Power, indicating secure attachment relationships to her parents and to God.

Self-image/Self-esteem

This interpersonal marker of the attachment pattern is evident in Scott King's descriptions of her attachment relationships to her parents and to God. Based on my earlier analysis, we are looking for both secure and anxious-avoidant dimensions of her attachment relationships to her parents and to God. Regarding this marker, Daniel (2015) writes that securely attached persons demonstrate "nuanced self-image and solid self-esteem," whereas anxious-avoidant persons demonstrate a "tendency to a defensively 'magnified' self-image to compensate for low self-esteem" (p. 115). What are some quotations from Scott King's autobiography that address the Self-image/Self-esteem marker?

Regarding her attachment relationships to her parents, the examples of their direct correlation to her self-image/self-esteem are sparse, yet there are glimpses of her parents' influence: "Isolated, in the rural South, black, and female, I didn't see much to suggest that I could have a bright future—except for my parents' coaching" (Scott King, (2017, p. 16). Early in her narrative, she declares herself "a proud Scott, shaped by my mother's discernment and my father's strength" (p. 9). Throughout her narrative, Scott King evidences a self-assuredness coupled with humility. For example, she reports feeling "an inner self in motion; she was excited and ready to go, but where? I didn't know" (p. 16). By age 13, she felt sufficiently secure in herself to ask herself questions about her identity, a developmentally appropriate task in adolescence (Gilmore & Meersand, 2014). She reports sitting "at the mirror for hours, staring, trying to figure out who I was. Why am I here? I know God made me, but why?" (Scott King, 2017, p. 16). Scott King was able to use the exploratory system (see Goodman, 2025, Chapter 2) to ask these penetrating questions because she had secure attachment relationships to her parents.

Scott King's parents were a few of the only blacks to own land in that region of Alabama. She comments on the effect this fact had on her: "This tradition of landownership helped to instill in us racial pride, self-respect, and dignity" (p. 15). She emphasized this point in speaking about her father's influence: "I sought to obtain that same kind of internal fortitude that my dad exemplified" (p. 9). Writing about the time toward the end of her life, Scott King discusses the importance and value of loving oneself:

> People really have to develop a true love for themselves. It helps to take account of one's self by writing down all the bad and good qualities you have and strive to eliminate the bad. Then say, "Even though I have those problems, I love me."
> (p. 301)

Likewise, she encourages her four children to "Always be your own best self" (p. 302). Finally, Scott King clearly felt sufficiently secure in her self-image to transcend self-interest. For in summing up her life, she writes, "It is a story of struggle. It is about finding one's purpose, a guide to overcoming fear and standing up for causes bigger than one's self" (p. 329). Thus, I conclude that Scott King's secure attachment relationships to her parents established a secure self-image in which she esteemed herself without lapsing into a defensively magnified self-image to compensate for low self-esteem.

Regarding Scott King's self-image/self-esteem in her attachment relationship to God, her narrative contains several examples of the ways in which this relationship sustained her self-image/self-esteem. In the beginning of her chapter on founding the King Center, she writes: "Whenever my life was guided by prayer, I felt good about what I was doing" (p. 185). Later, looking back on the course of her life, Scott King offers this advice to her readers:

> If it's in line with God's will, then I believe you will find fulfillment ... When I was in tune with the will and purpose of God, things may not have gone well, but I still felt good about what I was doing, and about myself.
>
> (p. 328)

She also references the peace that God gave her: "Over the years, as I prayed for strength, I felt a sense of relief. I was doing God's work, I knew, and He would take care of me and my family" (p. 3). Her self-image as a resilient, courageous woman called by God for a divine purpose is evident in this passage:

> I had a divine calling on my life, a charge, a challenge to serve not just black people, but all oppressed humankind. That calling will be with me to the end ... I came to understand what I was made of, what pressures I could withstand without breaking or running away. I was not a crystal figurine, fragile and fearful ... I am still amazed at what lies within me ... During that time [of the Bus Boycott] in Montgomery, I felt an inner strength; it told me that, if necessary, I could do it again. And again.
>
> (p. 3)

Thus, on this interpersonal marker, Scott King demonstrates a nuanced self-image and a solid self-esteem without exhibiting the tendency to magnify her self-image defensively to compensate for low self-esteem. We observe a correspondence between Scott King's self-image/self-esteem in relation to others as well as in relation to God, indicating secure attachment relationships both to her parents and to God.

Openness and Self-disclosure

The interpersonal marker of Openness and Self-disclosure is evident in descriptions of Scott King's attachment relationships to both her parents and to God. Based on my earlier analysis, we are looking for both secure and anxious-avoidant dimensions of her attachment relationships to her parents and to God. Regarding this marker, Daniel (2015) writes that securely attached persons "are pleased to share thoughts and feelings, but 'dose' these according to the situation," whereas anxious-avoidant persons "are reticent about sharing thoughts and feelings" (p. 115). What are some key passages in Scott King's autobiography that address the Openness and Self-disclosure marker?

Although Daniel (2015) categorizes both openness and self-disclosure as one interpersonal marker, I discovered that Scott King exhibited an openness to others and to God's voice but that she limited her self-disclosures to close friends only (perhaps common among public figures). Of course, she wrote an autobiography—the ultimate self-disclosure—but she felt conflicted about publishing it while she was alive. Barbara Reynolds, her writing assistant, suggested that "there are some things in this book I believe she did not want said in her lifetime" (Scott King, 2017, p. 355). For example, Scott King's portrayal of Reverend Jesse Jackson is particularly critical (see, e.g., pp. 228–229, 258). Thus, what follows are mostly examples of Scott King's openness to others and to God's voice rather than self-disclosures.

Regarding Scott King's attachment relationships to her parents, there are examples of her not being open or self-disclosing to them. As already mentioned in regard to the Attitude to Seeking and Receiving Help marker, she "agonized over asking my parents [for money], but decided against it; I wanted them to enjoy the fruits of their labor instead of financing my dreams" (p. 31). She also points out in the autobiography that she resembled her mother in her initial lack of openness to others: "I must admit, I'm a lot like her. I've never warmed up to people quickly. Once I feel comfortable, though, I'm very open" (p. 12). She directly addressed self-disclosure early in her narrative: "I always found it difficult to talk about myself" (p. 6), she notes, and yet she wrote two books about herself (the other being *My Life with Martin Luther King, Jr.*; Scott King, 1969). Scott King is also reticent to convey any grumbling: "You never knew the stresses and strains I underwent as a woman in a male-dominated culture, because I didn't complain" (Scott King, 2017, p. 4). Regarding her husband's repeated arrests, "I did not tell him of my deep pain ... I agonized over how unbearable life would be without him. I did not share these feelings" (p. 68).

On the other hand, in the Afterword, one of her closest friends, Myrlie Evers-Williams, writes: "We could talk to one another and be open and honest" (p. 340). Barbara Reynolds also quotes Scott King as telling her, "'We are an open book here. I have nothing to hide. Just promise me you will write the truth'" (p. 351). Scott King herself describes her gradual openness to white people in deeply racist rural Alabama:

> White teachers saw worth in me. In time, I saw past the terrible symbols of burning crosses, hateful words, and malicious intent and discovered that there were real, loving people under a skin color that so often meant trouble or heartache for our community. My white teachers laughed, cried, went to church, and attended county fairs. Underneath the skin—the skin that had been so foreboding to me—were people with good hearts and fair minds. It was important for me to understand this. As a child who had seen mostly the worst behavior of whites, it was critical for me to see a better side, and I feel now that these early contacts were divine connections. They reached me before the meanness that I had seen could create cement walls of enmity within my soul.
>
> (p. 19)

In the context of all these findings, I conclude that on this interpersonal marker, Scott King exhibited both secure and anxious-avoidant features in her secure attachment relationships to her parents. She seemed open to new experiences and people but limited her self-disclosures to only close friends.

Regarding Scott King's openness and self-disclosure in her attachment relationship to God, her narrative is replete with examples of turning to God in prayer for direction (pp. 3, 167), strength (pp. 3, 67, 189, 201, 327), and guidance (p. 327). These passages reflect an openness to listening to God's voice to lead and comfort her. Having learned the practice of meditation during her time at Antioch College, she would "sit quietly in the chapel at Antioch and try to deepen my relationship with God in the Quaker way" (p. 29). She also engages in self-disclosure to her Higher Power: "My private thoughts about the birth of my firstborn [in 1957] were a soliloquy, spoken to no one but God. Yet it appeared that God must have been listening" (p. 57). Scott King also discloses what she learned in meditation with God: "I publicly gave voice to the vision and path I believed God had put me on" (p. 86). Thus, on this interpersonal marker, Scott King demonstrates an openness to listening for God's voice and a capacity for self-disclosure to God in prayer that exceeded the openness and self-disclosure to her parents and significant others in her life. To some extent, we might say that Scott King demonstrates a compensation between her openness and self-disclosure to others and to God. She used her secure attachment relationship to God to compensate for her attachment relationships to her parents and to significant others on this interpersonal marker.

Dependence/Independence

This interpersonal marker of the attachment pattern is evident in Scott King's descriptions of her attachment relationships to her parents and to God. Based on my earlier analysis, I am looking in the autobiography for both secure and anxious-avoidant dimensions of her attachment relationships to her parents and to God. Regarding this marker, Daniel (2015) writes that securely attached persons "feel comfortable in committed relationships, but are also capable of autonomy," whereas anxious-avoidant persons "greatly value independence from others" (p. 115). What are some key quotations in Scott King's autobiography that address the Dependence/Independence marker?

Regarding Scott King's attachment relationships to her parents, her mother instilled in her the value of independence from others, especially men: "If you get an education and try to be somebody, you won't have to depend on anyone—not even a man" (Scott King, 2017, p. 13). Scott King writes of internalizing this value: "I could have my own goals that went beyond merely being dependent on a man—though I did want to marry and have children" (p. 13). She places this strong sense of independence in a specific social context: "We were self-reliant, as [self-]reliant as any black could be in the racist South" (p. 15). While doing domestic housework for a white woman in high school, she discovers that "I was not then, or ever, the submissive, subservient type. That job didn't last" (p. 19). Scott King also raised her children to value independence:

Liberated, independent women intimidate some men, and my daughters inherited these traits from me ... My girls knew Coretta, and Coretta was never a dependent woman. I had to learn to make it as a single parent at an early age ... I never wanted to damage my children by letting them depend on me.

(pp. 326–327)

Despite this strong independent streak, during high school away from home, she "had to stay with other families to be able to attend school. That was fine with me... I ... felt nurtured and embraced in Lincoln's halls" (p. 19). Thus, although it seems that Scott King was able to depend on others, she might have felt reluctant to depend on her parents, as evidenced by refusing to ask them for money in college (see p. 31). For this interpersonal marker, we observe a primary attachment strategy of security and a secondary attachment strategy of anxious-avoidance (see Goodman, 2025, Chapter 6) in her attachment relationships to her parents.

Regarding her dependence/independence in her attachment relationship to God, in her autobiography, she conveys a strong sense of dependence on her Higher Power coupled with a strong motivation to act independently on what she perceived as God's will to fulfill her "divine calling" (Scott King, 2017, p. 3). She adroitly explains this interplay between dependence on God and independent activity:

I took on tasks requiring skills and wisdom I didn't have until circumstances demanded them. All this kept me on my knees, calling on God. Over the years, as I prayed for strength, I felt a sense of relief. I was doing God's work, I knew, and He would take care of me and my family.

(p. 3)

After college, she characteristically "relied on my faith to show me the path forward, and on what I've come to think of as guardian angels" (p. 29). Similarly, Scott King "relied on God, engaging in serious prayer and meditation to help me settle a matter I felt strongly about in my heart. I couldn't involve my whole heart until I got a strong signal from God" (p 39). Thus, on this interpersonal marker, Scott King demonstrates a dependence on her Higher Power to guide her, direct her, and give her strength to fulfill her divine calling. On the other hand, Scott King demonstrates a strong sense of interpersonal independence instilled in her by her mother and communicated to her own children. We observe that, to some extent, Scott King demonstrates a compensation between her independence from others and her dependence on God. She uses her secure attachment relationship to God to compensate for her attachment relationships to her parents and to significant others on this interpersonal marker.

Conflict Management

This interpersonal marker of the attachment pattern is evident in Scott King's descriptions of her attachment relationships to her parents and to God. Based on my earlier analysis, we are looking for both secure and anxious-avoidant dimensions of her attachment relationships to her parents and to God. Regarding this marker, Daniel (2015) notes that securely attached persons demonstrate "constructive strategies for handling conflicts," whereas anxious-avoidant persons are "uncomfortable with potential conflicts, [and] attempt to ignore these" (p. 115). What are some key texts in her autobiography that address the Conflict Management marker? Notably, I found no recollections of incidents between Scott King and her parents, or between Scott King and God, that required conflict management.

Regarding Scott King's attachment relationships to her parents, there is little explicit indication that she ever had conflicts with her parents. At any rate, none of them made their way into her narrative. She does, however, recall her mother's strategy for handling conflicts:

> Mother had an expression: "Seldom visits make long friends." In other words, friendships will be longer lasting if you don't go visiting much. When you do, there's the tendency toward idle gossip and the potential to have conflicts and to fall out.
>
> (Scott King, 2017, p. 12)

This strategy seems to be one of conflict avoidance through absence of personal contact. Scott King seems to have adopted this strategy as a pastor's wife, explaining to her husband, "I'm perfectly satisfied to be home. I enjoy being by myself,' while my mother's words echoed in my head. *Seldom visits make long friends*" (p. 12; emphasis in original. Despite her mother's warnings about avoiding conflict by not getting too close to people, Scott King made her career out of promoting conflict resolution, enshrined in the King Center's Six Principles of Nonviolence and in the Kingian Six Steps of Nonviolence (pp. 208–209). Steps 3 and 4 illustrate this idea:

> 3. Make a personal commitment to solving the problem and resolving the conflict nonviolently, checking motives along the way. 4. Negotiate. Meet with the opposition, discuss differences, and try to come to a win-win resolution. If negotiations fail, only then do we go to step five.
>
> (p. 209)

She also believed in "a crucial article of faith in nonviolence that even the most violent of adversaries can be approached in a true spirit of reconciliation" (p. 247).

Did Scott King practice this "constructive strategy for handling conflicts," or was she "uncomfortable with potential conflicts, [and] attempt to ignore these" (Daniel, 2015, p. 115)? After learning that presidential candidate George McGovern had reneged on a promise to her, Scott King did not back down. She recalls saying:

> 'I know all of you think I'm nice and sweet, but if you renege on your promise to Walter, I am going to show up in Miami and set things straight.' In that phone conversation, I exposed an unusual side of myself. Rarely do I get so angry that

I resort to threats. However, once I get riled up enough to go that far, I do not make empty threats. Very quickly, McGovern called back and explained that he had made the change I wanted.

(p. 220)

Thus, although it seems that Scott King's mother urged her daughter to adopt a conflict-avoidant strategy, there is no evidence that she ever did that. She does not provide any evidence in the narrative for conflict with her parents, let alone conflict management. For this interpersonal marker, there is insufficient evidence to classify the quality of her attachment relationship to her parents, but she seemed to cultivate secure attachment relationships to others on this interpersonal marker, given the preponderance of evidence in the narrative.

Regarding Scott King's conflict management in her attachment relationship to God, as with her parents, there is little explicit indication that she ever had conflicts with her Higher Power. Even in her darkest hour, in the period following her husband's assassination, Scott King never indicates having a conflict with God. On the contrary, getting out of bed in the morning after crying:

[She] opened the door with a forceful determination I had never known before. I did not just open it; I thrust it open. But it required determination that came from beyond myself ... Sometimes I paused at the door, my hand on the knob, making sure I had my emotions in check. Then, with a prayer in my heart and a smile on my face, I could greet the morning.

(p. 173)

Scott King's attachment relationship to her Higher Power also inspired her approach to nonviolence that became her signature humanitarian contribution. She writes: "I began to consider myself a pacifist. Pacifism felt right to me; it accorded with what I had been taught as a Christian: to love thy neighbor as thyself" (p. 28). Thus, while not including examples of conflict between herself and God, Scott King did reveal the divine inspiration behind her conflict management strategies, which were constructive because they worked at an international level (e.g., getting corporations to divest holdings in South Africa as a nonviolent strategy to eliminate apartheid; see p. 208) as well as at a personal level (e.g., her assertive interaction with McGovern). Thus, on this interpersonal marker, Scott King demonstrates a secure attachment relationship to God. We observe a correspondence between her conflict management strategies with people and her inspiration for these strategies as coming from her Higher Power, indicating secure attachment relationships to her parents and to God.

Empathy

This interpersonal marker of the attachment pattern is evident in Scott King's descriptions of her attachment relationships to her parents and to God. Based on my earlier analysis, we are looking for both secure and anxious-avoidant dimensions of her attachment relationships to her parents and to God. Regarding this marker, Daniel (2015) writes that securely attached persons demonstrate "empathy with and care for others," whereas anxious-avoidant persons demonstrate "limited empathy and interpersonal 'coldness'" (p. 115). What are some passages in her autobiography that address the Empathy marker?

Regarding Scott King's attachment relationships to her parents, I begin obliquely with her comment about having a mother who explicitly cared for others: "She was always there when you needed her, and was a very giving person when you got to know her" (Scott King, 2017, p. 12). Scott King identifies with her mother's empathy with and care for others: "She would do anything in the world for you. I must admit, I'm a lot like her" (p. 12). Near the end of her mother's life, Scott King demonstrates empathy for her:

> I moved her from Alabama to Atlanta, to my home for a few months ... I [later] moved her to a nursing home associated with Georgia Baptist Hospital near the King Center, where it would be easy for me to visit her. As her health declined, I would sometimes sleep at this facility with her ... I tried to pamper her. I threw parties for her. I visited her practically every day.
>
> (p. 322)

Scott King (2017) comments on having a father who empathized with financial hardships of both black and white people:

> Dad would lend folks money out of his pocket. Sometimes the borrowers would pay a little on their accounts, and he would let them charge a bigger portion. When he died in 1998, shortly before turning one hundred, the amount people owed him for groceries and loans over a span of forty years added up to hundreds of thousands of dollars. He never let the mounting debt worry him.
>
> (p. 11)

Near the end of her father's life, Scott King demonstrates empathy for him:

> Dad kept on working at his general store way into his early nineties, until I decided to intervene and stop him, because he was becoming frail and not as mentally sharp. Many customers were taking advantage of his weakened state, cheating him.
>
> (p. 322)

I conclude from these passages that Scott King's secure attachment relationships to her parents cultivated empathic responses toward her parents, especially later in their lives when they were particularly vulnerable.

Scott King (2017) also demonstrates profound empathy for her husband's suffering, particularly on the many occasions when he was sentenced to prison: "I vicariously felt the weight of prison doors slamming behind me, too ... I understood what it meant to feel helpless and hopeful at the same time" (p. 74). Interestingly, she suggests that her faith helped her to express empathy for others. Following her husband's assassination, "just thinking about the parallels in his life with that of Jesus gave me some consolation, which I sorely needed" (pp. 162–163), she writes. Prayer was key to her experience of empathy: "Whenever my life was guided by prayer, I felt good about what I was doing, and I was able to reach out to other people with love and understanding" (p. 185). Scott King expresses empathy both to those who loved her and to those who hated her (see p. 19), no doubt a by-product of her secure attachment relationships to her parents and to God.

Regarding Scott King's empathy in her attachment relationship to God, early in her life, she describes expecting an unempathic response from God: "I was afraid of committing sins that would condemn me to burn in hell instead of joining God in that mysterious heaven hidden beyond the clouds" (Scott King, 2017, p. 17). Later, however, after joining the church, she directs the choir in the words of a hymn: "Yes, my Jesus cares" (p. 18). Notably, throughout her life, Scott King actualizes her empathic response to God by nurturing a oneness with God that perhaps transcends empathy. Four examples will suffice. Speaking in public for the first time, she observes that she "knew God was with me, because when I rose to speak, I felt the most powerful sense of His presence" (p. 86). During her husband's historic incarceration in Birmingham jail (1963), she recalls that:

> [she] knew that Martin's and my suffering would not be in vain ... It was not happenstance, but meaningful suffering to help people, both black and white, reach a higher purpose. Jesus had been crucified, but in the end He triumphed. I encouraged myself to hold onto my faith that what I was going through was meaningful, too.
>
> (p. 107)

Near the end of his life, as her husband prepared her for what would be his early and violent death, she writes of knowing that "Christians are often called by God to participate not only in the victory of a risen Christ, but in His agony and His suffering" (p. 154). Finally, describing feelings of collaboration with God, she writes that she "felt we were coworkers with God in His creative activity" (p. 182). Thus, on this interpersonal marker, Scott King demonstrates a secure attachment relationship to God. We observe a correspondence between her empathy for her parents and for all people and her empathic responses of oneness with her Higher Power.

Conclusion

In this chapter, I have analyzed the autobiographical narrative of Scott King (2017), using the nine interpersonal markers of attachment of Daniel (2015) to determine: (1) the quality of her attachment relationships to her parents and to God and (2) whether these two sets of attachment relationships (to parents and to God) support the correspondence hypothesis or the compensation hypothesis discussed in Chapter 3 of Goodman (2025). Based on a general reading of the narrative, I conclude that Scott King developed a primary attachment strategy of security in her attachment relationships to her parents and to God as well as a secondary attachment strategy of anxious-avoidance in her attachment relationships to her parents but not to God. Thus, generally speaking, and with only minor compensatory features, Scott King's narrative supports the correspondence hypothesis.

Examining Scott King's narrative more granularly, I then searched for key quotations that would support either a secure or anxious-avoidant attachment relationship to her parents and to God on each of the nine interpersonal markers of attachment of Daniel (2015), paying close attention to whether these two sets of attachment relationships corresponded to each other (i.e., secure/secure vs. anxious-avoidant/secure). A review of the analysis of each of these markers suggests that a correspondence in her secure attachment relationships to her parents and to God was evident on seven of the nine interpersonal markers. Only Openness and Self-disclosure and Dependence/Independence support the compensation hypothesis: Scott King was generally not open or self-disclosing to her parents or to most others, but she was open and self-disclosing to God. Similarly, she was independent from her parents and from most others but dependent on God while expressing her autonomy. Given all the evidence, I conclude that Scott King's autobiographical narrative supports the correspondence hypothesis; however, on two interpersonal markers, it appears that her secure attachment relationship to God compensated for the anxious-avoidant dimension of her attachment relationship to her parents.

Brief Treatment Plan for Scott King

Based on the preceding narrative analysis, how might I treat Scott King if she were to schedule a session of psychotherapy with me? Because I have read her autobiographical narrative prior to the first session, I have already formulated the hypothesis that she has a secure attachment relationship to her parents and to God. Thus, I do not anticipate a long-term treatment because I will not be working with her to change the quality of her attachment pattern from insecure to secure (see Goodman, 2025, Chapter 5). Instead, I foresee helping her to adjust to her current situation—as a grieving widow who is raising four children on her own. To what would I be helping her to adjust? Her husband eloquently wrote, "There are some things in our society, some things in our world, to which we should never be adjusted. There are some things concerning which we must always be maladjusted if we are to be people of good will" (King, 1967, p. 4). Could I help her to mourn the loss of her husband without trying to pathologize her anger toward the man—the government—who perpetrated this atrocity?

In the first phase of treatment, I would try to gain Scott King's trust. As a white man—someone from the same race and gender as the man who assassinated her husband and harassed her family as a child—how would I develop a therapeutic alliance (Wampold, 2001) with her? I already know that she has "never warmed up to people quickly" (Scott King, 2017, p. 12). Thus, I would be most careful in giving her all the time she needed to become comfortable with me. I would provide large doses of unconditional positive regard, empathy, and genuineness (Rogers, 1957), not only because of her personality disposition but also because of the cultural transference (La Roche, 1999) that she might bring with her, given her traumatic experiences with racism recounted in grim detail in her narrative (Scott King, 2017). I would also need to be aware of my own cultural countertransference as a white member of the dominant culture. Providing a safe haven and a secure base (see Goodman, 2025, Chapter 2) for Scott King to open up about her suffering and pain would go a long way toward facilitating her grieving process. I would also listen for and accept unconditionally any subtle indications of anger toward God, which were absent in the narrative. Perhaps she would be wondering: why would God take my husband away from me in the prime of our lives, and leave me to raise our four young children alone? This question obviously has no generic answer. Just sitting with her in her anguish might be sufficient to help her to move through the nonlinear stages of grief (Kübler-Ross, 1969).

In the second phase of treatment, given my knowledge of Scott King's secondary attachment strategy of anxious-avoidance, I would behave in a more animated, hyperactivating manner to provide her with a "gentle challenge" (Dozier, 2003, p. 254) to this strategy and thus gradually move her in the direction of greater attachment security. For example, I might highlight her rugged independence and ask her how it serves her now. I would look for the appropriate timing to interpret for her that she uses this "primary mode of relatedness" (Slade, 1999, p. 588) to protect herself from the pain of rejection that she fears she would experience if she were to rely on someone close to her for comfort and security. She alluded to this pain when, in a unique passage in her narrative, she complained that church members were not emotionally available to her during her mother's final days: "I could have been comforted even more by visits from my pastors and members of my church family, but it just didn't happen. This was a very lonely and extremely difficult time for me" (Scott King, 2017, p. 322). I would let this passage serve as a warning to me to be especially attentive and empathic and to engage her promptly in processing any "ruptures" (Safran & Muran, 1996, 2000) that will almost inevitably occur in our therapeutic relationship. In this manner, I would be providing her with an "emotionally corrective experience" (Alexander & French, 1946) in addition to assuring her of my cognitive understanding through the vehicle of interpretation. Given her secure attachment relationship to God, I am confident that she will continue to rely on her spiritual coping strategies (Pargament, 2011)—prayer, meditation, church attendance, community service—to provide her with the spiritual resilience to flourish in the wake of this horrendous tragedy. I recall Romans 8:28 (NIV, 1978), a Bible verse Scott King was fond of quoting: "All things work for the good of them that love the Lord" (p. 117).

References

Alexander, F., & French, T. M. (1946). *Psychoanalytic therapy: Principles and application.* Ronald.

Daniel, S. I. F. (2015). *Adult attachment patterns in a treatment context: Relationship and narrative.* Routledge.

Dozier, M. (2003). Attachment-based treatment for vulnerable children. *Attachment and Human Development, 5,* 253–257.

Freud, S. (1900). The interpretation of dreams. In J. Strachey (Ed. and Trans.), *The standard edition of the complete psychological works of Sigmund Freud* (Vols. 4–5, pp. 1–625). Hogarth Press.

George, C., Kaplan, N., & Main, M. (1985). Adult attachment interview. Unpublished manuscript. University of California.

Gilmore, K. J., & Meersand, P. (2014). *Normal child and adolescent development: A psychodynamic primer.* American Psychiatric Publishing.

Goodman, G. (2025). *Using psychoanalytic techniques to transform the attachment relationship to God: Our refuge and strength.* Routledge.

Granqvist, P., & Kirkpatrick, L. A. (2018). Attachment and religious representations and behavior. In J. Cassidy & P. R. Shaver (Eds.), *Handbook of attachment: Theory, research, and clinical applications* (pp. 917–940). Guilford Press.

King, M. L., Jr. (1967). The role of the behavioral scientist in the Civil Rights Movement. Invited Distinguished Address presented at the meeting of the American Psychological Association, Washington, DC. September 1.

Kübler-Ross, E. (1969). *On death and dying: What the dying have to teach doctors, nurses, clergy and their own families.* Scribner.

La Roche, M. J. (1999). Culture, transference, and countertransference among Latinos. *Psychotherapy: Theory, Research, Practice, Training, 36,* 389–397.

NIV (New International Version). (1978). *The holy Bible.* Zondervan.

Pargament, K. I. (2011). *Spiritually integrated psychotherapy: Understanding and addressing the sacred.* Guilford Press.

Rogers, C. R. (1957). The necessary and sufficient conditions of therapeutic personality change. *Journal of Consulting Psychology, 21,* 95–103.

Safran, J. D., & Muran, J. C. (1996). The resolution of ruptures in the therapeutic alliance. *Journal of Consulting and Clinical Psychology, 64,* 447–458.

Safran, J. D., & Muran, J. C. (2000). Resolving therapeutic alliance ruptures: Diversity and integration. *Journal of Clinical Psychology, 56,* 233–243.

Scott King, C. (1969). *My life with Martin Luther King, Jr.* Heny Holt and Company.

Scott King, C. (2017). *My life, my love, my legacy.* Henry Holt and Company.

Slade, A. (1999). Attachment theory and research: Implications for the theory and practice of individual psychotherapy with adults. In J. Cassidy & P. R. Shaver (Eds.), *Handbook of attachment: Theory, research, and clinical applications* (pp. 575–594). Guilford Press.

Wampold, B. E. (2001). *The great psychotherapy debate: Models, methods, and findings.* Erlbaum.

Westen, D., Nakash, O., Thomas, C., & Bradley, R. (2006). Clinical assessment of attachment patterns and personality disorder in adolescents and adults. *Journal of Consulting and Clinical Psychology, 74,* 1065–1085.

Chapter 3

Anne Frank

Anxious-Resistant Attachment— Higher Power as Compensation

Of all the autobiographical accounts of the four public figures whom I have analyzed for this book, none captivated me more than the writing of Anne Frank. A teenager writing in captivity during the occupation of the Netherlands during World War II, Frank is at various turns spunky, emotionally intense, keenly perceptive, wickedly sarcastic, both deeply pessimistic and optimistic, rageful, sweet, and passionate as well as compassionate. Frank strikes me as a cherished bundle of contradictions that cohabitate uneasily in her heart and soul. Her ruthless honesty in the face of adversity, and her ability to experience God in nature and even in the Holocaust, have inspired millions of people from all over the world to read her innermost thoughts and feelings contained in her diary (*The Diary of a Young Girl*; Frank, 2022) and in her semi-autobiographical short stories and unfinished novel (*Anne Frank's Tales from the Secret Annex*; Frank, 2003).

Anne Frank was born in Berlin on June 12, 1929. Of her brief 15 years of life, Frank spent two of them hiding from the Nazis and another six months in Bergen-Belsen concentration camp in northern Germany before she died of a typhus outbreak at the camp, probably in late February, 1945, only a month and a half prior to its liberation (Frank, 2022). Frank wrote both autobiographical narratives almost exclusively in hiding. She started writing in her diary on her thirteenth birthday, on June 12, 1942, and within one month, she and her father, mother, and older sister Margot went into hiding. Thus, Frank provides a brief sketch of her life prior to the family's move into what she calls the secret annex, a series of floors and rooms adjacent to her father Otto's pectin factory warehouse in Prinsengracht, Amsterdam. A custom-built bookcase guarded the entrance to this secret annex. Aside from the eight occupants of the secret annex—Anne Frank, her mother, father, and Margot; the van Daans (mother, father, and son Peter, two years older than Frank); and Dr. Dussel (a dentist)—a handful of non-Jews associated with Otto's business had access to this residence, supplying these Dutch Jews with provisions such as food and toiletries. This arrangement lasted almost 25 months, when, on August 4, 1944, a Nazi officer and three Dutch collaborators discovered the secret annex behind the bookcase, arrested all eight Jews living inside, and shipped them off to various concentration camps, where they all died—except for Anne Frank's father Otto, who survived the Auschwitz-Birkenau concentration camp when it was liberated on January 27, 1945. After the war, Otto was instrumental in retrieving Frank's diary from two of his business assistants and assembling its various entries into a coherent whole.

Based on the summation of Anne Frank's writings, which include extensive discussions of her relationships to her parents and to God, I conclude that Anne Frank had a complicated history of attachment relationships. Unlike the other three public figures I discuss in this book, I argue that Frank developed two qualitatively different attachment relationships to her parents. Her attachment relationship to her father was secure with anxious-resistant features, while her attachment relationship to her mother was anxious-resistant. Sometime during childhood, specific attachment relationships to multiple caregivers are composited into an internal working model, which serves as a template for predicting another person's ability to provide security and protection (Daniel, 2015). When a person develops two qualitatively different attachment relationships, as in the case of Anne Frank, the quality of the attachment relationship to the primary caregiver seems to dominate the quality of the internal working model, which is used to evaluate felt security generally. Thus, I demonstrate that Frank used a secure attachment relationship to God to compensate for her anxious-resistant attachment relationship to her mother. This secure attachment relationship to God, however, corresponds to her generally secure attachment relationship to her father (her presumed secondary attachment figure) and to a lesser extent, her maternal grandmother (her presumed tertiary attachment figure), who died just six months before Frank and her family went into hiding. Thus, Anne Frank's autobiographical material indicates both compensatory and corresponding features in her attachment relationship to God.

Although Frank uses God to compensate for her anxious-resistant attachment relationship to her mother, we do not observe a sudden spiritual awakening as in the case of Bill W. (see Chapter 4). Instead, Frank's spiritual awakening appears to take place gradually over the course of her two years in hiding. Perhaps in this sense, the correspondence pathway (see Goodman, 2025, Chapter 3) provides a "gentle take-off" for Frank's spiritual conversion, which is nevertheless stimulated by using her attachment relationship to God to compensate for her woefully inadequate attachment relationship to her mother. Over time, God becomes a surrogate attachment figure who provides comfort, security, and protection—vital states of mind that her mother cannot provide.

Although born in Berlin, Frank moved to Amsterdam at age 4 to escape Nazi persecution in 1933 Nazi Germany. Hitler had just come to power on January 30, and Otto wisely anticipated what was to become of German Jews (Frank, 2022). So as not to arouse suspicion, only Otto moved to Amsterdam in July of that year, followed by Frank's mother Edith, who joined her husband in September. Frank's sister Margot joined her parents in Amsterdam in December. Frank stayed behind with her beloved maternal grandmother, later joining the family in February, 1934 (Anne Frank House, n.d.). Thus, Frank was separated from her father, her secondary attachment figure, for seven months and her mother, her primary attachment figure, for five months. Given the fact that Frank was only 4 years old, these are not insignificant separations. Could these extended separations from her two most important attachment figures have caused her feelings of alienation from both her parents, but especially her mother? Frank (2022) writes: "I've hid anything having to do with me from Father, never shared my ideals with him, and deliberately alienated myself from him" (p. 342). Regarding her mother, Frank (2022) is even more blunt: "She's not a mother to me—I have to mother myself ... [I] can't seem to find anything of the sort in the woman I'm supposed to call 'Mother'" (p. 70). To underscore this alienation, Frank (2022) later writes: "Despite all my theories and efforts, I miss—every day and every hour of the day—having a mother who understands me" (p. 163). I argue that this feeling of alienation might have originated in the days, weeks, and months of anguish and longing for her mother and father during this months-long separation when Frank was only 4 years old.

Now supposedly safe from the Nazis in the Netherlands, the Franks lived for nine years in a middle-class Jewish neighborhood of Merwedeplein in Amsterdam (Frank, 2022). Frank attended a Montessori elementary school and later, the Jewish Lyceum, beginning at age 12. Frank was almost 11 years old when the Nazis invaded and occupied the Netherlands in May, 1940. Frank describes how she and all Jews in Amsterdam had to wear a yellow star whenever they went outside two years later, when Frank was almost 13. By this time, concentration camps were dotting the European landscape, and Otto knew that he and his family had to flee the country or go into hiding. In July, 1942, Frank's older sister Margot received a summons to report for work at a concentration camp, and on July 6, Otto moved the family into the secret annex adjacent to his pectin factory warehouse, along with another family, the van Daans. Dr. Dussel, a Jewish dentist, joined these two families in hiding four months later on November 17. These eight persons would comprise the characters in Frank's diary entries for the next two years.

Frank (2022) received her beloved diary as a thirteenth birthday present on June 12, 1942, almost four weeks before she and her family went into hiding. She anthropomorphized her diary, calling it "Kitty," and writes to it as if writing to a confidante. It was not until almost two years later, on March 28, 1944, that Frank learned through a radio broadcast from London that the Dutch government was interested in publishing first-person accounts such as diaries describing experiences of the Nazi occupation (Conrad, 2022). Frank welcomes this opportunity in her March 29 diary entry, seeking to revise her diary entries as a novel titled, *The Secret Annex*. Frank's original diary entries as well as her revisions for this novel resulted in versions A and B of Frank's diary, both later composited and published as *The Definitive Edition*. As the journalist Conrad (2022) notes, numerous critics have questioned the authenticity of *Diary of a Young Girl* "based on antisemitism, Holocaust denial and disbelief that a young person could write in a sophisticated manner." In 1980, the Netherlands Institute for War Documentation undertook an extensive handwriting analysis of the original diary entries and verified its authenticity. I believe that if Anne Frank had lived, she would have become one of the greatest post-war writers of her generation. Some might argue that with the publication of her diary and short stories, she already occupies this position. For example, the Boston Public Library ranks *Diary of a Young Girl* second (trailing only George Orwell's *1984* [Orwell, 1949]) on their list of the 100 most influential books of the twentieth century (Boston Public Library, January 28, 2013).

Anne Frank's Attachment Relationships to Her Parents

Anne Frank discusses her relationships to her parents extensively in her diary entries (Frank, 2022) and more obliquely in her short stories (Frank, 2003). Early on, Frank alerts the reader to conflicts in her relationship to her mother. Just a month after receiving her diary and less than a week after she went into hiding, Frank (2022) complains that "I feel myself drifting further away from Mother and Margot. I worked hard today and they praised me, only to start picking on me again five minutes later" (p. 35). Two months later, Frank writes of their relationship:

> I simply can't stand Mother, and I have to force myself not to snap at her all the time, and to stay calm, when I'd rather slap her across the face. I don't know why I've taken such a terrible dislike to her.
>
> (p. 58)

Once established, this "terrible dislike" emerges as one of the pervasive themes of Frank's diary. She is unrelenting in expressing her anger toward her mother. At rare moments, however, Frank does express a feeling of being understood: "Mother understood my anxiety and went with me" (p. 33). At this juncture, it is instructive to recall that caregivers of infants classified as anxious-resistant provide inconsistent, erratic care—sometimes they provide comfort when needed, while at other times, they are physically or emotionally unavailable when needed. Through Frank's eyes, we get a glimpse of a mother who can be understanding and praising at times and criticizing at other times. I argue that it is precisely this caregiving inconsistency that accounts for Frank's anxious-resistant attachment relationship to her mother.

Furthermore, Frank (2022) does not perceive her mother as able to provide a safe haven in hiding. In fact, Frank perceives her mother as just as much in need of a safe haven as she does: "We, by whom I mean the ladies—were also scared out of our wits. Brrr, I hate the sound of gunfire" (p. 243). Later, as the warehouse is being burglarized, Frank refers to the females living in the secret annex: "Four frightened women need to talk, so that's what we did until we heard a bang downstairs … We were too scared to think; all we could do was to wait" (p. 264). Obviously, Frank does not perceive her mother as a safe haven when her attachment system is activated. Frank does not view her mother as "stronger and wiser" (Bowlby, 1988, p. 120) to comfort her during stressful times; instead, her mother needs comforting herself.

By contrast, Frank's attachment relationship to her father seems generally secure. Perhaps the most compelling evidence in favor of this assessment comes when Frank's attachment system is clearly activated—when bombs are dropping outside the secret annex in the middle of the night. Frank shares a bedroom with Dr. Dussel, whom Frank portrays most unsympathetically. She therefore seeks comfort where she knows she can receive it:

> The planes dived and climbed, the air was abuzz with the drone of engines. It was very scary, and the whole time I kept thinking, "Here it comes, this is it." I can assure you that when I went to bed at nine, my legs were still shaking ... I stayed in Father's bed until one, in my own bed until one-thirty, and was back in Father's bed at two. But the planes kept on coming.
>
> (Frank, 2022, p. 126)

Frank sought refuge in her father's bed. Proximity-seeking when the attachment system is activated is a hallmark of a secure attachment relationship.

A traditional psychoanalyst might be tempted to interpret Frank's love for her father and hatred of her mother as the enactment of an unresolved Oedipus complex (Freud, 1900) from the preschool years. This theory would predict that Frank perceives her mother as a sexual rival for her father's love and attention. There is limited evidence for this view. Instead, Frank's older sister Margot seems to be the rival:

> I don't give a darn about [Mother and Margot] as people. As far as I'm concerned, they can go jump in a lake. It's different with Father. When I see him being partial to Margot, approving Margot's every action, praising her, hugging her, I feel a gnawing ache inside, because I'm crazy about him. I model myself after Father, and there's no one in the world I love more ... I long for something from Father that he's incapable of giving.
>
> (Frank, 2022, p. 69)

This passage seems to support the view that Frank perceives her father as the object of sexual love; however, as we have seen, she relies on him as a secure attachment figure and later develops unmistakable romantic and sexual feelings for Peter, the van Daans' son. A more likely scenario is that Frank turns to her father as a secure attachment figure when she realizes that her mother cannot provide her with the attachment security she needs. Frank herself provides some evidence for this point of view: "I cling to Father because my contempt of Mother is growing daily and it's only through him that I'm able to retain the last ounce of family feeling I have left" (p. 69). Thus, Frank turns to her father for attachment security because of her mother's pathetic inadequacy to provide this crucial feeling of attachment security for her.

At times, Frank (2022) recognizes the inadequacies of both her parents but questions whether it is only her perceptions of her parents that prevent her from feeling content: "The worst part is that Father and Mother don't realize their own inadequacies and how much I blame them for letting me down. Are there any parents who can make their children completely happy?" (p. 70). The preponderance of the evidence, however, suggests that Frank experiences her father as a safe haven and secure base—features of a secure attachment relationship—while she experiences her mother as inconsistent and unpredictable—features of an anxious-resistant attachment relationship.

Anne Frank's Secure Attachment Relationship to God

In this section, I argue that Anne Frank's narratives (Frank, 2003, 2022) illustrate the compensation hypothesis in the religion-as-attachment model (e.g., Granqvist & Kirkpatrick, 2018) because her secure attachment relationship to God compensated for her anxious-resistant attachment relationship to her mother. On the other hand, Frank's secure attachment relationship to God corresponds to her secure attachment relationship to her father, thus illustrating the correspondence hypothesis. Because Frank's generalized internal working model of attachment relationships seems to reflect an anxious-resistant approach to interpersonal interactions, her secure attachment relationship to God seems to be more compensatory than corresponding. Typically, persons who develop a secure attachment relationship to God through a compensation pathway (see, e.g., Bill W., Chapter 4) have developed anxious-avoidant attachment relationships to their parents and embrace atheism, only to discover God later in life during a major life crisis (see also Granqvist, 2020; Kirkpatrick, 2005). Frank, however, seems always to have believed in God, but during her experience in hiding, she deliberately begins to depend on God for protection and comfort. Frank's relationship to God is no longer perfunctory. In an early diary entry (October 29, 1942), Frank (2022) narrates an experience with her mother that depicts her apathetic communication with God at this point in her life:

> Mother pressed her prayer book into my hands. I read a few prayers in German, just to be polite. They certainly sound beautiful, but they mean very little to me. Why is she making me act so religious and devout?
>
> (p. 66)

Given the fact that it is Frank's mother foisting religion onto her, we are not surprised by Frank's reaction. The unconscious line of thinking might go something like this: "I am in conflict with my mother, and my mother is religious; therefore, in contrast to my mother, I will not be religious."

Unlike Bill W.'s compensatory pathway to a secure attachment relationship to God, Anne Frank gradually, during her two years in hiding, drew closer to a Higher Power and came to rely on this Higher Power. Frank builds this divine attachment relationship upon the foundation of her already secure attachment relationship to her father but also uses it to compensate for her anxious-resistant attachment relationship to her mother. Consider her diary entries as well as her short stories during her time in hiding. In a later diary entry (April 5, 1944), Frank (2022) considers a writing career after the war:

I want to go on living even after my death! And that's why I'm so grateful to God for having given me this gift, which I can use to develop myself and to express all that's inside me! When I write I can shake off all my cares. My sorrow disappears, my spirits are revived!

(p. 261)

Frank is crediting God with comforting her through the gift of writing. She expresses gratitude to God for having bequeathed to her the powerful gift of writing. Her attachment relationship to God certainly matured in the year and a half since she rebuffed her mother's attempted religious influence.

In an extraordinary passage from her unfinished novel, *Cady's Life* (Frank, 2003), Frank discusses through the protagonist Cady the moment that she went from perfunctorily communicating with God to meaningfully communicating with God. Cady is discussing her new feelings about God with her same-age friend Hans:

One of the first nights I was here, I got halfway through my prayers and realized that my mind was on very different matters. So I did something I'd never done before. I started thinking about the underlying meaning of the words and discovered that there's much more to this supposedly simple child's prayer than I ever suspected. Since that night, I've been saying other prayers, things that I myself thought were beautiful, not just a standard prayer. But a few weeks ago, I was halfway through my prayers again when a thought struck me like a bolt of lightning: "Why should God help me now, in my hour of need, when I all but ignored Him in better days?" This question kept haunting me, because I knew that it would only be fair if God were to ignore my prayers in return.

(p. 164)

Frank is struggling with the similarities and differences between her attachment relationship to her mother and her attachment relationship to God. In *Cady's Life*, Cady's mother visits Cady in a sanatorium (Cady is recuperating from a serious car accident) for only 15 minutes at a time, and only when Cady is asleep (p. 168). When Cady is awake for her mother's visit, the conversation is dull and perfunctory, just like her prayers to God. But Cady realizes in the passage above that she can cultivate a different relationship to God than the one she has to her mother.

Nevertheless, Cady wonders whether God will vindictively ignore her communications to Him for having ignored Him in the past. Frank (2003) resolves this issue for herself in Hans's reply:

When you were at home, leading your carefree life, you weren't reciting meaningless words on purpose, you just hadn't given God a lot of thought. Now that you're turning to Him because you're frightened and hurt, now that you're really trying to be the person you think you ought to be, surely God won't let you down. Have faith in Him, Cady. He has helped so many others!

(p. 164)

Frank now views God explicitly as an attachment figure to whom she is turning for explicitly attachment-activating reasons—"because you're frightened and hurt." Frank also mentions feeling alone as a third attachment-activating reason for turning to God as an attachment figure:

> I took God for granted. I mean, I never thought about Him, because all my wants and needs were taken care of. Now that I've had this accident and I'm often alone, I've had more than enough time to ponder all kinds of things.
>
> (p. 164)

She cannot turn to her mother for protection and comfort, but she can turn to God as compensation for her mother's inadequacy as an attachment figure.

Though having always believed in God and ritualistically prayed to God "like brushing my teeth" (Frank, 2003, p. 164), Anne Frank nevertheless describes a subtle spiritual awakening intertwined with the beauty of nature. During her two years in hiding, Frank arrives at her own image of God, with her own unique mode of relating to Him. Once again, she lets Hans in *Cady's Life* show the reader how she defines God for herself, independent of her parents' or Judaism's views of God:

> If you're asking what God is, my answer would be: Take a look around you, at the flowers, the trees, the animals, the people, and then you'll know what God is. Those wondrous things that live and die and reproduce themselves, all that we refer to as nature—that's God. He made them all just the way they are, and that's the only image of Him you need.
>
> (p. 164)

Frank suggests paradoxically that all living things comprise God, yet God created all living things. She seems content to live in this paradox.

Frank (2003) also draws the independent conclusion that although transcendent in nature, God is simultaneously immanent in her life—that He lives inside her. Cady writes in her diary:

> I believe that God speaks "through me" because He gives each person a little bit of Himself before sending them into the world ... This little bit of God is just as much a part of nature as the blossoming of flowers and the singing of birds.
>
> (p. 166)

Although there is no evidence that Frank ever read *Nature* by Ralph Waldo Emerson (1836) or *Walden* by Henry David Thoreau (1854), she would have been completely at home with the Transcendentalist movement, locating God in nature and believing that humanity is essentially good because God is good, and God resides in humanity. From an attachment perspective, it is noteworthy that Frank's God resides inside her because of her strong need for closeness to an attachment figure who will take care of her and not disappoint her like her mother. If God lives inside her, then there can be no separation anxiety to manage, no inconsistent caregiver availability to monitor. The immanent presence of God would be especially attractive to someone who has developed an anxious-resistant attachment relationship to an inconsistent, chronically disappointing primary caregiver.

Markers of an Anxious-Resistant Attachment Relationship

Daniel (2015) identifies two sets of markers that indicate an anxious-resistant attachment relationship: interpersonal and narrative markers. We know that Anne Frank (2022) edited her own diary entries in the hope that her diary would someday be published (Conrad, 2022); thus, her writing does not possess the spontaneity of an Adult Attachment Interview, which is designed to "surprise the unconscious" (George et al., 1985, p. 6) and yield a valid attachment classification. Thus, I will focus only on the interpersonal markers, which Daniel (2015) notes "are systematically and meaningfully connected in treatment providers' assessment of clients" (p. 113). I later use this information to formulate a brief treatment plan for Frank as if she had been referred to me for treatment. This treatment plan would guide me to implement the most effective set of intervention strategies for Frank.

I analyze the interpersonal markers of Anne Frank's attachment relationships to her mother and father and to God. Although Frank (2022) mentions her secure attachment relationship to her maternal grandmother, who took care of Frank for five months before she joined her parents in the Netherlands and who died six months before Frank went into hiding, I will not linger on this relationship because Frank infrequently mentions her and because this person is no longer physically available to serve as a safe haven or secure base. Frank does write that her beloved grandmother appears to her in a dream near the second anniversary of her grandmother's death and uses this dream as an opportunity to describe her grandmother in some depth. Later in her diary, "Grandma" appears to Frank as a "guardian angel" (p. 173) and even appears "in that [Shabbat] candle, and it's Grandma who watches over and protects me and makes me feel happy again" (p. 214). Thus, the memory of Frank's grandmother does provide her with attachment security at certain moments of her life.

I also do not routinely analyze these interpersonal markers in relation to Peter, her romantic interest. According to Kirkpatrick (2005) and other attachment researchers, the motivational system associated with pair bonding differs in important ways from the attachment system; for example, it includes a sexual component. Nevertheless, these two motivational systems are related to each other, and I sometimes demonstrate how Frank displays an anxious-resistant internal working model (see Goodman, 2025, Chapter 2) in her interactions with Peter in the secret annex.

Anne Frank's Attachment Relationships to Her Parents and to God

I present Table 3.1, which summarizes my findings of my analysis of the nine interpersonal markers of the attachment relationship by Daniel (2015). In the first column, I list these nine markers. In the second column, I include a key phrase from Daniel (2015) that most closely represents the specific attachment pattern suggested by the quotation. In the third column, I include a key quotation from Anne Frank's diary (Frank, 2022) or works of fiction (Frank, 2003) that supports each of the nine interpersonal markers related to her attachment relationships to her parents. Despite the stark difference in attachment quality in her relationships to her parents, I include mostly key quotations from her mother, whom I assume is Frank's primary caregiver. In the fourth column, I include a key phrase from Daniel (2015) that most closely represents the specific attachment pattern suggested by the quotation. Finally, in the fifth column, I include a key quotation that supports each of these markers related to her attachment relationship to God.

Proximity/Distance

Speculative though my analysis might be, the text provides ample evidence of this interpersonal marker to support my conjecture that Anne Frank developed an anxious-resistant attachment relationship to her mother, a secure attachment relationship to her father, and a secure attachment relationship to God. According to Daniel (2015), anxious-resistant persons "strive for proximity, but are not comfortable when it is achieved[, showing a] tendency to interpersonal 'fusion', [whereas secure persons] value and are comfortable with proximity" (p. 115). What follows are select key quotations that address the Proximity/Distance marker.

Despite living in such close quarters, Frank's physical proximity to her mother is not sufficient; she seems to be looking for interpersonal fusion with her mother: "At moments like these I can't stand Mother. It's obvious that I'm a stranger to her; she doesn't even know what I think about the most ordinary things" (Frank, 2022, p. 48). When Frank's mother tries to get emotionally close, however, Frank pushes her away:

> Mother came into the room, sat on my bed and asked very gently, "Anne, Daddy isn't ready. How about if I listen to your prayers tonight?" "No, Momsy," I replied. Mother got up, stood beside my bed for a moment and then slowly walked toward the door. Suddenly she turned; her face contorted with pain, and said, "I don't want to be angry with you. I can't make you love me!" A few tears slid down her cheeks as she went out the door. I lay still, thinking how mean it was of me to reject her so cruelly, but I also knew that I was incapable of answering her any other way. I can't be a hypocrite and pray with her when I don't feel like it. It just doesn't work that way.
>
> (p. 107)

Table 3.1 Nine interpersonal markers of attachment for Anne Frank

Interpersonal markers	Primary marker with parents	Key quotation/parents	Primary marker with God	Key quotation/God
Proximity/distance	Strive for proximity, but … not comfortable when it is achieved … Interpersonal fusion	"She doesn't even know what I think about the most ordinary things"	Values/is comfortable with proximity	"God is much closer than most people think"
Trust/expectation of others	Fear being abandoned or losing attention—expect the worst	"I only wish I could … receive encouragement from someone who loves me"	Trusting/positive expectations	"God has not forsaken me, and He never will"
Attitude to seeking and receiving help	Strong desire for help or support	"Everyone—and that includes you—closed their eyes and ears and didn't help me"	Open to seeking help	"Where can I find help? I simply have to go on living and praying to God"
Expression and regulation of emotions	Frequent and dramatic expressions, focus on and intensify negative emotions	"I'd rather slap [Mother] across the face"	Balanced expressions of positive and negative emotions	"A person who has courage and faith will never die in misery!"
Self-image/self-esteem	Low self-esteem with a strong need for interpersonal validation	"I know I'm far from being what I should; will I ever be?"	Nuanced self-image/solid self-esteem	"[God] gives each person a bit of Himself before sending them into the world"
Openness and self-disclosure	Reticent about sharing thoughts and feelings	"I've hid anything having to do with me from Father"	Pleased to share thoughts and feelings, dosed according to situation	"I'm so grateful to God for having given me this gift [her writing talent]"

(Continued)

Table 3.1 (Continued)

Interpersonal markers	Primary marker with parents	Key quotation/parents	Primary marker with God	Key quotation/God
Dependence/ independence	Feel dependent on others—seek out relationships	"I crawl into Father's bed nearly every night for comfort"	Feels comfortable in committed relationships, capable of autonomy	"I knew I couldn't count on others for support…I looked up … and trusted in God"
Conflict management	Great attention to conflicts, may be inclined to escalate these	"If only I weren't so involved in all these skirmishes!"	Constructive strategies for handling conflicts	"I slid to the floor … and began by saying my prayers, very fervently"
Empathy	Empathy with and care for others	"She didn't understand me, but I didn't understand her either"	Empathy with and care for others	"God … gives each person a little bit of Himself"

Source: Modeled after Daniel (2015, p. 115).

In fact, the overall impression Frank (2022) leaves us with in her diary is that she is preoccupied with her mother—her mother's interactions with sister Margot (p. 35), her mother's moods (p. 208), and even her mother's facial expressions (p. 107). Preoccupation with the caregiver is the signature feature of someone classified as anxious-resistant (see Goodman, 2025, Chapter 2).

By contrast, Frank (2022) seeks her father's proximity when her attachment system is activated: "I still haven't gotten over my fear of planes and shooting, and I crawl into Father's bed nearly every night for comfort" (p. 97). Frank also experiences a conflict with her roommate, Dr. Dussel, which she discusses with her father. She decides to confront Dr. Dussel and notes that her father "was sitting next door and that had a calming effect" (p. 120). Even this generally secure attachment relationship, however, leaves Frank sometimes wanting more: "I long for more than Father's affection, more than his hugs and kisses. Isn't it awful of me to be so preoccupied with myself?" (pp. 179–180).

Despite her generally secure attachment relationship to her father, there is evidence that Frank's generalized internal working model of her attachment relationships is anxious-resistant. For example, Frank (2022) writes of her nights in bed, "I see myself alone in a dungeon, without Father and Mother" (p. 153). Even more poignantly, she describes

> the feeling that I didn't belong to Momsy, Pim [term of endearment for her father] and Margot and that I would always be an outsider. I sometimes went around for six months at a time pretending I was an orphan.
>
> (p. 177)

Here, Frank identifies a pervasive feeling of alienation from her family that supports her "tendency to interpersonal 'fusion'" (Daniel, 2015, p. 115)—or at least her tendency to *desire* an interpersonal fusion that is impossible to achieve.

Even Frank's burgeoning romantic relationship with Peter, the van Daans' son, contains anxious-resistant features. She writes: "Oh, if only I could rest my head on his shoulder and not feel so hopelessly alone and deserted!" (Frank, 2022, p. 204). But when she finally receives the physical affection from Peter that she desires, she complains that "I don't think lying in each other's arms day in and day out is very satisfying, and I hope he feels the same" (p. 280). Because Peter is not seeking interpersonal fusion like Frank, she ultimately becomes disappointed in him:

> We talked about the most private things, but we haven't yet touched upon the things closest to my heart … I never broach the subjects I long to bring out into the open … I soon realized he could never be a kindred spirit.
>
> (p. 343)

In her unfinished novel, *Cady's Life*, however, Frank (2003) fulfills this fantasy of interpersonal fusion with Hans:

> "And now that we've discussed God, Cady, we've actually shared quite a few of our innermost thoughts. Give me your hand and let this be a sign that we'll always trust one another, and that if either of us should ever have any problems and want to talk about them, we'll know where to go!" Cady promptly held out her hand, and so they sat, hand in hand, for a long time, while a delightful calm came over both of them.
>
> (pp. 165–166)

The reality of her feelings about Peter, however, are clearly articulated in her diary: "He's disappointed me in many ways. I especially don't care for his dislike of religion" (Frank, 2022, p. 328).

Let us now investigate Anne Frank's attachment relationship to God on this interpersonal marker. In one of her earliest diary entries, prior to moving into the secret annex, Frank (2022) mentions one of her best friends, Hanneli Goslar. Frank does not mention Hanneli for over a year, then one night, she dreams that the Nazis have taken away Hanneli to a concentration camp. In the dream, Hanneli reproaches Frank for not helping her, prompting Frank to pray, "Merciful God, comfort her, so that at least she won't be alone" (p. 159). Frank indicates that God can make Hanneli feel His comforting presence. Frank also associates nature with closeness to God and comfort:

> The best remedy for those who are frightened, lonely or unhappy is to go outside; somewhere they can be alone, alone with the sky, nature and God. For then and only then can you feel that everything is as it should be and that God wants people to be happy amid nature's beauty and simplicity.
>
> (p. 206)

In her short story, "Fear," Frank (2003) expresses similar feelings about God's closeness during turmoil: "Anyone who's as frightened as I was should look to nature and realize that God is much closer than most people think. From that moment on, though countless bombs fell close by, I was never truly afraid again" (p. 116).

Finally, in her short story, "The Fairy," Frank (2003) underscores this point of God's constant presence in her life: "When you're alone with nature, your troubles will seem to melt away, I'm sure they will. You'll become thoughtful and glad and feel as if God hasn't forsaken you after all" (p. 140). Frank's deceased grandmother also becomes a supernatural presence that comforts her. In the short story, "The Guardian Angel," the Grandma reassures her granddaughter:

> I'm in Heaven, watching you from up above. I've become your guardian angel, and I'll always be at your side, just like I used to be. Go back to your work, my darling, and don't ever forget that Grandma is with you!
>
> (p. 108)

What distinguishes Frank's anxious-resistant attachment relationship to her mother from her secure attachment relationship to God (and her supernatural Grandma) is the pervasive feeling of comfort that she experiences when she seeks God's proximity. Thus, in these quotations referencing the interpersonal marker of Proximity/Distance, we observe a compensation between Frank's anxious-resistant attachment relationship to her mother and her secure attachment relationship to God.

Trust/Expectations of Others

This interpersonal marker of the attachment pattern is evident in Anne Frank's descriptions of her attachment relationships to her parents and to God (Frank, 2003, 2022). Based on my earlier analysis, we are looking for anxious-resistant dimensions of her attachment relationship to her mother and secure dimensions of her attachment relationships to her father and to God. Concerning this marker, Daniel (2015) writes that anxious-resistant persons "fear being abandoned or losing attention [and] expect the worst," whereas secure persons "are trusting and have positive expectations" (p. 115). I will now select key quotations that address the marker of Trust/Expectations of Others.

Regarding her attachment relationships to her parents, Frank (2022) implies that her parents are not meeting her expectations for trust: "The whole time I've been here [in the secret annex] I've longed unconsciously and at times consciously for trust, love and physical affection. This longing may change in intensity, but it's always there" (p. 67). In her short story, "Katrien," Frank (2003) writes that Katrien's mother thought that Katrien "was a strange child, and unfortunately Katrien could sense her disapproval. Her father, the farmer, was far too busy to concern himself with his only daughter" (p. 90). Similarly, in her short story, "Happiness," the protagonist laments the fact that

> I no longer have a mother (in fact I never knew her), and my father has little time for me. My mother died when I was two. My father farmed me out to a kindly couple who kept me for five years.
>
> (p. 109)

These fictional passages nevertheless reveal Frank's fear of losing—or having lost—the attention of both her parents. She expects the worst outcomes from both caregivers. In "Happiness," the protagonist loses both parents and lives in a boarding school until her father finally takes her back after five years (p. 109).

Despite the undifferentiated quality of both parental relationships in these short stories (i.e., both parents are disappointing attachment figures), Frank (2022) does differentiate these relationships in her diary. She reveals her enmeshed relationship with her mother in this July 12, 1942, diary entry:

> Every day I feel myself drifting further away from Mother and Margot. I worked hard today and they praised me, only to start picking on me again five minutes later … [Mother] bawled me out again, and the whole family wound up getting involved. I don't fit in with them, and I've felt that clearly in the last few weeks. They're so sentimental together, but I'd rather be sentimental on my

own. They're always saying how nice it is with the four of us, and that we get along so well, without giving a moment's thought to the fact that I don't feel that way. Daddy's the only one who understands me, now and again, though he usually sides with Mother and Margot.

(p. 35)

Repeatedly, Frank (2022) complains that her mother (and sometimes her father) do not "see" her or understand her. Her expectations of her mother to understand her are clearly negative. For example, Frank explains the nickname she chooses to use for her mother because of Frank's feelings of estrangement from her:

Despite all my theories and efforts, I miss—every day and every hour of the day—having a mother who understands me ... The kind of mom who doesn't take everything people say too seriously, but who does take me seriously. I find it difficult to describe what I mean, but the word 'mom' says it all. Do you know what I've come up with? In order to give me the feeling of calling my mother something that sounds like "Mom", I often call her "Momsy". Sometimes I shorten it to "Moms": an imperfect "Mom". I wish I could honor her by removing the "s".

(pp. 163–164)

Frank here seems to have resigned herself to having a disappointing mother, but the longing for maternal love often breaks through, as in this January 12, 1944, diary entry, in which she reflects on her relationship to her mother before going into hiding:

Every morning when I heard footsteps on the stairs, I hoped it would be Mother coming to say good morning. I'd greet her warmly, because I honestly did look forward to her affectionate glance. But then she'd snap at me for having made some comment or other and I'd go off to school feeling completely discouraged ... [I'd] want Mother to stop whatever she was doing and lend a willing ear. Then the time would come once more when I no longer listened for the steps on the stairs and felt lonely and cried into my pillow every night.

(pp. 177–178)

Frank clearly has a fear of being abandoned and losing her mother's attention, thoroughly consistent with the anxious-resistant description of the Trust/Expectations of Others marker.

Regarding Frank's attachment relationship to her father, she seems to trust him and hold positive expectations of his comfort and protection (Frank, 2022). She contrasts her loving feelings for her father to her feelings of hatred for her mother:

I finally told Daddy that I love "him" more than I do Mother ... I simply can't stand Mother, and I have to force myself not to snap at her all the time, and to stay calm, when I'd rather slap her across the face ... I should volunteer to help her, but I'm not going to because I don't love her and don't enjoy doing it. I can imagine Mother dying someday, but Daddy's death seems inconceivable.

(p. 58)

Frank continues in this vein throughout her diary. She usually feels seen and heard by her father. Here are a few brief quotations illustrating this conjecture: "Daddy's always so nice. He understands me perfectly" (p. 36). "Daddy usually comes to my defense. Without him I wouldn't be able to stick it out here [in the secret annex]" (p. 48). "If Father weren't so patient, I'd have long ago given up hope of ever meeting my parents' quite moderate expectations" (p. 49).

Despite Frank's trusting attitude and positive expectations of her father, a more generalized anxious-resistant internal working model of attachment relationships seems to override her secure attachment relationship to her father (Frank, 2022). At times, Frank places both parents in the same insecure attachment category. For example, Frank often complains that her father treats her older sister Margot differently: "When I see him being partial to Margot, approving Margot's every action, praising her, hugging her; I feel a gnawing ache inside, because I'm crazy about him ... I long for something from Father that he's incapable of giving" (p. 69). In another example, Frank allows her paternal disappointment to infiltrate her writing: "Father's not very open about his feelings, but he's the same sweetheart he's always been" (p. 68).

This anxious-resistant internal working model of attachment relationships sometimes even spoils her secure attachment relationship to her father: "Father and Mother don't realize their own inadequacies and how much I blame them for letting me down ... More often than not, I fail to meet expectations" (p. 70). In a rarely observed narrative marker (Daniel, 2015, p. 117) that indicates a collapse of her third-person narrative, Frank (2022) addresses her parents directly: "I only wish I could see some results or, just once, receive encouragement from someone who loves me. Don't condemn me" (p. 71). Looking for someone to comfort her after an injury, Frank ends up feeling disappointed:

> I bumped into the cupboard door so hard it nearly knocked me over, and was scolded for making such a racket. They wouldn't let me run water to bathe my forehead, so now I'm walking around with a giant lump over my right eye.
>
> (p. 139)

Frank is dramatizing how little comfort she feels she receives from her parents. An anxious-avoidant person would simply ignore such an injury. Because of Frank's generalized anxious-resistant internal working model of attachment relationships, she even questions her grandmother's love:

> Grandma was always so loyal and good. She would never have let any of us down. Whatever happened, no matter how much I misbehaved, Grandma

always stuck up for me. Grandma, did you love me, or did you not understand me either? I don't know.

(p. 165)

Frank's Trust/Expectations of Others marker of her attachment relationship to God, however, is always secure. There are a couple of instances in which Frank questions God's benevolence: "Sometimes I think God is trying to test me, both now and in the future" (p. 70), and "in spite of everything, I still don't have enough faith in God" (p. 165). Frank's diary entries in which she professes her trust in God are much more prevalent, however. Hearing and seeing the German planes flying back and forth above the secret annex, Frank declares that "my fear vanished. I looked up at the sky and trusted in God" (p. 190). Frank also displays her positive expectations of God's comfort for the future:

Everything is as it should be ... God wants people to be happy amid nature's beauty and simplicity. As long as this exists, and that should be forever, I know that there will be solace for every sorrow, whatever the circumstances. I firmly believe that nature can bring comfort to all who suffer.

(pp. 206–207)

Searching for meaning in her suffering and the suffering of the Jews at the hands of the Nazis, Frank trusts that God will turn evil into good through the teachings of Judaism:

Who has put us through such suffering? It's God who has made us the way we are, but it's also God who will lift us up again. In the eyes of the world, we're doomed, but if, after all this suffering, there are still Jews left, the Jewish people will be held up as an example. Who knows, maybe our religion will teach the world and all the people in it about goodness, and that's the reason, the only reason, we have to suffer.

(pp. 272–273)

Commenting about her life in the secret annex, Frank provides the final word about her trust in God and her positive expectations of Him: "My life here has gotten better, much better. God has not forsaken me, and He never will" (p. 257). Frank's narrative again strongly supports the idea of compensation. Although she fears losing her mother's attention and expects the worst care from her mother, which sometimes even extends to her attachment relationship to her father, Frank demonstrates an unwavering trust in God and has positive expectations that He will care for her and provide for her.

Attitude to Seeking and Receiving Help

This interpersonal marker of the attachment pattern is evident in Anne Frank's descriptions of her attachment relationships to her parents and to God (Frank,

2022). Based on my earlier analysis, we are looking for anxious-resistant dimensions of her attachment relationship to her mother and secure dimensions of her attachment relationships to her father and to God. Regarding this marker, Daniel (2015) writes that anxious-resistant persons have a "strong desire for help or support," whereas securely attached persons "are open to seeking help" (p. 115). Which parts of Frank's diary and short stories address the Attitude to Seeking and Receiving Help marker?

Regarding Frank's attachment relationship to her mother, Frank often expresses the wish that her mother would help her: "I'd ... want Mother to stop whatever she was doing and lend a willing ear" (Frank, 2022, p. 178). At times, Frank defensively writes that she does not need her mother's or anyone's help: "I don't need the support of Mother or anyone else" (p. 293). This attitude of desiring help yet not receiving it permeates her attachment relationships to both parents. Frank even finds her father inadequate to help her. In one of her most moving diary entries, Frank defiantly confronts her father in a letter, in which she vows to continue seeing Peter in his attic bedroom over her father's objections. She angrily writes, "When I was having problems, everyone—and that includes you—closed their eyes and ears and didn't help me" (p. 293). Frank's anger over failing to receive any emotional understanding from her parents sometimes boils over:

> "No one understands me!" This phrase is part of me, and as unlikely as it may seem, there's a kernel of truth in it. Sometimes I'm so deeply buried under self-reproaches that I long for a word of comfort to help me dig myself out again. If only I had someone who took my feelings seriously. Alas, I haven't yet found that person, so the search must go on.
>
> (pp. 327–328)

Frank yearns for help in the form of comfort, but she does not experience anyone in her proximity to give her this comfort. Even when her father tries to help, Frank (2022) criticizes his efforts: "Why didn't Father support me in my struggle? Why did he fall short when he tried to offer me a helping hand" (p. 341)? Frank seems to be floundering, and from her point of view, no one seems to notice or care about her. Feeling cut off from help from others, Frank often turns to herself: "Who else but me can I turn to for comfort? I'm frequently in need of consolation" (p. 70).

Frank (2022) does receive help from Peter, however: "I have help, since Peter helps me through many a rough patch and rainy day" (pp. 248–249). Even this relationship, however, eventually sours in disappointment: "Peter is kind and good, and yet I can't deny that he's disappointed me in many ways" (p. 328). The overall impression is that help is available, yet Frank ends up feeling disappointed in this help. The clinical description of anxious-resistant persons of Daniel (2015) perfectly captures this dynamic:

> [anxious-resistant persons] often clearly and insistently seek care and attention. However, when it is given to them, they will receive it with a mixed, critical

attitude, as if it is not quite good enough or does not correspond to what they actually asked for (Lopez, 2009; Wallin, 2007).

(pp. 82–83)

Frank (2022) compensates for this bitter disappointment in seeking and receiving help by relying on her secure attachment relationship to God. Several diary entries illustrate Frank's positive attitude toward seeking and receiving help from God. Frank often acknowledges her own helplessness but then prays for help from God. For example, Frank's childhood friend Hanneli appears to her in a dream. Believing that the Nazis have sent Hanneli to a concentration camp, Frank admits that, "I can't help her. I can only stand by and watch while other people suffer and die. All I can do is pray to God to bring her back to us" (p. 158). She punctuates her faith in God's help at the end of this diary entry: "I'll always pray for her!" (p. 159). Frank continues to worry about all the Jews whom the Nazis are rounding up: "The most you can do is pray to God to perform a miracle and save at least some of them. And I hope I'm doing enough of that!" (pp. 165–166). Frank makes it clear where she finds help: "Where can I find help? I simply have to go on living and praying to God" (p. 175). She eventually views even her romantic relationship to Peter as help provided by God: "Now God has sent someone to help me: Peter" (p. 178). Frank's narrative strongly supports the idea of compensation: her anxious-resistant attachment relationship to her mother and her generalized internal working model of anxious-resistance to all her caregivers as emotionally inconsistent and ultimately unsatisfying helpers ultimately give way to seeking and receiving help from God as a compensatory secure attachment relationship.

Expression and Regulation of Emotions

This interpersonal marker of the attachment pattern is evident in Anne Frank's descriptions of her attachment relationships to her parents and to God (Frank, 2003, 2022). Based on my earlier analysis, we are looking for anxious-resistant dimensions of her attachment relationship to her mother and secure dimensions of her attachment relationships to her father and to God. Regarding this marker, Daniel (2015) notes that anxious-resistant persons demonstrate "frequent and dramatic expressions [of emotions, but] focus on and intensify negative emotions," while securely attached persons demonstrate "balanced expressions of both positive and negative emotions" (p. 115). What aspects of Frank's diary address the Expression and Regulation of Emotions marker?

Regarding Anne Frank's attachment relationships to her parents, she writes about a wide range of emotions that she experiences in the secret annex. Frank often intensifies her negative emotions and even causes drama among both her family and the guests in the secret annex. Frank (2022) exhibits some awareness of her ever-changing moods: "If you were to read all my letters in one sitting, you'd be struck by the fact that they were written in a variety of moods" (p. 153).

This variety of moods is an unpleasant experience for Frank: "I was suffering then (and still do) from moods that kept my head under water (figuratively speaking)" (p. 167). Despite her disdain for negative moods, she nevertheless enjoys causing drama:

> I've discovered a trick, and the effect is overwhelming, just like pricking someone with a pin and watching them jump. Here's how it works: I start talking about politics. All it takes is a single question, a word or a sentence, and before you know it, the entire family is involved!
>
> (p. 250)

At other times, however, Frank's mother is the source of her negative emotions: "Yesterday Mother and I had another run-in and she really kicked up a fuss. She told Daddy all my sins and started to cry, which made me cry too, and I already had such an awful headache" (p. 58). Frank's headache symptom might represent suppressed anger felt toward her mother (Liu et al., 2011). Later in this same diary entry, however, Frank's anger toward her mother breaks through her suppression: "I simply can't stand Mother, and I have to force myself not to snap at her all the time, and to stay calm, when I'd rather slap her across the face" (Frank, 2022, p. 58). In addition, Frank holds onto her angry feelings toward her mother. She describes a specific interaction with her mother before the family went into hiding: "Strangely enough, even though Mother has wounded me thousands of times, this particular wound still stings whenever I think of how angry I was" (p. 169). Frank is focusing on and intensifying her negative emotions toward her mother, just by thinking about this painful interaction. Frank adds that she has "never forgiven her for" (p. 169) this incident. She recalls that she "must have cried for hours" afterwards (p. 169). Here is a final example of Frank's intense negative feelings for her mother:

> I'm seething with rage, yet I can't show it. I'd like to scream, stamp my foot, give Mother a good shaking, cry and I don't know what else because of the nasty words, mocking looks and accusations that she hurls at me day after day, piercing me like arrows from a tightly strung bow, which are nearly impossible to pull from my body.
>
> (pp. 91–92)

The reader will notice how she characterizes her interactions with her mother so melodramatically—tell-tale signs of an anxious-resistant attachment relationship. Interestingly, however, Frank also seems to regulate her rage sufficiently to avoid actually *doing* anything to her mother.

Frank's Expression and Regulation of Emotions seem no more controlled in her father's presence (Frank, 2022). Frank becomes so frustrated with all the adults living in the secret annex that she blurts out in her writing, "I'd like to scream at Mother,

Margot, the van Daans, Dussel and Father too: 'Leave me alone, let me have at least one night when I don't cry myself to sleep with my eyes burning and my head pounding'" (p. 92). She discusses her emotions with her father, but she seems to lack any control over them: "Father and I had a long talk yesterday afternoon. I cried my eyes out" (p. 295). She complains to her father that "all I ever got were admonitions not to be so noisy. I was noisy only to keep myself from being miserable all the time" (p. 293). Like an anxious-resistant child, Frank uses whatever means available to her to get the attention she craves, including making noise that she knows will get the desired responsiveness. Frank, however, often pays for her negative attention-seeking. She berates herself for having "let myself be guided entirely by my feelings ... I'm still torn with guilt about the mean letter I wrote [Father] when I was so upset" (p. 342). It appears that Frank would like to have more rational control of her expression of emotions. At other times, however, she just lets the rage fly:

> I'm supposed to grin and bear it. But I can't! I have no intention of taking their insults lying down. I'll show them that Anne Frank wasn't born yesterday. They'll sit up and take notice and keep their big mouths shut when I make them see they ought to attend to their own manners instead of mine. How dare they act that way! It's simply barbaric ... I'll give them a taste of their own medicine, and then they'll change their tune! ... If you only knew, Kitty, how I seethe when they scold and mock me. It won't take long before I explode with pent-up rage.
>
> (p. 51)

Conversely, Frank (2003, 2022) demonstrates more positive and more regulated emotions when she discusses God or addresses God directly. In her short story, "Happiness," Frank associates a positive emotional state with communion with an inner spirituality:

> Once you've found your own inner happiness, you'll never lose it. I don't mean this in terms of material things, but in a spiritual sense. I believe that once your own inner happiness has been found, it might go underground for a while, but it will never be lost.
>
> (p. 112)

She then explains that she uses her inner spirituality to compensate for her troubles:

> I'd been too wrapped up in my own troubles. But once I looked up and saw the beauty of my surroundings, that little voice inside me suddenly stopped itemizing the bad things. All I could do or think or feel was that it was beautiful, that it was the only real truth ... Later on I understood that I had found my own inner happiness for the first time that afternoon. No matter what the circumstances are, that happiness will be with you always.
>
> (pp. 112–113)

Frank seems to use her secure attachment relationship to God to change her mood from negative to positive:

> I long for freedom and fresh air, but I think we've been amply compensated for their loss. On the inside, I mean. This morning, when I was sitting in front of the window and taking a long, deep look outside at God and nature, I was happy, just plain happy.
>
> (p. 207)

Frank even uses the word "compensated" to explain this change in mood that her communion with God has brought her.

In an extraordinary diary entry on March 7, 1944, Frank (2022) shares that she has grown tired of the ritualistic prayers she was taught and has created her own way of communicating to God in prayer:

> I lie in bed at night, after ending my prayers with the words "Ich danke dir für all das Gute und Liebe und Schöne" ["Thank you, God, for all that is good and dear and beautiful"], and I'm filled with joy. I think of going into hiding, my health and my whole being as das Gute; Peter's love (which is still so new and fragile and which neither of us dares to say aloud), the future, happiness and love as das Liebe; the world, nature and the tremendous beauty of everything, all that splendor, as das Schöne.
>
> (p. 221)

She then describes the effect of this prayer on her emotional well-being: "At such moments I don't think about all the misery, but about the beauty that still remains ... A person who has courage and faith will never die in misery!" (p. 221). In summary, Frank's diary entries support a compensation for her dysregulated emotions associated with her mother, and to a lesser extent, her father and others in the secret annex, with her secure attachment relationship to God, as evidenced by her underscoring the positive emotions associated with this relationship based on her faith and the sacred beauty of nature.

Self-image/Self-esteem

This interpersonal marker of the attachment pattern is evident in Anne Frank's descriptions of her attachment relationships to her parents and to God (Frank, 2003, 2022). Based on my earlier analysis, we are looking for anxious-resistant dimensions of her attachment relationship to her mother and secure dimensions of her attachment relationships to her father and to God. Regarding this marker, Daniel (2015) writes that anxious-resistant persons demonstrate "low self-esteem with a strong need for interpersonal validation," whereas securely attached persons demonstrate "nuanced self-image and solid self-esteem" (p. 115). What are some quotations from Frank's diary entries and short stories that address the Self-image/Self-esteem marker?

Regarding Anne Frank's attachment relationship to her mother, she reveals how her hatred of her mother affects her feelings about herself. For example, in her October 3, 1942, diary entry, after declaring that she does not love her mother and can imagine her mother's death, she reflects on what she has just written: "It's very mean of me, but that's how I feel" (Frank, 2022, p. 58). She includes meanness in her self-image because of her negative feelings toward her mother. Incidentally, perceiving herself as mean toward her mother suggests that she also loves her mother; I doubt that she would perceive herself as mean if she were to imagine Hitler's death. Thus, she experiences ambivalent feelings toward her mother, which is expected from someone classified as anxious-resistant. Over a year later, in her January 2, 1944, diary entry, Frank shares her guilt more extensively, having reviewed her earlier diary entries about her mother:

> I said to myself, "Anne, is that really you talking about hate? Oh, Anne, how could you?" ... I was suffering then (and still do) from moods that kept my head under water (figuratively speaking) and allowed me to see things only from my own perspective, without calmly considering what the others—those whom I, with my mercurial temperament, had hurt or offended—had said, and then acting as they would have done.
>
> (p. 167)

Later in the same diary entry, Frank continues to disparage herself and express feelings of guilt over her anger toward her mother while still justifying it:

> I didn't want to see what was going on, and I felt very sorry for myself ... But there's one thing I can't do, and that's to love Mother with the devotion of a child. I soothe my conscience with the thought that it's better for unkind words to be down on paper than for Mother to have to carry them around in her heart.
>
> (p. 168)

Just four days later, Frank (2022) continues to discuss her feelings toward her mother and how her mother's behavior affects her. She imagines "a mother as a woman who, first and foremost, possesses a great deal of tact, especially toward her adolescent children, and not one who, like Momsy, pokes fun at me when I cry" (p. 169). Again and again, Frank's negative feelings toward her mother contribute to her negative self-image. "I forgive Mother too," she writes, "But every time she makes a sarcastic remark or laughs at me, it's all I can do to control myself. I know I'm far from being what I should; will I ever be?" (p. 180).

In the short story, "Katrien," Frank (2003) continues this theme with a girl protagonist who feels scorned by her mother. The daughter "wasn't at all like the cheerful, lively girl [the mother] longed to have" (p. 91). Wondering how her daughter spent the morning, the mother blurts out, "You're such a lazy little thing and I hate laziness!" (p. 91). The mother's accusation prompts the girl to win her mother's validation by planning to "buy her mother a new thimble, a nice shiny silver thimble. She had just enough money. Then Mother would see that she wasn't a Lazy Bean after all" (p. 92). This strong need for interpersonal validation from her mother, a marker of an anxious-resistant attachment pattern, is clearly evident in this story.

Regarding Frank's attachment relationship to her father, Frank seems to view her father as the only person who keeps her self-esteem afloat, given the adversarial relationship with her mother. Early in her stay in the secret annex, she writes, "If Father weren't so patient, I'd have long ago given up hope of ever meeting my parents' quite moderate expectations" (Frank, 2022, p. 49). Frank senses that she is not meeting her parents' expectations, which clearly bothers her, yet her father's patience gives her hope that she will succeed in at least meeting his expectations in the future. Just three weeks before her arrest by the Nazis, Frank concludes that "Father's the only one who's given me a sense of confidence and made me feel as if I'm a sensible person" (p. 341).

Despite having a more benign relationship to her father, Frank (2022) nevertheless questions her father's love for her. While denying feelings of jealousy over Margot's relationship to her father, Frank wonders whether he loves her as a unique person in the family:

> [Father] doesn't realize that he treats Margot differently than he does me: Margot just happens to be the smartest, the kindest, the prettiest and the best. But I have a right to be taken seriously too. I've always been the clown and mischief maker of the family; I've always had to pay double for my sins: once with scolding and then again with my own sense of despair ... I'm not jealous of Margot; I never have been. I'm not envious of her brains or her beauty. It's just that I'd like to feel that Father really loves me, not because I'm his child, but because I'm me, Anne.
>
> (p. 69)

Frank is seeking her father's validation beyond whatever he is already providing her, and her inability to secure this additional validation produces a feeling of despair—no doubt because of her negative self-image as a "clown and mischief maker" (p. 69).

Later in her diary, Frank (2022) develops romantic feelings for Peter and clashes with her father over this relationship because her father wants her to put a stop to her make-out sessions with Peter. Feeling betrayed by her father's lack of support for this relationship, Frank angrily confronts her father, who is deeply offended and hurt by her remarks. Observing the devastation that she has wrought to her father's demeanor, Frank berates herself:

> Oh, I've failed miserably. This is the worst thing I've ever done in my entire life ... To accuse [Father], who's so good and who's done everything for me—no,

that was too cruel for words ... I've been far too smug. Not everything that Mistress Anne does is good! Anyone who deliberately causes such pain to someone they say they love is despicable, the lowest of the low! ... I should be deeply ashamed of myself, and I am.

(p. 296)

Thus, even in the context of her secure attachment relationship to her father, Frank's Self-image/Self-esteem can sink to the lowest depths.

We observe that Frank's "low self-esteem and strong need for interpersonal validation" (Daniel, 2015, p. 115) is not relationship-specific but rather infiltrates her generalized internal working model of attachment relationships. Aside from a few early remarks about having "a throng of admirers who can't keep their adoring eyes off me" (Frank 2022, p. 12) prior to her going into hiding, Frank's self-esteem is low, and her desire for validation from others is great. Frank often makes self-deprecating remarks. For example, two months after moving into the secret annex, Frank writes, "A few nights ago, I was the topic of discussion, and we all decided I was an ignoramus" (p. 44). Frank often denigrates her looks in her diary entries, sometimes recruiting others to validate or invalidate her beliefs. For example, she "once asked Margot if I was ugly" (p. 63). The prospect of needing glasses stimulates her self-reproach: "I've become very nearsighted and should have had glasses ages ago (Ugh, won't I look like a dope!)" (p. 118). Considering whether to publish her diary after the war, Frank doubts "whether anyone will ever be interested in this drivel. They'll probably call it 'The Musings of an Ugly Duckling'" (p. 274).

In fact, Frank (2022) takes a dim view of herself throughout her diary, irrespective of specific relationships. At various times, Frank views herself as "the Annex's bundle of nerves" (p. 137), "an idiot" (p. 173), "foolish" (p. 209), "crazy" (p. 231), "not beautiful, intelligent, or clever" (p. 249), self-condemned (pp. 340–341), suffering from "cowardice" (p. 153), and "selfishly wrapped up again in my own problems and pleasures" (pp. 158–159), thinking "of no one but myself" (p. 167). Frank's low self-esteem and strong need for validation from others sometimes even prompt her to want to be someone else altogether:

In bed at night, as I ponder my many sins and exaggerated shortcomings, I get so confused by the sheer amount of things I have to consider that I either laugh or cry, depending on my mood. Then I fall asleep with the strange feeling of wanting to be different than I am or being different than I want to be, or perhaps of behaving differently than I am or want to be.

(pp. 82–83)

Frank's relationship-specific anxious-resistant Self-image/Self-esteem interpersonal marker became generalized as low self-esteem and a strong need for interpersonal validation from everyone. In her short story, "Katrien," the protagonist plans to purchase a "big bag of candy" for a group of girls who had been calling her "Lazy Bean" because "then they'd be sure to like her and ask her to play with them, and then they'd see that she was good at games too, and never again would she be called anything but Katrien" (Frank, 2003, p. 92). Katrien needs validation even from the bullies.

Regarding Anne Frank's Self-image/Self-esteem interpersonal marker in her attachment relationship to God, her narrative illustrates how she tries to use this relationship to compensate for her low self-image/self-esteem—with mixed results. Angry and despondent over others' derision of her in the secret annex, Frank wants to ask God

> to give me another personality, one that doesn't antagonize everyone. But that's impossible. I'm stuck with the character I was born with, and yet I'm sure I'm not a bad person. I do my best to please everyone, more than they'd ever suspect in a million years.
>
> (Frank, 2022, p. 91)

Frank views her attachment relationship to God as ineffectual in this regard, for God cannot change her personality. We also observe Frank's strong need for interpersonal validation in doing her best to please everyone. Frank also reproaches herself for falling short despite God's bounty: "He's given me so much, which I don't deserve, and yet each day I make so many mistakes!" (p. 165). Frank seems to be comparing what she has to what she deserves and concludes that her cosmic moral account is in arrears. On the other hand, Frank believes that "if God lets me live [after the war], I'll achieve more than Mother ever did" (p. 273). She has a sense that God will help her to live a successful life that exceeds that of her Mother—Frank's standard bearer of what a woman can achieve in their culture and historical epoch. Belief in God and religion helps Frank in "upholding your own sense of honor and obeying your own conscience" (p. 336). Her validation ultimately comes from a God Who "speaks 'through me' because He gives each person a bit of Himself before sending them into the world. It's this part of us that distinguishes between good and evil and answers our questions" (*Cady's Life*; Frank, 2003, p. 166). Thus, on this interpersonal marker, Frank demonstrates solid self-esteem in her attachment relationship to God, which compensates for her low self-esteem and strong need for interpersonal validation from her mother and other significant others. She uses her secure attachment relationship to God to compensate for her anxious-resistant attachment relationship to her mother on this interpersonal marker.

Openness and Self-disclosure

This interpersonal marker of the attachment pattern is evident in Anne Frank's descriptions of her attachment relationships to her parents and to God (Frank, 2022). Based on my earlier analysis, I am looking in her diary for anxious-resistant dimensions of her attachment relationship to her mother and secure dimensions of her attachment relationships to her father and to God. Regarding this marker,

Daniel (2015) writes that anxious-resistant persons "share thoughts and feelings, but not always adapted to the context," whereas securely attached persons "are pleased to share thoughts and feelings, but 'dose' these according to the situation" (p. 115). What are some key passages in Frank's diary entries and short stories that address the Openness and Self-disclosure marker?

In the short story, "Katrien," the protagonist's mother angrily confronts her about her whereabouts:

> "You've been gone all morning and haven't done a single bit of work. Where have you been?" "Out front." ... "You're such a scaredy-cat. Can't you tell me where you've been, or is that such a big secret?" The poor child was crying so hard she couldn't answer. Suddenly she stood up, knocking over her chair, and, sobbing, raced out of the room and up to the attic, where she slumped down on a pile of gunny sacks in the corner and quietly cried her eyes out. Her mother shrugged and cleared the table.
>
> (Frank, 2003, pp. 91–92)

Katrien is demonstrating an anxious-avoidant attachment pattern on the Openness and Self-disclosure marker because she is "reticent about sharing thoughts and feelings" (Daniel, 2015, p. 115), which is contrary to our expectation of the anxious-resistant pattern with the maternal attachment figure.

In real life, Frank (2022) demonstrates this same reticence about sharing thoughts and feelings with her mother. Early on in her diary, when she discloses that she "can't stand" her mother, Frank expresses the hope that "Mother will never read this or anything else I've written [in my diary]" (p. 58). Thus, from the beginning, Frank seems to be at least partially aware of the tension between having a strong desire for validation from her mother and having a strong desire for sharing her thoughts and feelings, regardless of the interpersonal context. Assuming that she still wants validation from her mother, she forcefully restricts her urge to self-disclose.

There are moments, however, when Frank cannot seem to help herself, and she does illustrate the anxious-resistant attachment pattern of "shar[ing] thoughts and feelings, but not always adapted to the context" (Daniel, 2015, p. 115). Frank (2022) shares that:

> more than once, after a series of absurd reproaches, I've snapped at Mother: "I don't care what you say. Why don't you just wash your hands of me—I'm a hopeless case?" Of course, she'd tell me not to talk back and virtually ignore me for two days. Then suddenly all would be forgotten and she'd treat me like everyone else. It's impossible for me to be all smiles one day and venomous the next. I'd rather choose the golden mean, which isn't so golden, and keep my thoughts to myself.
>
> (pp. 92–93)

Frank seems to be making a conscious effort to keep her thoughts and feelings to herself in relation to her mother, at which she is only partially successful. Her mantra seems to be, in relation to her mother, "to remain silent and aloof" (p. 108) because "it's better for unkind words to be down on paper [in my diary] than for Mother to have to carry them around in her heart" (p. 168).

One senses from reading Frank's diary entries, however, that Frank struggles to keep her negative thoughts and feelings regarding her mother to herself. For example, Frank (2022) reports, "Mother slapped me last night, which I deserved. I mustn't carry my indifference and contempt for her too far. In spite of everything, I should try once again to be friendly and keep my remarks to myself!" (p. 238). Frank does not disclose why her mother slapped her, but the context suggests that she openly shared her negative feelings about her mother directly with her mother. Given all the evidence, it appears that Frank adopts an anxious-avoidant strategy on the Openness/Self-disclosure marker with respect to her attachment relationship to her mother, but an anxious-resistant strategy nevertheless sometimes breaks through.

Regarding the Openness/Self-disclosure interpersonal marker with respect to her father, Frank (2022) is reticent about sharing her thoughts and feelings even with him despite her secure attachment relationship to him. She writes, "Father has noticed I'm not my usual self, but I can't tell him what's bothering me" (p. 190). Over a month later, she underscores her reticence about self-disclosure: "What affected me even more was the realization that I was never going to be able to confide in Father. I didn't trust anyone but myself" (p. 220). Again, over four months after that, Frank shares the same sentiment: "I've hid anything having to do with me from Father, never shared my ideals with him, and deliberately alienated myself from him. I couldn't have done it any other way" (p. 342). On the other hand, Frank does disclose a conflict she is having with Dr. Dussel to her father: "That evening, when I managed to get hold of [my father], I told him what had happened and we discussed what my next step should be" (p. 120).

Overall, however, Frank appears reticent to share her thoughts and feelings with everyone, including her sister:

> Every day I'm growing ... less willing to share a single thought with Margot; I'm closed up tighter than a drum. Above all, I have to maintain my air of confidence. No one must know that my heart and mind are constantly at war with each other.
>
> (Frank, 2022, p. 230)

Throughout her diary entries, Frank reveals a deep conflict about openness and self-disclosure. On the one hand, she insists that she is "honest and [I] tell people right to their faces what I think, even when it's not very flattering" (p. 248). More frequently, however, she writes about hiding her thoughts and feelings from the world: "I've been putting on an act for the last year and a half, day in, day out.

I've never complained or dropped my mask, nothing of the kind" (pp. 293–294). Ironically, she is writing about this lack of openness to her father in a letter she gives him. Despite her reticence about sharing herself with not only her family members but also with everyone, we nevertheless observe Frank's strong desire to share herself:

> Can you tell me why people go to such lengths to hide their real selves? Or why I always behave very differently when I'm in the company of others? Why do people have so little trust in one another? I know there must be a reason, but sometimes I think it's horrible that you can't ever confide in anyone, not even those closest to you.
>
> (p. 180)

Frank seems conflicted about her reticence to share her thoughts and feelings with her family members and with everyone else, yet she mostly succeeds in hiding herself away except for in her diary entries. Thus, Frank seems to favor an anxious-avoidant strategy with this interpersonal marker.

What about her attachment relationship to God? Does Frank (2022) also communicate a reticence about sharing her thoughts and feelings with God? There is limited evidence in the narrative that Frank feels pleased to share her thoughts and feelings with God. In a diary entry devoted to her interest in a writing career after the war, Frank admits:

> I'm so grateful to God for having given me this gift [her writing talent], which I can use to develop myself and to express all that's inside me! When I write I can shake off all my cares. My sorrow disappears, my spirits are revived!
>
> (pp. 260–261)

Frank realizes that despite her reticence about self-disclosure, her God-bestowed writing talent requires her to self-disclose, which she acknowledges improves her emotional well-being. The evidence, though sparse, suggests that Frank uses her secure attachment relationship to God to compensate for her lack of openness and self-disclosure with the others in her life.

Dependence/Independence

This interpersonal marker of the attachment pattern is evident in Anne Frank's descriptions of her attachment relationships to her parents and to God (Frank, 2022). Based on my earlier analysis, we are looking in the diary entries for anxious-resistant dimensions of her attachment relationship to her mother and secure dimensions of her attachment relationships to her father and to God. Regarding this marker, Daniel (2015) writes that anxious-resistant persons "feel dependent on others—seek out relationships," whereas securely attached persons "feel comfortable in committed relationships, but are also capable of autonomy" (p. 115). What are some key quotations in Frank's diary that address the Dependence/Independence marker?

Like anyone going through adolescence, Anne Frank (2022) is experiencing conflicts over dependence and independence. Allen and Tan (2018) suggest that even securely attached adolescents typically appear more anxious-avoidant on the Adult Attachment Interview (AAI) because they are seeking greater autonomy from their caregivers in preparation for living lives largely independent of them during adulthood. We observe this conflict in many of Frank's diary entries, where she declares total independence from her parents, and then she still "crawl[s] into Father's bed nearly every night for comfort" (Frank, 2022, p. 97). As early as November 7, 1942, Frank alludes to this conflict:

> I'll have to become a good person on my own, without anyone to serve as a model or advise me, but it'll make me stronger in the end. Who else but me is ever going to read these letters? Who else but me can I turn to for comfort? I'm frequently in need of consolation.
>
> (p. 70)

At this point in her adolescent development, Frank recognizes her dependence on others ("in need of consolation") and simultaneously laments her need to become independent from others ("I'll *have* to become a good person on my own"; emphasis added). Earlier in the same diary entry, Frank claims that she has "cut myself adrift from [my family]. I'm charting my own course, and we'll see where it leads me. *I have no choice*" (p. 70; emphasis added). Frank seems to be wishing for an alternate situation in which she could continue to depend on her family for support. She continues to express sadness about her growing need for independence:

> I'm no longer the baby and spoiled little darling whose every deed can be laughed at. I have my own ideas, plans and ideals, but am unable to articulate them yet ... Despite everything, I'll keep going, that I'll find my own way and choke back my tears.
>
> (pp. 70–71)

As Frank's desire for independence grows, she seems to perceive her entire family as standing in the way:

> At times like these, Father, Mother and Margot don't matter to me in the least. I wander from room to room, climb up and down the stairs and feel like a songbird whose wings have been ripped off and who keeps hurling itself against the bars of its dark cage. "Let me out, where there's fresh air and laughter!" a voice within me cries.
>
> (p. 151)

Yet she continues simultaneously to express her ambivalence regarding independence: "All I want to do is scream 'Let me be, leave me alone!' Who knows, perhaps the day will come when I'm left alone more than I'd like" (p. 190)! Despite implicating her entire family in her growing need for independence, Frank spends an enormous amount of time talking about and focusing on her relationship to her mother in her diary entries, which suggests an ongoing dependence on her. Frank also recognizes this conflict: "I realized I could manage without my mother, completely and totally, and *that hurt*" (p. 220; emphasis added). At other times, however, Frank experiences no ambivalence over her autonomy. Writing about her mother, Frank declares:

> I know what I want, I know who's right and who's wrong, I have my own opinions, ideas and principles, and though it may sound odd coming from a teenager, I feel I'm more of a person than a child—I feel I'm completely independent of others. I know I'm better ... than Mother.
>
> (p. 232)

Making comparisons to her mother suggests an ongoing dependence on her. An autonomous Anne Frank would not feel the need to make such comparisons.

Regarding Frank's attachment relationship to her father on this interpersonal marker, we observe a similar ambivalence. Frank remarks that "I'm becoming more and more independent of my parents" (Frank, 2022, p. 273), yet she simultaneously complains that "[Father's] been trying not to treat me like a child, but now he's much too cold" (p. 238). Frank wants to feel independent while simultaneously missing the familiar dependence and childlike relationship to her father. Asserting her independence in the letter she wrote to her father after he confronted her about going to the attic to make out with Peter, Frank sounds as though she is trying to convince herself as much as she is trying to convince her father:

> I've struggled long and hard and shed many tears to become as independent as I am now. You can laugh and refuse to believe me, but I don't care. I know I'm an independent person, and I don't feel I need to account to you for my actions ... Now the battle is over. I've won! I'm independent, in both body and mind. I don't need a mother anymore, and I've emerged from the struggle a stronger person ... Now that it's over, now that I know the battle has been won, I want to go my own way, to follow the path that seems right to me. Don't think of me as a fourteen-year-old, since all these troubles have made me older; I won't regret my actions, I'll behave the way I think I should! Gentle persuasion won't keep me from going upstairs ... Whatever you do, just leave me alone!
>
> (pp. 293–294)

That Frank would spend so much time and effort explaining her feelings to her father belies her dependence on him, seeking out the attachment relationship to him. Of course, after seeing her father's reaction to the letter, Frank is stricken with guilt and self-reproaches (p. 296), further demonstrating her dependence on his approval of her.

Regarding her attachment relationship to God, Frank demonstrates a resolute dependence on God, Who in exchange grants her autonomy and freedom from fear.

> I stood at the top of the stairs while German planes flew back and forth, and I knew I was on my own, that I couldn't count on others for support. My fear vanished. I looked up at the sky and trusted in God.
>
> (Frank, 2022, p. 190)

Thus, Frank demonstrates that her dependence on God compensates for her dependence on her parents, from whom she struggles to become independent but never quite succeeds. She never struggles to become independent from God but instead openly welcomes God into her life.

Conflict Management

This interpersonal marker of the attachment pattern is evident in Anne Frank's descriptions of her attachment relationships to her parents and to God in her diary and her short stories (Frank, 2003, 2022). Based on my earlier analysis, we are looking in her diary entries for anxious-resistant dimensions of her attachment relationship to her mother and secure dimensions of her attachment relationships to her father and to God. Regarding this marker, Daniel (2015) writes that anxious-resistant persons give "great attention to conflicts, [and] may be inclined to escalate these," whereas securely attached persons demonstrate "constructive strategies for handling conflicts" (p. 115). What are some key texts in her diary entries and short stories that address the Conflict Management marker?

Regarding Frank's attachment relationship to her mother, her diary entries show that Frank often showcases her conflicts with her mother (Frank, 2022). In a rage, she sometimes makes outrageous statements designed to force her mother to deny their veracity and provide Frank with reassurance. Frank recounts the contours of these conflicts:

> If Mother adds her advice, the pile of sermons becomes so thick that I despair of ever getting through them. Then I talk back and start contradicting everyone until the old familiar Anne refrain inevitably crops up again: "No one understands me!"
>
> (p. 327)

At other times, Frank stops talking altogether during conflicts and then cries, thus drawing more attention to herself. In her short story, "Katrien," Frank (2003) describes a conflict between the girl protagonist, Katrien, and her ridiculing mother: "You couldn't get a word out of [Katrien] when she was like this, and she was liable to break into tears at the drop of a hat" (p. 92). When Frank's mother comes into her bedroom to say her nighttime prayers with her instead of her father, Frank refuses, thus causing her mother anguish. Rather than tactfully explaining to her mother that she will say her prayers with her that night but prefers that her father perform this task in the future, Frank (2022) instead escalates the conflict with her refusal, justifying her behavior by rationalizing that "I can't be a hypocrite and pray with her when I don't feel like it. It just doesn't work that way" (p. 107). Frank then becomes emotionally dysregulated as she continues to justify her behavior, suggesting that her refusal has more to do with revenge than hypocrisy:

> She's the one who's rejected me. She's the one whose tactless comments and cruel jokes about matters I don't think are funny have made me insensitive to any sign of love on her part. Just as my heart sinks every time I hear her harsh words, that's how her heart sank when she realized there was no more love between us ... Everyone expects me to apologize, but this is not something I can apologize for, because I told the truth, and sooner or later Mother was bound to find out anyway.
>
> (pp. 107–108)

This diary entry illustrates an angry Anne Frank, eager to escalate this conflict by not making any effort to meet her mother halfway or at least explain to her mother what is troubling her about her mother's behavior. Instead, she seeks retribution in the hope that her mother will eventually feel what Frank is feeling and thus stop the offending behavior.

Frank (2022) highlights one conflict with her mother as particularly painful—"one incident I've never forgiven her for" (p. 169)—which occurred prior to the family's going into hiding. Frank's mother and sister were laughing at her because she could not go shopping with them downtown:

> Tears of rage rushed to my eyes, and Margot and Mother began laughing at me. I was so furious that I stuck my tongue out at them, right there on the street ... I rode my bike home and must have cried for hours. Strangely enough, even though Mother has wounded me thousands of times, this particular wound still stings whenever I think of how angry I was.
>
> (p. 169)

Rather than trying to work out this conflict with her mother, Frank instead broods over it, using it as fuel to energize her ongoing feud with her mother. It is as though Frank were passively waiting for her mother to approach her and make things right with her—a classic anxious-resistant strategy that, according to Daniel (2015), reflects "a general feeling of helplessness and lack of control" produced by an inability "to control whether necessary care and protection [were] given to them" (p. 82). Wallin (2007) notes that anxious-resistant persons often use this helplessness to coerce care from another person: "Don't' you think I'm to be pitied sometimes?" (Frank, 2022, p. 117). Walking around the secret annex with a scowl just might elicit the care from her mother for which she is so desperately longing.

Regarding Frank's attachment relationship to her father, she at least confronts him directly when she disagrees with his prohibition of make-out sessions with Peter. Rather than work out the conflict constructively, however, Frank writes him the scathing letter quoted from earlier, which she ends with the stinging line, "Just leave me alone!" (Frank, 2022, p. 294). The approach infuriates her father, who later tells her, "'I've received many letters in my lifetime, but none as hurtful as this ... You've done us a great injustice!'" (p. 295). Frank's father's reaction to his daughter's letter suggests that Frank's letter escalated the conflict, an indicator of an anxious-resistant attachment relationship. Over two months later, Frank seems to have rejected her father, having resorted to hiding herself rather than trying to resolve her conflicts with him: "I've hid anything having to do with me from Father, never shared my ideals with him, and deliberately alienated myself from him. I couldn't have done it any other way" (p. 342). The inevitability of this decision is probably related to her ongoing feelings of guilt about her letter: "I'm still torn with guilt about the mean letter I wrote him when I was so upset" (p. 342). Presumably, Frank's withdrawal from her father would only draw her father's attention to her, not away from her.

Frank's anxious-resistant pattern of conflict management seems generalized to others in the secret annex. She seems to regret her active role in the daily conflicts in the secret annex: "If only I weren't so involved in all these skirmishes!" (Frank, 2022, p. 149). In fact, however, Frank seems to relish these conflicts by actively provoking them:

> I've discovered a trick, and the effect is overwhelming, just like pricking someone with a pin and watching them jump. Here's how it works: I start talking about politics. All it takes is a single question, a word or a sentence, and before you know it, the entire family is involved!
>
> (p. 250)

Frank derives some pleasure out of escalating these conflicts, even though she often feels scapegoated during conflicts.

In her attachment relationship to God, Frank (2022) does not directly acknowledge conflict. In an early diary entry (November 7, 1942), Frank writes, "Sometimes I think God is trying to test me, both now and in the future" (p. 70), but she never follows up on this idea. During experiences of internal conflict, Frank turns to God to manage: "I slid to the floor in my nightgown and began by saying my prayers, very fervently. Then I drew my knees to my chest, lay my head on my arms and cried, all huddled up on the bare floor" (p. 260). Thus, Frank seems to use her secure attachment relationship to God as a constructive way to manage her internal conflict, which contrasts with her conflict management strategy of dramatization and escalation, as evidenced in her relationships to her parents and to others in the secret annex. It is likely that she also used her secure attachment relationship to God to compensate for these escalating conflicts with her parents and other secret annex residents. She does not manage conflicts with God, however, because she does not appear to have conflicts with God.

Empathy

This interpersonal marker of the attachment pattern is evident in Anne Frank's descriptions of her attachment relationships to her parents and to God (Frank, 2022). Based on my earlier analysis, we are looking in her diary entries for anxious-resistant dimensions of her attachment relationship to her mother and secure dimensions of her attachment relationships to her father and to God. Regarding this marker, Daniel (2015) writes that anxious-resistant persons are "preoccupied by others, but inclined to misattribute and project," whereas securely attached persons demonstrate "empathy with and care for others" (p. 115). What are some passages in her diary that address the Empathy marker?

Regarding Frank's empathy in her attachment relationship to her mother, the evidence suggests that Frank sometimes struggles to empathize with her mother. Frank casts her gaze toward her mother in most of her diary, but Frank's lack of empathy toward her mother can perhaps be summarized in one sentence: "Mother's against me and I'm against her" (Frank, 2022, p. 252). Frank does not ask herself why she might feel as though her mother is against her. She recognizes that "mother is sad, because she still loves me" (p. 253) but denies how her mother's sadness might be affecting her because "she no longer means anything to me" (p. 253). This example would support the anxious-avoidant dimension of empathy ("limited empathy and interpersonal 'coldness'"; Daniel, 2015, p. 115); however, the context of these words suggests that Frank is enraged with her mother and is defending against having feelings toward her.

Most of the evidence, however, points to Frank's strong empathy for her mother despite their ongoing conflict. When Frank rebuffed her mother's attempt to say Frank's prayers with her, Frank comments on her compassionate feelings about her mother:

> I felt sorry for Mother—very, very sorry—because for the first time in my life I noticed she wasn't indifferent to my coldness. I saw the sorrow in her face when she talked about not being able to make me love her.
>
> (Frank, 2022, p. 107)

She also explains that she calls her mother "Momsy" because she is not the kind of mother that Frank wants; however, "it's a good thing she doesn't realize this, since it would only make her unhappy" (p. 164). In perhaps the most poignant example of Frank's empathy toward her mother, she writes:

> It's true, she didn't understand me, but I didn't understand her either. Because she loved me, she was tender and affectionate, but because of the difficult

situations I put her in, and the sad circumstances in which she found herself, she was nervous and irritable, so I can understand why she was often short with me.
(p. 167)

Just 10 days later, Frank recognizes that her mother does not really know her thoughts and decides to keep it that way because "I'd like to spare her that grief, especially since I know that everything would remain the same" (p. 177). Thus, we observe compassion and care regarding her mother's feelings, mixed with a possible misattribution of her mother's expected reaction if she were to find out about her daughter's thoughts. Overall, though, Frank seems empathic toward her mother.

Regarding Frank's empathy in her attachment relationship to her father, we observe her empathy most poignantly after she processes her father's reaction to her confrontational letter regarding her make-out sessions with Peter in the attic. She writes, "Poor Pim, I might have known what the effect of such an epistle would be" (Frank, 2022, p. 294). Her empathy toward her father takes the form of self-condemnation." "To accuse Pim, who's so good and who's done everything for me—no, [writing that letter] was too cruel for words" (p. 296). Over two months later, Frank is still berating herself for having written this letter: "I'm still torn with guilt about the mean letter I wrote him when I was so upset" (p. 342). Thus, we observe that Frank expresses empathy toward her father, mixed with self-reproaches and a focus on herself. Overall, though, Frank seems empathic toward her father.

Although there are moments of limited empathy and interpersonal "coldness" (Daniel, 2015, p. 115), Frank (2022) nevertheless demonstrates deep compassion for others, both inside and outside the secret annex. There are too many examples to cite; only several shall suffice. Before going into hiding, Frank depicts some of her classmates in decidedly unempathic terms. For example, she describes Rob Cohen as "an obnoxious, two-faced, lying, sniveling little goof who has an awfully high opinion of himself" (p. 10). For the most part, however, Frank exhibits uncommon empathy for others, even her sworn enemy, Mrs. van Daan. Frank describes an incident in which the dentist Dr. Dussel is working on a hysterical Mrs. van Daan, who is yelling and flailing about in the makeshift dentist's chair. Frank observes that she and the other secret annex residents "roared with laughter. Of course, that was very mean of us. If it'd been me, I'm sure I would have yelled even louder" (p. 86). In a heartbreaking passage, Frank demonstrates empathy for the Jews the Nazis are rounding up to go to concentration camps, but as we observed with her father, Frank's empathy is tinged with feelings of guilt and self-reproach:

We're so worried about those we hold dear, whom we can no longer help. I feel wicked sleeping in a warm bed, while somewhere out there my dearest friends are dropping from exhaustion or being knocked to the ground. I get frightened myself when I think of close friends who are now at the mercy of the cruelest monsters ever to stalk the earth and all because they're Jews.
(p. 80)

Frank (2022) also recognizes the limitations of feeling empathy for others. In reflecting on her relationship to Peter, Frank considers "how nice it would be if someone were to confide everything to me. But now that it's reached that point, I realize how difficult it is to put you in someone else's shoes and find the right answer" (p. 335). It hurts Frank to see Peter "so lonely, so scornful, and so wretched" (p. 336). Thus, it appears that Frank has an enormous capacity to feel empathy for others in general.

Regarding Frank's empathy in her attachment relationship to God, there are no instances of Frank's feeling what God might be feeling; however, in Frank's mind, God empathizes with His creation, especially the persecuted. Frank has a dream about her friend Hanneli, who beseeches her for help (Frank, 2022). As part of her empathic response toward her friend, Frank prays to God, Who she believes will help Hanneli: "Merciful God, comfort her, so that at least she won't be alone. Oh, if only you could tell her I'm thinking of her with compassion and love, it might help her go on" (p. 159). Frank sincerely believes in God's capacity for empathy and is asking God to communicate Frank's empathy to her friend. Hanneli continues to occupy Frank's mind as she asks for divine intervention:

> Dear God, watch over her and bring her back to us. Hanneli, you're a reminder of what my fate might have been. I keep seeing myself in your place ... Thinking about the suffering of those you hold dear can reduce you to tears; in fact, you could spend the whole day crying. The most you can do is pray to God to perform a miracle and save at least some of them.
>
> (pp. 165–166)

Frank clearly believes that God has the empathy and power to deliver at least some Jews from the Holocaust. In early 1945, as Frank, an emaciated 15-year-old, lay dying of typhus fever in the Bergen-Belsen concentration camp in northern Germany, did she continue to believe in God's benevolence and empathy for her and the other six million Jews who perished in the Holocaust? We will never know.

Perhaps Frank's most revealing comments about empathy in her attachment relationship to God appear in her short stories. For example, in "Give!," Frank declares that God creates everyone the same and that differences in social status are inconsequential in God's sight:

> Everyone is born equal; we all come into the world helpless and innocent. We all breathe the same air, and many of us believe in the same God. And yet ... and yet, to many people this one small difference [social status] is a huge one! It's huge because many people have never realized what the difference is, for if they had they would have discovered long ago that there's actually no difference at all!
>
> (Frank, 2003, p. 118)

Frank is implying that by creating all human beings equal, God empathizes with everyone, regardless of their social status. She continues in this vein, declaring that "the world has plenty of room, riches, money and beauty. God has created enough for each and every one of us. Let us begin by dividing it more fairly!" (p. 119). This passage demonstrates not only God's empathy by providing for everyone but also Frank's empathy for persons who have been short-changed from participating in the world's abundance.

In *Cady's Life*, Frank (2003) suggests that God has created goodness even in the hearts of criminals:

> As Hans said, "Our sense of what's good and right also comes from God." "Does everyone really have this? What about criminals? I'm pretty sure they do too ….do even the worst criminals, the ones the world looks upon as wicked to the core, still have a bit of goodness deep down inside that might shine through someday?"
>
> (pp. 166–167)

Earlier in this story, Frank, through the character of Hans, explains that:

> God has created mankind and every living thing just as they are. Our souls and our sense of what's good and right also come from Him. So the answer to your questions comes from within yourself, as well as from God, since He made you the way you are.
>
> (p. 165)

The story's protagonist Cady later writes in her diary: "I believe that God speaks 'through me' because He gives each person a little bit of Himself before sending them into the world" (p. 166). Frank implies that God lives inside everyone—even criminals and persons of low social status—in the form of conscience and goodness. Frank's beliefs about God include a profound empathy for humankind based on His steadfast presence in every human soul. The evidence therefore strongly suggests that Frank believes that God deeply cares about people and understands their pain. According to Frank, God also listens to her prayers and can act on these prayers by performing miracles. Thus, on this interpersonal marker, Frank demonstrates secure attachment relationships to her mother and father and to God. We observe that her empathy in relation to her attachment relationship to God corresponds with her empathy in relation to her attachment relationships to her parents.

Conclusion

In this chapter, I analyzed Anne Frank's autobiographical narratives (i.e., diary entries and short stories (Frank, 2003, 2022)), using nine interpersonal markers of attachment of Daniel (2015) to determine: (1) the quality of her attachment relationships to her parents and to God and (2) whether these two sets of attachment relationships (to parents and to God) support the correspondence hypothesis or the compensation hypothesis discussed in Chapter 3 of Goodman (2025). Based on a general reading of these narratives, I conclude that Frank developed a secondary strategy of anxious-resistance in her attachment relationship to her parents and a primary strategy of security in her attachment relationship to God. Thus, I conclude that Frank's narratives support the compensation hypothesis; however, there is also room to consider the correspondence hypothesis if we believe that Frank coopted facets of her secure attachment relationship to her father in the process of developing her secure attachment relationship to God.

Examining Frank's narratives more closely, I searched for key quotations to support an anxious-resistant attachment relationship to her mother and secure attachment relationships to her father and to God. I used the nine interpersonal markers of Daniel (2015) to support the compensation hypothesis (i.e., anxious-resistant to secure). A review of the analysis of each of these markers indicates that Frank uses her secure attachment relationship to God to compensate for her anxious-resistant attachment relationship to her mother on all nine interpersonal markers except for empathy (she exhibited empathy in all relationships). Regarding Frank's attachment relationship to her father, the correspondence hypothesis was supported by only three interpersonal markers—Proximity/Distance, Self-image/Self-esteem, and Empathy—but even the Self-image/Self-esteem marker contained some anxious-resistant features. Thus, the evidence suggests that her attachment relationship to her father contains significant anxious-resistant features, which means that Frank's secure attachment relationship to God compensated for the attachment relationships not only to her mother but also to her father. This more granular evidence does not support the conclusion that the quality of Frank's attachment relationship to her father corresponds to the quality of her attachment relationship to God, as I initially hypothesized from my general narrative analysis. In Frank's mind, God provides the safe haven and secure base as well as the consistent feeling of being known and loved that she lacks in both her parental attachment relationships. Even Frank's beloved father commented after the war that he had no idea about the contents of his daughter's mind: "The Anne that appeared before me [in her diary] was very different from the daughter I had lost. I had had no idea of the depth of her thoughts and feelings" (Anne Frank House, n.d.). Her father's ignorance about his daughter's internal world supports Frank's contention that she "hid anything having to do with me from Father, never shared my ideals with him, and deliberately alienated myself from him" (Frank, 2022, p. 342). I contrasted this attitude toward her father with the attitude of openness and trust in God: "'I've been saying other prayers, things that I myself thought were beautiful, not just a standard prayer'" (Frank, 2003, p. 164). Frank ultimately found her refuge in God. Unfortunately, Frank did not have the opportunity to use this secure attachment relationship to God to change her anxious-resistant attachment relationships to her parents, but it clearly helped her to accept her circumstances in hiding.

Brief Treatment Plan for Anne Frank

Based on the preceding narrative analysis, how might I treat Anne Frank if she were to schedule a session of psychotherapy with me? To answer this question, I would like to take liberties with Frank's history. Frank was arrested on August 4, 1944, but if the Nazis had never discovered the secret annex, Frank would have been liberated with the rest of the Netherlands nine months later at the end of the war. She probably would have welcomed speaking to a psychologist about her ordeal in the secret annex, the deprivation of food, air, sunlight, and privacy, and her ongoing conflicts with her mother and, to a lesser extent, her father. Would she have wanted to continue her romantic relationship with Peter? I suspect that Frank would have eagerly discussed all these issues and more with me.

Frank's most obvious symptom that would drive her into treatment is anxiety. She refers to herself as "the Annex's little bundle of nerves" (Frank, 2022, p. 137). We also learn that Frank has "been taking valerian [a plant-based remedy] every day to fight the anxiety and depression" but that she does not find it helpful because "it doesn't stop me from being even more miserable the next day" (p. 146). I would therefore imagine that Frank would be quite willing to try talk therapy, given the disappointing results of valerian and her love of talking (p. 16).

It is often challenging to develop a working alliance with adolescents because they often mistrust adults, but I suspect that it would be relatively easy to establish a therapeutic alliance with Frank. She is eager to share her thoughts and feelings with anyone who will listen to her without judgment. Being a man, I would also have the advantage of being able to "borrow" some of the good feeling she has for her father in the initial phase of treatment. At the same time, however, I would be wary of an eventual "fall from grace," where I might become the insensitive, critical mother, a time when the therapeutic alliance would be tested. As a clinical supervisor once told me, "Weather the storms." I need to "survive [my] destruction by the subject" (Winnicott, 1969, p. 713) to convince Frank of my trustworthiness as a safe haven and secure base. I need to demonstrate through my steadfast reliability and modulated emotional reactions to her provocations that she cannot destroy my caregiving through retaliation against her, through withdrawal of my emotional investment in her, or through my outright abandonment of her. I need to exist independently of her, not as her mother or father or as a teddy bear that occupies a potential space between reality and illusion (Winnicott, 1971), but as a new person outside her control who nevertheless wants to relate to her authentically as a person with my own intentions and feelings (Goodman, 2013). Essentially, I would be introducing Frank to a separate person eager to engage with her on a therapeutic adventure of self-and-other discovery.

After this initial phase of treatment, I would begin the second phase of treatment by introducing a "gentle challenge" (Dozier, 2003, p. 254) to my interactions with her. In Chapter 6 of Goodman (2025), I suggest that anxious-resistant attachment represents a hyperactivating strategy for overdramatizing the anxiety stimulated by the threat of rejection and abandonment. To ensure the emotional care needed by the infant, she must compensate for the caregiver's inconsistent responsiveness through exaggerated cues for attention and comfort. I would therefore behave in a manner that would gently challenge this hyperactivating strategy by behaving in a less animated, deactivating manner. Of course, this behavior might trigger Frank's hypersensitivity to my mood, exposing me to an accusation of being "cold" and "clinical." This deactivating behavior might even activate Frank's feelings of helplessness in the therapeutic relationship to elicit more active, involved care from me.

Wallin (2007) discusses two types of anxious-resistant patients—the helpless type and the angry type. Following Ainsworth and her colleagues (Ainsworth et al., 1978), Wallin suggests that anxious-resistant adults enact attachment strategies observed in the Strange Situation similar to these two subtypes of anxious-resistant infants. C2 (helpless) infants display helpless behavior upon reunion to evoke care from their caregivers, while C1 (angry) infants display angry, ambivalent behavior to accomplish the same goal. Having thoroughly read diary and short stories (Frank, 2003, 2022), I believe that Frank usually uses helplessness to evoke the care she needs. Occasionally, Frank expresses rage, but she limits it to the letter to her father and to her diary entries and short stories rather than directly toward the person with whom she feels enraged: "I'm seething with rage, yet I can't show it" (Frank, 2022, p. 91). More often, though, Frank leads with helplessness:

> The little toe on my right foot got stuck in the vacuum cleaner. It bled and hurt, but my other ailments were already causing me so much trouble that I let this one slide, which was stupid of me, because now I'm walking around with an infected toe.
>
> (p. 139)

Can you imagine Frank walking around the secret annex with an infected toe, probably limping in an exaggerated manner, trying to evoke a reaction from someone, anyone?

If the therapeutic goal is to change Frank's attachment pattern from anxious-resistant to secure, then I would need to validate her nascent belief in her own self-sufficiency and point out that she is less helpless than she believes. I would also help her gradually to understand the unconscious purpose of her helplessness—to guarantee the other's care of her emotional needs. Of course, her focus typically rests exclusively on the caregiver to meet her needs rather than on herself. I might mention her awareness of her own exhaustion in trying to meet Peter's emotional needs:

> Peter's beginning to lean on me and I don't want that, not under any circumstances. It's hard enough standing on your own two feet, but when you also have to remain true to your character and soul, it's harder still.
>
> (p. 335)

She struggles to believe that anyone could meet her legitimate emotional needs without having to resort to helpless or passive-aggressive behavior, which makes it harder for her to be available to meet the emotional needs of others like Peter.

As already mentioned, adolescence is a phase of development in which even securely attached adolescents typically appear hyper-independent on the AAI because they are seeking greater autonomy from their caregivers in preparation for living lives largely independent of them during adulthood (Allen & Tan, 2018). Frank (2022) is beginning to understand this process of developing autonomy: "I'm becoming more and more independent of my parents" (p. 273). Psychotherapy could help promote her autonomy-seeking in the context of feeling adequately cared for.

Frank's secure attachment relationship to God could come in handy in this regard. She demonstrates that she has the capacity to rely on God when human relationships fail her. Can she come to perceive others who have disappointed her—her mother, her father, and Peter—as children of God who are nevertheless deeply flawed and needing grace and forgiveness? After all, God loves Frank with all her flaws. In *Cady's Life* (Frank, 2003), Hans tells Cady:

> God has created mankind and every living thing just as they are. Our souls and our sense of what's good and right also come from Him. So the answer to your questions comes from within yourself, as well as from God, since He made you the way you are.
>
> (p. 165)

In therapy, Frank would develop the insight that God also created the disappointing people in her life, who have their own private pain to which she has no visible access. She might use her feelings of love and gratitude to God to begin to accept her parents and Peter as flawed persons who nevertheless love her as best they can, given their own personal histories. Frank could use the model of her secure attachment relationships to God and to me to repair her conflicted relationships to these persons.

What experiences might I have in working with Anne Frank? Which countertransference reactions might I anticipate that would communicate something about her unconscious experience and help me to navigate my therapeutic relationship with her? Over the course of reading Frank's work, I developed a strong desire to befriend her. I admire her pluck, her vulnerability, and her perseverance through horrendous circumstances. I would need to be aware not to allow my admiration of her to cause me to protect her from what she might perceive as uncomfortable truths about herself such as her use of helplessness to elicit care. I might be tempted to avoid her anger with me by placating her, which would be sacrificing my own intentionality at the altar of her approval of me as a therapist. Of course, this avoidance is a form of withdrawal from her and a signal that I am unable to tolerate her anger, which would mean that I have not survived her destruction. She would eventually relegate me to yet another caregiver who could not tolerate all the parts of her personality, including the destructive ones. I would be depriving her of the opportunity to integrate her angry, deprived self-representation with her loving, empathic self-representation, and relatedly, her angry, depriving representation of me with her loving, empathic representation of me. I would need to avoid getting entangled in conflict and respond instead with consistency and acceptance of all that she is and all that she desires to be. Can I perceive my own need to be liked by Frank as an unconscious communication from Frank that she desperately wants me to like her and thus provide her with the attention and care that she needs?

Finally, I also want to be continuously aware that Frank and I do not share the same religious background. How might Frank feel about working with a Christian? In my private practice, I have treated many Jews who have taught me about their religion, culture, and customs. In each of these therapeutic relationships, I remained open to learning from them rather than imposing my own understanding of their religion. Thus, I feel capable of creating the same context for learning in my therapeutic relationship with Frank. Despite her experiences with Nazis and Christian Nazi sympathizers, I expect that Frank would be open to working with a Christian therapist. She does not equate "Christian" with "Nazi." In fact, Frank (2022) views Jews and Christians as sharing the same fate: "The Christians in Holland are also living in fear because their sons are being sent to Germany. Everyone is scared … Jews and Christians alike are waiting, the whole world is waiting, and many are waiting for death" (pp. 90–91). She also expresses anger toward Peter because he "scoffs at Jesus Christ" (p. 336). Thus, as long as I remain open to her religious understandings, culture, and customs, our different religious backgrounds might actually enhance our work together, confirming for her that "God is much closer than most people think" (Frank, 2003, p. 116).

References

Ainsworth, M. D. S., Blehar, M. C., Waters, E., & Wall, S. (1978). *Patterns of attachment: A psychological study of the strange situation*. Erlbaum.

Allen, J. P., & Tan, J. S. (2018). The multiple facets of attachment in adolescence. In J. Cassidy & P. R. Shaver (Eds.), *Handbook of attachment: Theory, research, and clinical applications* (3rd ed., pp. 399–415). Guilford Press.

Anne Frank House. (n.d.). *The diary*. Available at: www.annefrank.org

Boston Public Library. (2013, January 28). The 100 most influential books of the 20th century. Available at: www.goodreads.com/list/show/31302.Boston_Public_Library_The_ 100_Most_Influential_Books_of_the_20th_Century

Bowlby, J. (1988). *A secure base: Parent-child attachment and healthy human development*. Basic Books.

Conrad, R. (2022). Having Anne Frank's version of her diary could change how we see it. *The Washington Post*, June 26. https://link-gale-com.proxy.library.emory.edu/apps/doc/ A708334749/BIC?u=emory&sid=bookmark-BIC&xid=ea0ba08a

Daniel, S. I. F. (2015). *Adult attachment patterns in a treatment context: Relationship and narrative*. Routledge.

Dozier, M. (2003). Attachment-based treatment for vulnerable children. *Attachment and Human Development, 5,* 253–257.

Emerson, R. W. (1836). *Nature.* James Munroe and Company.

Frank, A. (2003). *Anne Frank's tales from the secret annex: A collection of her short stories, fables, and lesser-known writings* (revised edition) (G. van der Stroom, Ed.; S. Massotty, Trans.). Bantam Dell. Kindle Edition.

Frank, A. (2022). *The diary of a young girl: The definitive edition* (Y. Ooisi, Trans.). EFE Books. Kindle Edition.

Freud, S. (1900). The interpretation of dreams. In J. Strachey (Ed. and Trans.), *The standard edition of the complete psychological works of Sigmund Freud* (Vols. 4–5, pp. 1–625). Hogarth Press.

George, C., Kaplan, N., & Main, M. (1985). Adult Attachment Interview. Unpublished manuscript. University of California.

Goodman, G. (2013). Encopresis happens: Theoretical and treatment considerations from an attachment perspective. *Psychoanalytic Psychology, 30,* 438–455.

Goodman, G. (2025). *Using psychoanalytic techniques to transform the attachment relationship to God: Our refuge and strength.* Routledge.

Granqvist, P. (2020). *Attachment in religion and spirituality: A wider view.* Guilford Press.

Granqvist, P., & Kirkpatrick, L. A. (2018). Attachment and religious representations and behavior. In J. Cassidy & P. R. Shaver (Eds.), *Handbook of attachment: Theory, research, and clinical applications* (pp. 917–940). Guilford Press.

Kirkpatrick, L. A. (2005). *Attachment, evolution, and the psychology of religion.* Guilford Press.

Liu, L., Cohen, S., Schulz, M. S., & Waldinger, R. J. (2011). Sources of somatization: Exploring the roles of insecurity in relationships and styles of anger experience and expression. *Social Science and Medicine, 73,* 1436–1443.

Lopez, F. G. (2009). Clinical correlates of adult attachment organization. In J. H. Obegi & E. Berant (Eds.), *Attachment theory and research in clinical work with adults* (pp. 94–117). Guilford Press.

Orwell, G. (1949). *1984.* Secker & Warburg.

Thoreau, H. D. (1854). *Walden.* Oxford University Press.

Wallin, D. J. (2007). *Attachment in psychotherapy.* Guilford Press.

Winnicott, D. W. (1969). The use of an object. *International Journal of Psycho-Analysis, 50,* 711–716.

Winnicott, D. W. (1971). *Playing and reality.* Basic Books.

Chapter 4

Bill W.

Anxious-Avoidant Attachment— Higher Power as Compensation

As co-founder of Alcoholics Anonymous (AA; Anonymous, 2000) and co-founder of the self-help movement in the United States (Flora et al., 2010), Bill W. is arguably one of the most iconic figures in American history, yet one unfamiliar to most. Bill W. also pioneered the integration of psychological and spiritual principles into a practical—and effective—group and individual intervention for alcoholics. A recent meta-analysis (Kelly et al., 2020) concluded that AA groups were at least as effective as popular psychotherapy treatment models such as cognitive-behavior therapy (CBT). In addition, Wikipedia currently lists 43 12-step programs at least partially patterned after AA (https://en.wikipedia.org/wiki/List_of_twelve-step_groups). I explore Bill W.'s humble beginning in rural Vermont and trace his steps to Wall Street and a spiritual conversion experience documented in his posthumous autobiography, *Bill W.: My First 40 Years* (Anonymous, 2000). An avowed atheist for most of these 40 years, how did Bill W. create one of the most successful ecumenical spiritual movements of the past 100 years? Does his life illustrate what William James (1902) described as the "sick soul," who comes to spirituality after having been broken? How do "sick souls" establish their Higher Power as a secure attachment figure to compensate for rejecting, inconsistent, or negligent attachment figures from childhood? How would a therapist leverage this spiritual conversion to help him to develop secure attachment relationships to significant others?

Through studying an account of his life written in his own words (Anonymous, 2000), I conclude that Bill W. developed an anxious-avoidant attachment relationship to his parents and to God. Moreover, Bill W.'s anxious-avoidant attachment relationship to God—a secondary attachment strategy (see Goodman, 2025, Chapter 6) that manifested itself in his atheistic convictions—changed to a secure attachment relationship to God when his stress levels had reached a threshold of desperation that broke through this secondary attachment strategy (Granqvist & Kirkpatrick, 2018) and forced him to manifest secure attachment behaviors such as proximity-seeking and contact-maintenance to God (see Goodman, 2025, Chapter 6). Bill W.'s narrative prototypically illustrates the compensation hypothesis in the religion-as-attachment model (e.g., Granqvist & Kirkpatrick, 2018) because the secure attachment relationship to God compensated for the anxious-avoidant attachment relationships to his parents, especially his mother. Did this spiritual conversion to a secure attachment relationship to God produce a conversion to his anxious-avoidant attachment relationships to his parents? How could a therapist facilitate healing in these parental attachment relationships?

In this chapter, I first identify the interpersonal markers of Bill W.'s anxious-avoidant attachment relationships to his parents and his secure attachment relationship to his Higher Power and then explore how Bill W.'s spiritual awakening catalyzed his later achievements such as creating the 12 steps of AA, which became a blueprint for all 12-step programs. Third, and finally, as a prime example of someone who might have come to me for therapy, I formulate a treatment plan for Bill W. as a prototypical representative of anxious-avoidantly attached persons like him.

Bill W. (Anonymous, 2000) was born in East Dorset, Vermont, in 1895—fittingly, in the back of a bar. His father, Gilman, was a marble quarryman; he later moved to British Columbia to manage a quarry. His mother, Emily, was a frustrated housewife and mother; she later moved to Boston to become an osteopathic physician. Bill W.'s parents divorced when he was 10 years old, which created "a shock which I will never forget" (p. 12). With both parents moving away, Bill W. was raised by his maternal grandparents, Gardner and Ellen. At the age of 12, they sent Bill W. away to Burr and Burton Seminary, a boarding school in Manchester, Vermont, seven miles away from their home, visiting them on weekends. Despite his separation from his family, Bill W. considered boarding school a "lovely place to be" (p. 26).

While at boarding school, the 16-year-old Bill W. fell deeply in love with Bertha Bamford, the daughter of a prominent minister (Anonymous, 2000). She died suddenly from complications of surgery, leaving Bill W. with "an old-fashioned nervous breakdown, which meant, I now realize, a tremendous depression ... My whole career and my whole life utterly collapsed" (p. 30). A year later, however, Bill W. met Lois Burnham, four years his senior. They were later to get married and spend the rest of their lives together. Norwich University Military College and World War I, however, threatened to interfere with their marital plans. At age 21, Bill W. became a coast artillery officer in the US Army, and just before shipping out to France, he and Lois married.

Also just prior to shipping out, the Army sent Bill W. to Fort Rodman, Massachusetts, where he completed his training (Anonymous, 2000). Despite his knowledge of a family history of alcoholism ("I'd been told how many of my ancestors went down with it"; p. 42), Bill W. took his first drink of alcohol, a Bronx cocktail, during this final training. What did this drink, and the three that followed it, do to him? According to Bill W.:

> that strange barrier that had existed between me and all men and women, even the closest, seemed to instantly go down. I felt that I belonged where I was, I belonged to life, I belonged to the universe, I was a part of things at last.
>
> (p. 43)

So began a love affair with "John Barleycorn," as Bill W. personified alcohol (p. 102), at other times referring to him as a "devil" and a "demon" (p. 113).

After World War I, Bill W. moved to Brooklyn, New York, with Lois and attended Brooklyn Law School at St. Lawrence University, dropping out at age 28 one exam short of completing his degree (https://the12traditions.com/217/bill-wilson-and-law-school/). He never finished because he failed a final exam while inebriated. Bill W. then took an interest in Wall Street and became a successful securities investigator (Anonymous, 2000). He and Lois would travel to corporations up and down the Eastern seaboard to ask questions and observe their operations and then report back to the wealthy stakeholders who had sent him. He was paid handsomely for this work and was able to buy his own shares in the corporations whose stock values he believed would rise. According to Bill W., "when 1928 blew around I was a tycoon, see, and they thought I was just wonderful. Meanwhile, the drinking—up and up and up" (p. 72).

Bill W.'s alcohol consumption became so excessive that he entered Charles B. Towns Hospital, a rehab facility in Manhattan, on four separate occasions between 1933 and 1934 (Anonymous, 2000). In those days, the treatment for alcoholism consisted of a "sedative, an occasional shot of whiskey, which was taken down to nothing in about three days; meanwhile they plied you with castor oil and belladonna [a toxic plant that induces vomiting]" (p. 106). The physicians at Towns Hospital used these methods, however, to treat only the symptoms of alcoholism. Even the hospital's owner, Charlie Towns, "didn't talk too much about curing alcoholism" (p. 107).

On December 14, 1934, during his final rehab stay at Towns Hospital, Bill W. had a vision (Anonymous, 2000). Desperate and pondering suicide, Bill W. spoke these words: "'I'll do anything, anything at all. If there be a Great Physician, I'll call on him ... If there be a God, let him show himself'" (p. 145). According to Bill W., he suddenly "stood upon [a mountain] summit where a great wind blew. A wind, not of air, but of spirit. Then came the blazing thought, 'You are a free man'" (p. 145). After this spiritual experience, Bill W. never took another drop of alcohol.

With his collaborator, Dr. Bob, Bill W. became the co-founder of Alcoholics Anonymous (AA) on June 10, 1935—the date when Dr. Bob took his last drink of alcohol and six months after Bill W. had taken his (Anonymous, 2000). In December of 1938—four years after his mountaintop experience—Bill W. created the 12-step program of recovery, the blueprint for this organization that many later programs of addiction recovery adopted (Thomsen, 1975). I will later analyze these 12 steps for clues about the quality of Bill W.'s attachment relationship to God, even though he did not refer to the 12 steps in his autobiography because the autobiography covers his life only up to the spiritual conversion that saved his life.

Bill W.'s Attachment Relationships to His Parents

Bill W. (Anonymous, 2000) discusses his relationships to his parents and grandparents mostly in the first 31 pages of his autobiography. At that point in his narrative, at age 17, he meets his future wife, Lois Burnham, who "came along and picked me up as tenderly as a mother does a child. I was attracted to her" (p. 32). Thus, he no longer seems to need parental figures and almost never mentions them again. The narrative suggests that Bill W. developed an anxious-avoidant attachment to his mother as well as an anxious-avoidant attachment to his father that nevertheless included secure attachment features. When his parents divorced when Bill was 10, his maternal grandparents took care of him, and it seems likely that he developed a secure attachment relationship to his maternal grandfather, although this attachment pattern seems to be relationship-specific (see Goodman, 2025, Chapter 2). As I demonstrate below, Bill W.'s anxious-avoidant attachment relationships to his parents deeply affected his "primary mode of relatedness" (Slade, 1999, p. 588) in most of his subsequent interactions as well as his spiritual worldview; he became an atheist in young adulthood.

Bill W. paints an emotionally barren picture of his mother and her family line: "Mother was never especially communicative on intimacies. She was, as I have explained, of that rather dour Griffith stock" (p. 10). At age 7 or 8, his mother was, by his recollection,

> a disciplinarian, and I can remember the agony of hostility and fear that I went through when she administered her first good tanning with the back of a hairbrush. Somehow I never could forget that beating. It made an indelible impression upon me, for I really think that she was angry.
>
> (Anonymous, 2000, pp. 8–9)

This recollection of corporal punishment associated with maternal anger directed toward him might also qualify Bill W. for a disorganized attachment relationship to his mother, but other examples make clear that Bill W. formed an anxious-avoidant attachment relationship to her. Reflecting on this relationship at the time of writing, Bill W. concludes:

> There was a sort of barrier between Mother and me which has only in recent years dissolved. I loved Father, but I admired and respected Mother. Probably I was always lacking in the right sort of love for her, as I think she was at times for me.
>
> (p. 13)

For example, after Bill W.'s aforementioned high school sweetheart died suddenly at age 16, and he had withdrawn from all school activities in a deep depression, "my mother came up, terribly angry, from Boston [where she was living]" (p. 31). From Bill W.'s perspective, his mother showed him no compassion, instead behaving in a reproachful manner toward him. Bill W. also shares that his mother was having "nervous breakdowns, sometimes requiring that she go away for extended periods to the seashore, and on one occasion to the sanitarium" (p. 10). Thus, Bill W.'s mother was often physically as well as emotionally unavailable to her young son.

Another example of Bill W.'s attachment relationship to his mother demonstrates that, even in an attachment-activating situation like her son's physical pain (see Goodman, 2025, Chapter 2), the response of Bill W.'s mother was not sensitive to his needs (Anonymous, 2000). While in college, Bill W. slipped on ice and dislocated his elbow. Instead of going to a local physician for treatment, Bill W.

> absolutely insisted on going all the way [from Northfield, Vermont] to Boston [a nearly three-hour trip] to let my mother, then an osteopathic physician down there, look after it. Mother marveled that I hadn't had the thing reduced at school.
>
> (p. 33)

In Chapter 6 of Goodman (2025), I discuss secondary attachment strategies that break down under stressful conditions, uncovering what we would consider to be secure attachment strategies such as proximity-seeking. In this incident, Bill W. was probably in so much anguish that proximity-seeking broke through his defensive, anxious-avoidant strategy of ignoring his attachment needs; thus, he reached out to his mother. It is hard not to notice his mother's reaction: rather than feeling compassion or vicarious distress, she expressed astonishment that he would travel so far to seek her attention and ministrations.

Bill W. describes his father differently from his mother, at least until his father abandoned the family to live in British Columbia when Bill W. was 10 (Anonymous, 2000). He characterized his father's entire family idealistically: "My father's people were very amiable and were noted on all sides for their humanity. They were popular folk. They were easygoing folk. They were tolerant folk" (p. 5). He similarly idealized his father:

> In those days I had a fine companionship with my dad, who used to play ball with me in the yard every night, and on Sundays we would rent a covered buggy—I don't believe that's exactly the name of it, having a flat top with tassels all around—and drive about in some estate and with a great deal of satisfaction.
>
> (pp. 8–9)

Contrasting his relationship to his mother, Bill W. wrote, "I loved Father" (p. 13). Even when Bill W. created nitroglycerine from a chemistry set in a backyard woodshed, his father, though "horrified" (p. 8), nevertheless disposed of the explosive chemical without any apparent reproach of his scientifically minded son. Despite episodic memories of his father's being a loving and playful attachment figure, Bill W. nevertheless points out that "my father never became an alcoholic, [but] he was at times a pretty heavy drinker" (p. 10). Perhaps Bill W.'s idealization of his father included minimizing the extent of his father's alcohol consumption, which would also render him emotionally unavailable at times.

What thus far appears to be a mostly secure attachment relationship to his father soon changes to an anxious-avoidant attachment relationship after Bill W.'s father moves to British Columbia to manage another marble quarry (Anonymous, 2000). From the time his father left the family to the time of the writing of the autobiography, "I have not seen my own father more than a dozen times" (p. 10). Later in the autobiography, Bill W. revises the number of visits: "I don't believe that in all the years I had seen my father half a dozen times" (p. 103). His father quickly remarried and had a daughter (p. 11), which, in addition to the geographical distance, provided little motivation for his father to visit his son. Furthermore, his father left it up to his mother to tell Bill W. that he had left the country: "Mother told us that Father had gone for good" (p. 13). Overall, "the wound of my father's and mother's separation and subsequent divorce" left a 10- or 11-year-old Bill W. "particularly [suffering]" (pp. 14–15). Bill W. does not recall when or how he learned that his parents' divorce had been finalized. Adding salt to his wound, though, his mother took his younger sister with her to Boston; she left Bill W. in the care of his maternal grandparents.

I want to highlight this later attachment figure for Bill W.: his maternal grandfather. Without his maternal grandfather, it is possible that Bill W.'s life trajectory might have ended quite differently. Bill W.'s grandfather became his primary attachment relationship at around age 10, after both his parents moved away (Anonymous, 2000). By Bill W.'s account, this attachment relationship seemed to be secure. Importantly, he felt his grandfather's love for him: "[The Griffiths] were capable of great love for their own, and this is certainly a factor in my grandfather's relation to me" (p. 7). His grandfather's love that continued throughout his childhood, Bill W. reciprocated:

> All during this period my grandfather was really the soul of kindness. He loved me deeply, and I loved him as I have few other people. One of my earliest recollections, dating back to the time before we went to Rutland, was that of sitting on his knee and later at his knee, while he read me books of travel.
> (p. 19)

His maternal grandfather was a validating presence, much as his father had been before he abandoned the family: "My grandfather ... warmly approved all my activities" (p. 21). Bowlby (1982) postulated that the principal function of the attachment system is protection (see Goodman, 2025, Chapter 2), and indeed, Bill W. describes this grandfather as "my protector" and a provider who was "generous with my spending money" (p. 30). Bill W. regarded him as a safe haven, a key attachment behavior. After experiencing multiple panic attacks at college, Bill W. writes that he "was sent back to my grandfather, which was just where I wanted to go" (p. 34). Perhaps because of his anxious-avoidant attachment relationship to his mother, Bill W. describes his inability to feel the same love for his maternal grandmother that he felt toward his grandfather: "She was very sweet and good to me, but somehow she never evoked the love and adulation that I gave my grandfather" (p. 66). Thus, after the age of 10, Bill W. does seem to find attachment security in his relationship to his maternal grandfather.

When at age 17, Bill W. met Lois Burnham, his future wife, she also became an attachment figure to him, manifesting some of the hallmarks of an attachment relationship such as loving feelings and separation protest (see Zeifman & Hazan, 1997, 2018): "Lois appeared, and she lifted me out of this despond and we fell deeply in love ... I ... couldn't bear leaving her. At the unconscious level, I have no doubt she was already becoming my mother" (Anonymous, 2000, p. 35). As mentioned earlier, Bill W. underscores Lois's sensitive caregiving behavior and unconditional acceptance of his proximity-seeking, two key predictors of a secure attachment relationship: "Lois came along and picked me up as tenderly as a mother does a child" (p. 32). Shortly before his spiritual conversion and permanent sobriety from alcohol, Bill W. reflected on the consistency and trustworthiness of his attachment relationship to Lois: "I thought of Lois, how magnificent, how devoted, how unwavering she had been. Fair weather or foul, it had always been the same. Never had she failed me" (p. 143). Even during the darkest hour of his alcoholism, Bill W. sought her proximity, which she gladly provided: "We had drawn closer together as the menace [alcoholism] grew nearer" (p. 144). Even after the Wall Street Crash of 1929, "Lois was always there, and even now [in an alcoholic stupor] she was beside me" (p. 144). Perhaps some of Bill W.'s account idealizes his attachment relationship to Lois, but overall, she seems to have provided attachment security for him.

I want to identify one additional, surrogate attachment figure for Bill W.—one that served a valuable position in his "psychic equilibrium," to borrow the fitting term of Rizzuto (1979, p. 88). That surrogate attachment figure is alcohol. Following Granqvist (2020), humans can become attached to nonliving entities such as teddy bears and imaginary friends. So too can humans become attached to habitual behaviors and psychoactive substances that provide temporary pleasure, relief, comfort, and security. Alcohol is always available; it can never reject you or abandon you. It can instantly (though temporarily) replace feelings of sadness or resentment or anxiety or guilt with feelings of pleasure or numbness or excitement or ecstasy. It can help you to forget your failures. All is right with the world while drinking—until the intoxication wears off. Referring to his relationship to alcohol as a "commitment" (p. 112), Bill W. (Anonymous, 2000) explains that while drinking alcohol,

> That strange barrier that had existed between me and all men and women, even the closest, seemed to instantly go down. I felt that I belonged where I was, I belonged to life, I belonged to the universe, I was a part of things at last.
> (p. 43)

A feeling of belonging is aligned with feelings of comfort and acceptance, two hallmarks of an attachment relationship (see Goodman, 2025, Chapter 2). This attachment relationship to alcohol even superseded the one to his wife. His perpetual drunkenness made Lois "kind of an also-ran. Poor girl, it's been her lot ever since" (p. 77). Finally, Bill W. often personifies his attachment relationship to alcohol, referring to it as "John Barleycorn" (p. 102), "Barleycorn" (pp. 92, 113, 123), "this devil" (p. 113), and "the demon" (pp. 86, 113). Alcohol therefore became an entity with sentient qualities that he came to depend on as a child depends on his caregiver for security.

Bill W.'s Attachment Relationship to God

In this section, I will argue that Bill W.'s (Anonymous, 2000) narrative prototypically illustrates the compensation hypothesis in the religion-as-attachment model (e.g., Granqvist & Kirkpatrick, 2018) because the secure attachment relationship to God compensated for the anxious-avoidant attachment relationships to his parents, especially his mother. As an atheist, Bill W. denied an attachment relationship to a Higher Power, which we can conceptualize as avoidance and dismissal of this relationship. In Chapter 3 of Goodman (2025), I discussed that believing in God is the default setting for most children unless (1) they are socialized not to believe in God and (2) they have insecure attachment relationships to their parents. In Chapter 6 of Goodman (2025), I discussed that under conditions of extreme stress, secondary attachment strategies such as deactivating the attachment system to avoid feelings of rejection and abandonment ("I couldn't care less if you leave me; you don't matter to me anyway") can break down, and the primary attachment strategy of activating the attachment system (through proximity-seeking and contact-maintenance behaviors) can then be observed. Bill W.'s life represents the prototype of this phenomenon. He experienced a sudden, life-changing spiritual conversion (p. 145), which resulted in his sobriety from alcohol, close relationships with other persons in recovery from alcohol, including the co-founder of AA, Dr. Bob (p. 163), and a sustained belief and trust in a Higher Power (pp. 146–147), which he called "this great and sudden gift of grace" (p. 146).

The evidence of Bill W.'s (Anonymous, 2000) atheism is clear from the narrative. He refers to his god as "science" (p. 133); elsewhere, he declares that "man is god" (p. 135). After having spoken to his childhood friend Ebby, who had stopped drinking alcohol through the Christian-influenced Oxford Groups, Bill W. considers recovery, only without the God part: "After all, a conservative atheist like me ought to be able to get on without anything like that!" (p. 139). Bill W. seemed to be aware that despite his atheism, he might have always believed in God *unconsciously*: "I was not a conscious believer in God at the time—I had no defined belief" (p. 50). He seems to understand that in retrospect, he had been defending against a conscious awareness of a Higher Power until the point of his spiritual conversion.

At the point of spiritual conversion, Bill W. (Anonymous, 2000) called on God—the God in Whom he did not believe—to intervene on his behalf:

> I remember saying to myself, "I'll do anything, anything at all. If there be a Great Physician, I'll call on him." Then, with neither faith nor hope I cried

out, "If there be a God, let him show himself." The effect was instant, electric. Suddenly my room blazed with an indescribably white light. I was seized with an ecstasy beyond description ... I became acutely conscious of a presence which seemed like a veritable sea of living spirit. I lay on the shores of a new world ... For the first time I felt that I really belonged. I knew that I was loved and could love in return. I thanked my God who had given me a glimpse of His absolute Self. Even though a pilgrim upon an uncertain highway, I need be concerned no more, for I had glimpsed the great beyond.

(pp. 145–146)

We observe that Bill W. suddenly becomes aware of his perception of a Higher Power and seems to characterize this relationship to this Higher Power as a secure attachment by noticing that he felt he "really belonged" and felt he was "loved and could love in return." These are hallmark characteristics associated with secure attachment. He had previously identified alcohol as exclusively giving him the feeling of belonging (see p. 43).

Interestingly, Bill W. (Anonymous, 2000) emphasizes that faith is not a prerequisite for a spiritual conversion experience. Though in the preceding passage, he notes that he had no faith at the moment of spiritual conversion, I would argue that it took faith to call out to a heretofore nonexistent God. Elsewhere, he elaborates on his thoughts about the role of faith in the spiritual conversion experience. He declares, "Out of no faith, faith had suddenly appeared. No blind faith either, for it was fortified by the consciousness of the presence of God" (p. 147). He seems to be suggesting that the faith appeared after the awareness of God's presence, not before, because he had "been incapable of faith and so, God's help" (p. 147). Summarizing the key elements of his spiritual awakening to other alcoholics, Bill W. returns to this theme:

Provided their personal hopelessness was great enough, an appeal to any higher power at all would bring results. They only needed to cry out in the dark for whomever or whatever might be there. No faith would be required. That would be part of the gift itself.

(p. 155)

Perhaps Bill W.'s experience mirrors that of the man who asks Jesus to heal his son from epilepsy: "I do believe; help me overcome my unbelief!" (Mark 9:24; NIV, 1978). Bill W.'s calling out in desperation for a sign from God was the act of faith required for this spiritual conversion process to unfold. It was at this moment when the secondary attachment strategy broke down, and a secure attachment to a Higher Power, which included proximity-seeking accompanied by feelings of trust, belonging, and love, could be established. From Bill W.'s perspective, his faith was a pure act of grace, the acceptance of a gift of priceless value, freely given by a Higher Power, which Bill W. could have never earned.

Markers of an Anxious-Avoidant Attachment Relationship

As mentioned in previous chapters, Daniel (2015) identifies two sets of markers that indicate an anxious-avoidant attachment relationship: interpersonal and narrative markers. Even though Bill W. dictated this autobiography, which was published posthumously (Anonymous, 2000, p. ix), an editor made edits throughout the manuscript, thus rather spoiling the text for any analysis of narrative markers. Thus, I will focus only on the interpersonal markers, which Daniel (2015) notes "are systematically and meaningfully connected in treatment providers' assessment of clients" (p. 113). I will later use this information to formulate a brief treatment plan and intervention strategy for Bill W. as if he had been referred to me for treatment.

In keeping with the structure of these autobiographical chapters, I will analyze the interpersonal markers of only Bill W.'s attachment relationships to his parents and his Higher Power and ignore his attachment relationships to his maternal grandfather, his wife, and alcohol (as a surrogate attachment figure), even though I argued earlier that he established attachment relationships to all three. The focus will remain on the attachment relationships to his parents from early childhood and his attachment relationship to God.

Bill W.'s Attachment Relationships to His Parents and to God

As in previous chapters, I present Table 4.1, which summarizes the findings of my analysis of the nine interpersonal markers of the attachment relationship (Daniel, 2015). In the first column, I list these nine markers. In the second column, I include a key phrase from Daniel (2015) that most closely represents the specific attachment pattern suggested by the quotation. In the third column, I include a key quotation from Bill W.'s (Anonymous, 2000) autobiography that supports each of the nine interpersonal markers related to his attachment relationships to his parents. In the fourth column, I include a key phrase from Daniel (2015) that most closely represents the specific attachment pattern suggested by the quotation. Finally, in the fifth column, I include a key quotation that supports each of these markers related to his attachment relationship to God.

Proximity/Distance

Because Proximity/Distance relies on visual observation, this interpersonal marker is difficult to assess in text; thus, my analysis is speculative. Based on my earlier analysis, we are looking for anxious-avoidant dimensions of Bill W.'s attachment relationships to his parents and secure dimensions of his attachment relationship to God after his spiritual awakening. According to Daniel (2015), securely attached

Table 4.1 Nine interpersonal markers of attachment for Bill W.

Interpersonal markers	Primary marker with parents	Key quotation/parents	Primary marker with God	Key quotation/God
Proximity/distance	Prefers distance/uncomfortable with proximity	"There was a sort of barrier between Mother and me"	Values/is comfortable with proximity	"I was surrounded and, indeed, filled with that life-giving presence"
Trust/expectation of others	Ignores feelings of insecurity	"I was always lacking in the right sort of love for her, as … she was for me"	Trusting/positive expectations	"I'd been incapable of faith … Faith had suddenly appeared"
Attitude to seeking and receiving help	Prefers to handle things by himself	"I hid the wound and never talked about it with anybody, even my sister"	Open to seeking help	"If there be a Great Physician, I'll call on him"
Expression and regulation of emotions	Limited expression of emotions, false positivity	"I am deliriously happy"	Balanced expressions of positive and negative emotions	"As I became more quiet a great peace stole over me"
Self-image/self-esteem	Defensively "magnified" self-image to compensate for low self-esteem	"I began a desperate struggle to become number one"	Nuanced/solid self-esteem	"Ego deflation at great depth was the key to the riddle … God-confidence was the thing"
Openness and self-disclosure	Reticent about sharing thoughts and feelings	"I hid liquor about as a squirrel would cherish nuts"	Pleased to share thoughts and feelings, dosed according to situation	"[An alcoholic must be] capable of being honest enough to admit his own defeat"

				"Their lives had been transformed by … dependence upon God for His guidance"
Dependence/ independence	Greatly values independence from others	"It was a wonder I didn't kill some of the farmers about, as it was a very high-powered gun"	Feels comfortable in committed relationships, capable of autonomy	
Conflict management	Uncomfortable with potential conflicts, attempts to ignore these	"All during college I had backed away from drinking … But here it was"	Constructive strategies for handling conflicts	"People ought to confess their sins 'one to another.'"
Empathy	Limited empathy and interpersonal "coldness"	"I cut the head out of my bed (my grandfather didn't care for this so much)"	Empathy with and care for others	"One alcoholic turning the message to another could ready the sufferer"

Source: Modeled after Daniel (2015, p. 115).

Note: [a]These interpersonal markers reflect Bill W.'s attachment relationship to God after his spiritual conversion experience.

persons "value and are comfortable with proximity," whereas anxious-avoidant persons "prefer distance and are uncomfortable with proximity. [They c]onsider self 'different'" (p. 115). What follows are select key quotations that address the Proximity/Distance marker.

Even in his earliest memory, Bill W. is alone—not in proximity to his parents (Anonymous, 2000). Instead, he is "looking out of the window from my crib just as the sunset developed over the great mountain and becoming very conscious of it for the first time. It is an impression which never left me" (p. 3). As mentioned earlier, Bill W.'s father abruptly left home when Bill W. was age 10—without telling him. He writes, "[Since he left] I have not seen my own father more than a dozen times" (p. 10) or perhaps "half a dozen times" (p. 103). Soon after his father's abandonment of him, his mother "set about to making a career and embarked upon a career" in Boston, and "excepting for brief vacation periods, I saw little of her for the next years" (p. 13). Thus, both of Bill W.'s parents rejected him and created distance between them and him. By age 12, Bill W. was living weekdays at Burr and Burton Seminary, a boarding school (p. 23); thus, he experienced rejection by his maternal grandparents. Bill W. could not graduate from high school because he had failed German, so his "mother came up, terribly angry, from Boston" (p. 31). Rather than showing compassion and understanding, Bill W.'s mother showed anger and disappointment, no doubt making him feel further rejected.

Because Bill W. (Anonymous, 2000) indicates that he did not believe in God ("a conservative atheist like me ought to be able to get on without anything like that!"; p. 139), we cannot analyze his attachment relationship to God except to comment that a nonrelationship to God represents the ultimate distancing of oneself from God. This denial of God's existence could be interpreted as one strategy in the anxious-avoidant attachment relationship model to deactivate the attachment system (see Goodman, 2025, Chapter 3).

We can instead turn our attention to Bill W's (Anonymous, 2000) attachment relationship to God during and after his spiritual awakening. During his spiritual awakening, Bill W.

> became acutely aware of a presence which seemed like a veritable sea of living spirit .... I seemed possessed by the absolute ... For the first time I felt that I really belonged. I knew that I was loved and could love in return.
>
> (pp. 145–146)

Bill W.'s feelings of presence, possession, belonging, and love all suggest proximity to his Higher Power rather than distance. Even the day after his spiritual awakening, "I was surrounded and, indeed, filled with that life-giving presence which had made my assurance that all was so well so complete" (p. 149). The presence of God was palpable to him; God was no longer distant or nonexistent. Thus, in these quotations referencing the interpersonal marker of Proximity/Distance, we observe a compensation between Bill W.'s anxious-avoidant attachment relationships to his parents and his secure attachment relationship to God.

Trust/Expectations of Others

This interpersonal marker of the attachment pattern is evident in Bill W.'s descriptions of his attachment relationships to his parents and to God (Anonymous, 2000). Based on my earlier analysis, we are looking for anxious-avoidant dimensions of his attachment relationships to his parents and secure dimensions of his attachment relationship to God. Concerning this marker, Daniel (2015) writes that securely attached persons "are trusting and have positive expectations," whereas anxious-avoidant persons "fear rejection or ridicule, but try to ignore feelings of insecurity" (p. 115). I will now select key quotations that address the marker of Trust/Expectations of Others.

Regarding his attachment relationships to his parents, Bill W. (Anonymous, 2000) characterizes his father's abandonment and his mother's disclosure of this event during a picnic on North Dorset Pond as "a shock which I can never forget ... an agonizing experience" (pp. 12–13). His trust in his parents to provide a safe haven had been permanently shattered. His mother's departure to Boston to pursue a medical degree shortly thereafter (p. 13) probably solidified Bill W.'s expectation that his parents would always reject him. Bill W. describes "a barrier between Mother and me ... Probably I was always lacking in the right sort of love for her, as I think she was at times for me" (p. 13). This expectation of rejection and subsequent fear of disappointing others followed him into the army, when he qualified for officer training and selected coast artillery. Those who chose this branch of the army were considered cowards because they would likely not see hand-to-hand combat. Bill W. describes feeling ashamed of his choice because "I had let my ancestors down!" (p. 41). Thus, we observe that from early in life, Bill W. developed the expectation that others would reject him and that he would continue to disappoint the significant people in his life. These quotations demonstrate anxious-avoidant attachment relationships to his parents.

Analyzing Bill W.'s (Anonymous, 2000) attachment relationship to God after his spiritual awakening, we observe a completely different attitude. Bill W. expresses a profound trust in God's protection and care: "I had done all right and had given my life to God" (p. 137). Later, he elaborates on this trust: "No matter how wrong things seemed to be, there would be no question of the ultimate rightness of God's universe ... Even though a pilgrim upon an uncertain highway, I need be concerned no more" (p. 146). Prior to his spiritual awakening, "I'd been incapable of faith ... Yet, out of no faith, faith had suddenly appeared ... Despair had turned into utter security" (p. 147). Thus, the narrative strongly supports the idea of compensation: although Bill W. developed the expectation of rejection from his parents and disappointment from his family, his description of his attachment relationship to God reflects a profound trust and expectation of care, demonstrating that a secure attachment relationship to his Higher Power compensated for anxious-avoidant attachment relationships to his parents.

Attitude to Seeking and Receiving Help

This interpersonal marker of the attachment pattern is evident in Bill W.'s descriptions of his attachment relationships to his parents and to God (Anonymous, 2000). Based on my earlier analysis, we are looking for anxious-avoidant dimensions of his attachment relationships to his parents and secure dimensions of his attachment relationship to God. Regarding this marker, Daniel (2015) writes that securely attached persons "are open to seeking help," whereas anxious-avoidant persons "prefer to handle things themselves" (p. 115). Which parts of Bill W.'s book address the Attitude to Seeking and Receiving Help marker?

Regarding Bill W.'s (Anonymous, 2000) attachment relationships to his parents, perhaps the most poignant example of this marker takes place after his mother informed him at age 10 of his father's departure. Instead of reaching out for support and care, Bill W. "hid the wound and never talked about it with anybody, even my sister, let alone my Grandfather and Grandmother Griffith" (p. 13). Interestingly, Bill W. does not even mention his mother as a possible confidant of his feelings. Did he not seek help in this situation because he knew that it would not be forthcoming? This quotation also supports the interpersonal marker, Openness and Self-disclosure. Bill W. also discusses his budding interest in science and chemistry, having set up a makeshift laboratory in the woodshed (p. 8). As mentioned earlier, he was casually mixing explosive chemicals such as sulphuric acid and nitric acid to make nitroglycerine when his father "found that I had mixed certain acids … [and] dug a very large hole" (p. 8) to bury these chemicals. What was a boy under the age of 10 doing with these chemicals in the first place? Why had Bill W. not asked for help in setting up his laboratory or guidance in conducting his experiments? He was pursuing this interest strictly on his own, which could have resulted in fatal consequences if he had inadvertently blown up himself and his family.

When feeling particularly distressed, however, Bill W. did seek help from his mother, but only as a young adult (Anonymous, 2000). As previously mentioned, in college, Bill W. slipped on ice and dislocated his elbow, which had already sustained damage from an earlier baseball injury. Instead of going to a local orthopedist, he traveled to Boston to allow his mother to tend to the elbow (p. 33). As I discussed earlier, his secondary attachment strategy of anxious-avoidance broke down under this distressing situation, uncovering a secure attachment strategy of help-seeking.

Regarding this interpersonal marker, Bill W. (Anonymous, 2000) evidenced a secure attachment relationship to God. In the days leading up to his spiritual awakening, Bill W. was contemplating seeking God. This period of contemplation immediately followed a conversation he had had with his childhood friend and fellow alcoholic Ebby, who had become sober from alcohol through his association with the Oxford Groups. Bill W. writes,

Yes, if there was any great physician that could cure the alcohol sickness, I'd better seek him now, at once. I'd better find what my friend had found ... If getting well required me to pray at high noon in the public square with the other sufferers, would I swallow my pride and do that?

(p. 139)

Thus, we observe again the breakdown of a secondary attachment strategy in an extremely distressing situation—the threatened loss of sanity due to alcohol addiction—and the revelation of the underlying secure attachment strategy of help-seeking. The most compelling example of help-seeking from God comes from Bill W.'s already quoted spiritual awakening: "I remember saying to myself, 'I'll do anything, anything at all. If there be a Great Physician, I'll call on him.' Then, with neither faith nor hope I cried out, 'If there be a God, let him show himself'" (p. 145). At his lowest point in life, which alcoholics often refer to as "rock bottom," Bill W. sought help from a Higher Power. He continued to seek help from his Higher Power and even codified help-seeking from a Higher Power in the 12 Steps of AA. Again, Bill W.'s narrative strongly supports the idea of compensation: although Bill W. acted alone and never asked for help from his parents as a child, this secondary anxious-avoidant attachment strategy finally broke down at his lowest point, revealing the secure attachment strategy of seeking help from God. Thus, a secure attachment relationship to his Higher Power compensated for anxious-avoidant attachment relationships to his parents.

Expression and Regulation of Emotions

This interpersonal marker of the attachment pattern is evident in Bill W.'s descriptions of his attachment relationships to his parents and to God (Anonymous, 2000). Based on my earlier analysis, we are looking for anxious-avoidant dimensions of his attachment relationships to his parents and secure dimensions of his attachment relationship to God. Regarding this marker, Daniel (2015) notes that securely attached persons demonstrate "balanced expressions of both positive and negative emotions," whereas anxious-avoidant persons demonstrate "limited expression of emotions; false positivity; suppression of negative emotions" (p. 115). What aspects of his autobiography address the Expression and Regulation of Emotions marker?

Regarding Bill W.'s (Anonymous, 2000) attachment relationships to his parents, we observe difficulties with emotion regulation in both parents. According to Bill W., his mother had "nervous breakdowns" and once required a stay at a "sanitarium," while his father was "at times a pretty heavy drinker" (p. 10). It is likely that neither parent could regulate their emotions without breaking down or relying on alcohol to numb painful feelings. As for young Bill W., all we have available to us are his descriptions of events; we were not there to observe his emotion regulation skills. Based on how he wrote about certain experiences, however, we can surmise how he expressed and managed his emotions. In Chapter 3 on Anne Frank, the narrative is brimming over with a wide range of emotions that make the reader feel what she is feeling. With very few exceptions, Bill W. writes about traumatic events as if he were reporting the weather; however, Bill W. does express his emotions when his mother tells him that his father has abandoned the family:

> Then it was that Mother told us that Father had gone for good. To this day I shiver every time I recall that scene on the grass by the lakefront. It was an agonizing experience for one who apparently had the emotional sensitivity that I did.
>
> (p. 13)

He also expressed negative emotions when his mother "administered her first good tanning with the back of a hairbrush": "I can remember the agony of hostility and fear that I went through" (p. 9). The expression of negative emotions in this attachment-activating situation seems to break through the anxious-avoidant tendency to constrict his emotional life.

Although Bill W. views himself as emotionally sensitive, he seems to be emotionally constricted when recounting other childhood events that might elicit a strong emotional reaction within ourselves. For example, Bill W. writes that his sister Dorothy "went off to live with [my mother], and it fell to the lot of Grandfather and Grandmother Griffith to bring me up" (p. 14). His sister got to live with his mother, while he was abandoned again—this time by his other parent. Yet there is no expression of emotion associated with this traumatic event. Similarly, 12-year-old Bill W. was shipped off to Burr and Burton Seminary, boarding there "five days a week" (p. 23). Yet, Bill W. provides no commentary about his feelings about this move away from his beloved maternal grandfather. He seems to have concluded that this was just his lot in life—to be cast off by attachment figures.

Bill W. (Anonymous, 2000) seemed more adept at expressing his emotions around nonattachment figures. At boarding school, while trying out for the baseball team, he got hit in the head while trying to catch a ball. He recounts the aftermath of this incident:

> The moment they saw I wasn't hurt, they all commenced to laugh at my awkwardness, and I remember the terrible spasm of rage that came up in me. And I remember how I jumped up and shook my fist and said, "I'll show you! I'll be captain of your baseball team." And there was another laugh.
>
> (p. 23)

Because this social awkwardness was so intense, Bill W. enlisted the help of alcohol to help him suppress this feeling. While waiting to be deployed to France in World War I to fight the Germans, Bill W. took his first drink of alcohol at age 21:

> Well, my self-consciousness was such that I simply had to take that drink. So I took it, and another one, and then, lo, the miracle! That strange barrier that

had existed between me and all men and women, even the closest, seemed to instantly go down.

(p. 43)

Despite his miserable family circumstances, Bill W. declared that he was "deliriously happy" (p. 30) as a 16-year-old boy in love for the first time, an illustration of false positivity in his emotional life. He described his "early childhood mood swings" as "childishness and grandiosity" (p. 110)—false positivity. Thus, we observe a limited expression of emotions around his attachment figures, the deliberate suppression of negative emotions with the aid of alcohol, and false positivity, all of which suggest anxious-avoidant attachment relationships to his parents.

Regarding this interpersonal marker, Bill W. (Anonymous, 2000) evidenced a secure attachment relationship to God, expressing positive emotions toward God, coupled with a balanced regulation of these emotions through self-reflection. Bill W. wrote that during his spiritual awakening:

every joy I had known was pale by comparison. The light, the ecstasy. I was conscious of nothing else for a time ... As I became more quiet a great peace stole over me, and this was accompanied by a sensation difficult to describe.

(p. 145)

And later, he remarks, "These feelings and convictions, no matter what the vicissitude, have never deserted me since" (p. 146).

Although Bill W.'s (Anonymous, 2000) autobiography ends shortly after the recounting of this spiritual awakening, he does continue writing books about alcoholism recovery for AA members. One of these books, *Alcoholics Anonymous* (Anonymous, 2010, pp. 59–60), includes the 12 steps of AA, which other 12-step programs have been following all over the world as a suggested program of recovery. Two of these 12 steps—steps 4 and 10—suggest that regulating emotions through self-reflection and honesty with oneself is a necessary part of establishing a secure attachment relationship to a Higher Power. Thus, in his anxious-avoidant attachment relationships to his parents, Bill W.'s expression of his emotions is constricted, suppressing negative emotions unless the precipitating event is sufficiently stressful to merit a reaction. On the other hand, he openly expresses his emotions in relation to God, which are genuine and positive (despite episodes of depression later in life [see p. 166]). On this interpersonal marker, therefore, Bill W. used his secure attachment to his Higher Power to compensate for inadequate attachment relationships to his parents.

Self-image/Self-esteem

This interpersonal marker of the attachment pattern is evident in Bill W.'s descriptions of his attachment relationships to his parents and to God (Anonymous, 2000). Based on my earlier analysis, we are looking for anxious-avoidant dimensions of his attachment relationships to his parents and secure dimensions of his attachment relationship to God. Regarding this marker, Daniel (2015) writes that securely attached persons demonstrate "nuanced self-image and solid self-esteem," whereas anxious-avoidant persons demonstrate a "tendency to a defensively 'magnified' self-image to compensate for low self-esteem" (p. 115). What are some quotations from Bill W.'s autobiography that address the Self-image/Self-esteem marker?

Regarding Bill W.'s (Anonymous, 2000) attachment relationships to his parents, the examples of their direct correlation to his self-image/self-esteem are nonexistent; however, we observe this defensively magnified self-image in temporal contiguity to his parents' divorce. For example, soon after his parents abandoned him at age 10, Bill W. became infatuated with being the best at everything he attempted: "I felt I had to be able to … bat like Ty Cobb, walk a tightrope like the folks in the circus, shoot like Buffalo Bill" (p. 18). He also became proficient in Morse code, which "created quite a sensation in the town and marked me out for distinction, something for which, of course, I increasingly craved, until at last that became an obsession" (p. 20). After his maternal grandfather mentioned that no one other than Australians could make boomerangs, Bill W. saw "a challenge to be an absolutely number-one figure in the world. I would be the first white man to do this, so I thought" (p. 22). After succeeding at making a functioning boomerang, he reflects that

> that episode in a sense sets the keynote for my whole career. From then on, it was always number one, number one, number one. I came out of my shyness, I came out of—seemingly came out of a good deal of my inferiority. And then I began a desperate struggle to become number one.
>
> (pp. 22–23)

This grandiosity no doubt concealed his suffering "with the wound of my father's and mother's separation and subsequent divorce" (pp. 14–15). His parents' divorce "certainly did something to me which left a very deep mark indeed" (p. 15), and he carried this mark throughout his childhood and beyond, perhaps blaming himself for his parents' divorce, as many children do (e.g., Healy et al., 1993).

To avoid the low self-image and self-esteem, Bill W. (Anonymous, 2000) compensated with fantasies of grandiosity, the opposite of what he was really feeling about himself: "Again I felt I was nobody" (p. 32), and "I declared myself to be no good" (p. 35). Bill W. eventually used alcohol to compensate for his low self-image/self-esteem: "Without liquor, I felt the old awkwardness and inferiority" (p. 44). Bill W. sums up the role of alcohol in his life like this: "My drinking had been motivated by the desire for the grandiose … This terrible urge to [want] distinction and power, prompted by my childhood inferiorities, could be magnified by alcohol" (p. 94). Thus, I conclude that Bill W.'s anxious-avoidant attachment relationships to his parents established an insecure self-image in which he lacked self-esteem, from whose awareness he protected himself with grandiose fantasies of power and prestige, later aided and abetted by alcohol as a surrogate attachment figure.

Regarding Bill W.'s (Anonymous, 2000) self-image/self-esteem in his attachment relationship to God, his narrative contains a couple of the ways in which this relationship compensated for his low self-image/self-esteem. Thinking about the process of recovery that occurred among some of his alcoholic friends and him, Bill W. realized that

> before they could receive the gift [of sobriety], their self-confidence had to be destroyed—absolutely destroyed. Ego deflation at great depth was the key to the riddle. The sociologists and psychologists who would restore self-confidence had been mistaken. God-confidence was the thing, not self-confidence.
>
> (p. 154)

Unwittingly, Bill W. advocates for the compensation hypothesis himself—only a relationship to God can restore shattered self-esteem. Bill W. later adds that "they were talking about morality and spirituality; about God-centeredness versus self-centeredness; they were talking about personal conversion [i.e., establishment of a personal relationship to a Higher Power]" (p. 157). Thus, on this interpersonal marker, Bill W. demonstrates "solid self-esteem" (Daniel, 2015, p. 115) in his secure attachment relationship to God—what he might call "God-esteem"—to compensate for his low self-esteem originating from his anxious-avoidant attachment relationships to his parents.

Openness and Self-disclosure

The interpersonal marker of Openness and Self-disclosure is evident in Bill W.'s descriptions of his attachment relationships to his parents and to God (Anonymous, 2000). Based on my earlier analysis, we are looking for both anxious-avoidant dimensions of his attachment relationships to his parents and secure dimensions of his attachment relationship to God. Regarding this marker, Daniel (2015) writes that securely attached persons "are pleased to share thoughts and feelings, but 'dose' these according to the situation," whereas anxious-avoidant persons "are reticent about sharing thoughts and feelings" (p. 115). What are some key passages in Bill W.'s autobiography that address the Openness and Self-disclosure marker?

Throughout his narrative, Bill W. (Anonymous, 2000) characterizes his childhood and early adult life as one grand exercise in keeping secrets, perhaps even from himself. Of course, his parents also practiced this secret-keeping. First, his father left without telling Bill W. or his sister where he was going, and then his mother initially lied to him that he had "gone away on a business trip" (p. 12). Young Bill W. learned early to keep his own secrets: "I hid the wound [of my father's abandonment] and never talked about it with anybody, even my sister, let alone Grandfather and Grandmother Griffith" (p. 13). It is interesting that he does not mention his mother as a potential confidant. She does not even appear to be a possibility for him. Bill W. also mentions his mother's "covert trip to Bennington, Vermont, to see a fearsome man called Lawyer Barber. Somehow I learned that the divorce was complete" (p. 15). By using the word "covert," I presume that Bill W. knew nothing about the true nature of this trip until much later.

Discussing the worst years of his alcoholism, Bill W. did not even tell his parents what was going on with him: "I don't believe that in all the years I had seen my father half a dozen times. But even Mother had little idea of the sad estate in[to] which I had fallen" (p. 103). In summary, Bill W.'s parents kept family secrets from Bill W., and whenever he was suffering, Bill W. usually kept it to himself, not involving his parents. As a Wall Street businessman, Bill W. also tried keeping his alcoholism a secret: "Whenever possible I bought a fifth of gin in the morning and nibbled at it discreetly during business hours while I watched the market" (p. 85). He kept secrets even from his beloved wife Lois: "I began to steal from Lois's slender purse, and on some occasions I would hock articles filched from the house" (p. 103). To prevent Lois from knowing that he was drinking alcohol in their own home, Bill W. would leave bottles of gin "outside and sneaking out for them or hiding them in the lower areaway … I hid liquor about as a squirrel would cherish nuts" (p. 95). Lack of openness—in fact, a profound secretiveness—became a way of life for Bill W. In the context of all these findings, I conclude that on this interpersonal marker, Bill W. exhibited anxious-avoidant features in his attachment relationships to his parents. Sharing his thoughts and feelings proved too risky to do, exposing him to expected rejection.

Regarding Bill W.'s (Anonymous, 2000) Openness and Self-disclosure in his attachment relationship to God, his narrative is filled with these characteristics during and after his spiritual awakening. In his most desperate moment, as we have seen, Bill W. calls out, "I'll do anything, anything at all. If there be a Great Physician, I'll call on him" (p. 145). This openness to sharing his pain with his Higher Power catalyzed the spiritual awakening. Afterward, he told his physician, Dr. Silkworth, Lois, his childhood friend Ebby, and many others about his spiritual awakening. He even enshrined self-disclosure to a Higher Power in steps 5 and 11 of his 12-step program of recovery (see below for a more complete treatment of this subject). This openness with God seemed to transform his openness with others. His fascination with the Oxford Groups' practice "to confess their sins 'one to another'" (p. 127) later permeated his ideas for the 12 steps. People confess their sins not only to God but also in front of other persons—an illustration of being open and self-disclosing to both God and people. According to Bill W., every alcoholic must be capable of "being honest enough to admit his own defeat" (p. 155). Thus, on this interpersonal marker, Bill W. demonstrates an openness to his Higher Power coupled with a capacity for self-disclosure to God in prayer that exceeded the openness and self-disclosure to his parents and significant others prior to his spiritual awakening. In other words, Bill W. demonstrates a compensation between his openness and self-disclosure to others prior to his spiritual awakening and to God after his spiritual awakening. He used his secure attachment relationship to God to compensate for his anxious-avoidant attachment relationships to his parents on this interpersonal marker.

Dependence/Independence

This interpersonal marker of the attachment pattern is evident in Bill W.'s descriptions of his attachment relationships to his parents and to God (Anonymous, 2000). Based on my earlier analysis, I am looking in the autobiography for both secure and anxious-avoidant dimensions of his attachment relationships to his parents and to God. Regarding this marker, Daniel (2015) writes that securely attached persons "feel comfortable in committed relationships, but are also capable of autonomy," whereas anxious-avoidant persons "greatly value independence from others" (p. 115). What are some key quotations in Bill W.'s autobiography that address the Dependence/Independence marker?

Regarding Bill W.'s (Anonymous, 2000) attachment relationships to his parents, Bill W. seemed to live an independent existence. Examining one of his earliest memories, recall that Bill W. "is looking out of the window from my crib just as the sunset developed over the great mountain" (p. 3). There are no persons in this memory—only Bill W. During childhood, Bill W.'s lack of parental supervision is astonishing, even taking into consideration the historical period in which he lived. Attempting to replicate a stunt performed by Buffalo Bill at a circus, 11-year-old Bill W. started shooting with a gun lumps of coal he had tossed into the air: "It was a wonder I didn't kill some of the farmers about, as it was a very high-powered gun" (p. 18). How did he gain access to a gun? "My grandfather bought me [the rifle]" (p. 15). Where were his parents? "Somehow I learned that the divorce was complete" (p. 15).

Similarly, 12-year-old Bill W. was fixated on making a boomerang, originating from his maternal grandfather's challenge. Bill W. explains:

> I got out all the books I could lay my hands on at the public library. I found out all I could about boomerangs ... I worked at all hours in the shop on boomerangs ... During this long period of constructing boomerangs, I completely lost interest in everything else. My interest in school went to nothing ... This went on for a period of almost six months.
>
> (pp. 21–22)

Thus, by this young age, Bill W. was all by himself, doing whatever he wanted to be doing—and doing it all by himself. He does not involve his maternal grandfather or anyone else in his work. There is no collaboration. This independent streak continued into adulthood. Training for combat in World War I, Bill W. remarks, "I had this terrific sense of patriotism. I had this terrific sense of freedom" (p. 39). He enjoyed being on his own, although by this time, he was dating his future wife, Lois. Nevertheless, as regards his parents, Bill W. had a strained relationship with his mother and, after the divorce, saw little of her (p. 10) and even less of his father (pp. 10, 103). Again, from a young age, Bill W. functioned autonomously from his parents, greatly valuing his independence. Thus, we observe an anxious-avoidant attachment strategy used in Bill W.'s attachment relationships to his parents.

It is noteworthy that, amid his fierce autonomy from his parents, Bill W. (Anonymous, 2000) nevertheless forged a highly dependent and destructive relationship to his surrogate attachment figure: alcohol. Describing the downward spiral, Bill W. writes, "The demon [alcohol] was now moving into full possession" (p. 86). He discusses his relationship to alcohol as "an obsession" that "condemned me to drink against my will" (p. 105). So powerful was this attachment that Bill W. was seeking "instruments that would exorcise this devil" (p. 113).

Before his spiritual awakening, Bill W. (Anonymous, 2000) acted completely independent of God because he was an atheist (e.g., p. 139). After his spiritual awakening, however, Bill W. paradoxically developed a dependent relationship to God while simultaneously functioning autonomously enough to found an international nonprofit organization, AA. Recounting his friend Ebby's spiritual conversion, Bill W. writes that "[Ebby] would not get over drinking by himself or by any resource of psychology or psychiatry"; rather, "with much reluctance, [he] actually tried to pray" (p. 131). Regarding his own surrender to a Higher Power, Bill W. remembers "the blazing thought, 'You are a free man'" (p. 145). Bill W. is illustrating a duality between utter dependence on God and complete liberation from alcohol. In other words, Bill W.'s secure attachment relationship to God is now compensating for his addictive relationship to his surrogate attachment figure: alcohol. After his spiritual awakening, Bill W. now sought "dependence upon God for His guidance in all things" (p. 156). Now, "God-confidence was the thing, not self-confidence" (p. 154). Thus, on this interpersonal marker, Bill W. demonstrates a dependence on his Higher Power to guide him and direct him to found AA and become a spokesperson for what became a worldwide self-help movement for people struggling with addiction and seeking a spiritual solution. We observe that Bill W. uses his secure attachment relationship to God to compensate for his anxious-avoidant attachment relationships to his parents and his addictive relationship to alcohol. After December 11, 1934, Bill W. never took another drink (Anonymous, 2013).

Conflict Management

This interpersonal marker of the attachment pattern is evident in Bill W.'s descriptions of his attachment relationships to his parents and to God (Anonymous, 2000). Based on my earlier analysis, we are looking for both secure and anxious-avoidant dimensions of his attachment relationships to his parents and to God. Regarding this marker, Daniel (2015) notes that securely attached persons demonstrate "constructive strategies for handling conflicts," whereas anxious-avoidant persons are "uncomfortable with potential conflicts, [and] attempt to ignore these" (p. 115). What are some key texts in his autobiography that address the Conflict Management marker?

Regarding Bill W.'s (Anonymous, 2000) attachment relationships to his parents, the narrative shows that Bill W. tended to ignore conflicts during his childhood. After his mother beat him with a hairbrush, Bill W. developed feelings of animosity toward her but did not speak of them—with her or with anyone else: "Somehow I never could forget that beating. It made an indelible impression upon me, for I really think that she was angry" (p. 9). Of the conflicts between his parents, Bill W. "never knew exactly what took place" (p. 10), preferring to ignore what was going on in the household. The family atmosphere was probably not conducive to discussing conflict: "Mother was never especially communicative on intimacies" (p. 10). When his mother told him that his father had abandoned the family, instead of asking questions or expressing protest, Bill W. "hid the wound and never talked about it with anybody" (p. 13), thus ignoring the conflict. Though aware of conflict with his mother, there is no evidence that Bill W. addressed it with his mother: "There was a sort of barrier between Mother and me which has only in recent years dissolved" (p. 13). Having been offered alcohol for the first time, Bill W. took his first drink, ignoring his family pedigree of alcoholism: "All during college I had backed away from drinking. I'd been told how many of my ancestors went down with it ... I was frightened by liquor. But here it was" (pp. 42–43). I view Bill W.'s alcoholism as an inability to manage conflict by applying an ineffective strategy to ignore it through manifesting an altered state of consciousness. Thus, for this interpersonal marker, Bill W. seems to reflect an anxious-avoidant strategy of conflict management, not only with his mother but also with himself.

Regarding Bill W.'s (Anonymous, 2000) conflict management in his attachment relationship to God, there was no conflict with God because God did not exist for Bill W. (p. 139). So, how did his strategy of conflict management change after his spiritual awakening? Just prior to his conversion, Bill W. became intrigued by his rehab physician Dr. Silkworth's description of the natural course of alcoholism, which included "a period of obliquity, of rebellion, of this-can't-be-me-ism, which was a bar to any progress whatever" (p. 111). Clearly, Bill W. counted himself as having gone through this process and was ready for the next phase of the disease—"that in-between stage, where the pain is rising more sharply and the patient has periods of wanting to want to stop" (p. 111). Later, Bill W. learned from the Oxford Groups (The Layman with a Notebook, 1933)—an ecumenical Christian community whose spiritual practices influenced Bill W.'s creation of the 12 steps of AA—that conflict could be managed by confession of "sins 'one to another'" and "restitution, the restoration of good personal relationships by making amends for harms done" (p. 127). We learn in the anonymously written "Afterword" that even after his spiritual awakening, Bill W. experienced long, severe bouts of depression, which led him to twice weekly psychotherapy in 1944 with Dr. Harry Tiebout, a psychoanalytic psychiatrist in New York. Whether he experienced conflict with his Higher Power over his chronic depression, we do not know. We do know that Bill W. viewed God as having the power to resolve his conflict with alcohol: "Providence was preparing a table to be set in the presence of our ancient enemy, Barleycorn" (p. 113; see also p. 123). Thus, while ignoring or avoiding conflict with his parents, we observe that Bill W. found a constructive strategy for managing his conflicts with others after he became sober that included confessing wrongs to others in the presence of God, indicating a secure attachment relationship (see also the 12 Steps below). In other words, he compensated for ignoring conflicts with his parents by resolving conflicts with others, prompted by his secure attachment relationship to God.

Empathy

This interpersonal marker of the attachment pattern is evident in Bill W.'s descriptions of his attachment relationships to his parents and to God (Anonymous, 2000). Based on my earlier analysis, we are looking for both secure and anxious-avoidant dimensions of his attachment relationships to his parents and to God. Regarding this marker, Daniel (2015) writes that securely attached persons demonstrate "empathy with and care for others," whereas anxious-avoidant persons demonstrate "limited empathy and interpersonal 'coldness'" (p. 115). What are some passages in his autobiography that address the Empathy marker?

Regarding Bill W.'s (Anonymous, 2000) empathy in his attachment relationships to his parents, there is not much evidence in the narrative that supports or refutes the presence of this interpersonal marker. His comment that he "was always lacking in the right sort of love for [his mother], as I think she was at times for me" (p. 13) represents an empathic understanding of his interactions with his mother, but he is viewing this childhood relationship from a post-sobriety vantage point. It is difficult to know whether he experienced empathy toward his parents as a child because we were not there, and his childhood memories, like all childhood memories, underwent revision with repeated recall since these interactions occurred (see Lee et al., 2017). There are two moments that might count as unempathic. First, he made explosives in his backyard woodshed (Anonymous, 2000, p. 8) that could have annihilated his neighborhood; second, he secured the lumber for his boomerang "by cutting the head out of my bed (my grandfather didn't care for this so much)" (p. 22). Rather than caring about what his parents must have been going through with their divorce, Bill W. was instead inwardly focused on the "wound of my father's and mother's separation and subsequent divorce" (pp. 14–15). Bill W. also seems unempathic toward his peers: "I had many playmates, but I think I regarded all of them as competitors" (p. 15). Without regard to how his childhood peers might perceive him, Bill W. believed that "always, always, when I set my mind on it, I could become the number-one man" (p. 24). Thus, I conclude from these passages that Bill W.'s attitude toward his parents and toward others seemed to lack empathy, consistent with an anxious-avoidant attachment relationship. We must note, however, that the evidence supporting or not supporting empathy is sparse.

Regarding Bill W.'s (Anonymous, 2000) empathy in his attachment relationship to God, God did not exist (p. 139); therefore, he did not have an empathic response to God. After his spiritual awakening, however, Bill W. demonstrated profound empathy for his fellow alcoholics as a messenger of God. Bill W. had to feel understood, however, before he could understand others (see Fonagy et al.,

2002). Undergoing treatment for alcoholism at the Towns Hospital beginning in the fall of 1933, Bill W. felt that his rehab physician, Dr. Silkworth, "understood [alcoholism], and I understood myself" (p. 105). Dr. Silkworth demonstrated the empathy

> [t]o come in and be with us in the caves in which we lived. I never knew anything about his personal sufferings, yet he must have had them ... The doctor's treatment rested squarely on his ability to make an identification with us alcoholics. One which I suspect ran to great depth.
>
> (p. 112)

During a later stay at Towns Hospital, Bill W. received a visit from his childhood friend Ebby, whose empathy for his situation profoundly affected him:

> As a fellow sufferer he could, and did, identify himself with me as no other person could. As a recent dweller in the strange world of alcoholism he could, in memory, reenter it and stand by me in the cave where I was. Everybody else had to stand on the outside looking in. But he could enter, take me by the hand, and confidently lead me out ... One alcoholic had been talking to another as none other could.
>
> (p. 153)

Bill W. later enshrined this empathic connection among alcoholics in step 12 of his 12-step program of recovery. Analyzing the course of his own recovery, Bill W. (Anonymous, 2000) concludes:

> That had been the missing link: one alcoholic talking to another, bearing hopelessness in one hand and hope in the other ... One alcoholic turning the message to another could ready the sufferer for his gift [of recovery] as nobody else could.
>
> (pp. 154–155)

Bill W. now extended his own empathy to the world of alcoholics:

> As each dedicated himself to carrying the message to still another, and those released to still others, such a society could pyramid to tremendous proportions. Why, it could reach every single alcoholic in the world capable of being honest enough to admit his own defeat. There must be millions of them, the alcoholics who still didn't know.
>
> (p. 155)

Thus, on this interpersonal marker, Bill W. demonstrates a secure attachment relationship to God. We observe that he compensated for his lack of empathy for his parents with an empathic attitude toward other alcoholics, which he views as part of a spiritual connection to his Higher Power, Who "restore[d him] to sanity" (step 2; Anonymous, 2010, p. 59). In the following section, I analyze Bill W.'s (Anonymous, 2010) 12 steps of AA and connect each step to the nine interpersonal markers (Daniel, 2015).

The 12 Steps of Alcoholics Anonymous and Secure Attachment to God

As mentioned earlier, four years after this spiritual awakening, Bill W. created the 12 steps of AA (Anonymous, 2010, pp. 59–60), which became the blueprint for all subsequent self-help programs of addiction recovery. I want to highlight the features of these 12 steps that reflect a secure attachment relationship to a Higher Power. I will be using the nine interpersonal markers (Daniel, 2015) to demonstrate how these 12 steps reflect core features of a secure attachment relationship to God. I will discuss each step in turn.

Analysis of the 12 Steps

1. We admitted we were powerless over alcohol—that our lives had become unmanageable

By admitting powerlessness, the person is breaking through their denial of the addiction and instead practicing openness and self-disclosure, perhaps for the first time. The person is disclosing to themselves that they have no control over their lives (Daniel, 2015, p. 115; marker #6). The person also admits to themselves that they are not independent of alcohol; in fact, they are highly dependent on alcohol. Valorizing their independence from alcohol and from people is over (marker #7). Finally, by acknowledging the unmanageability of a person's life, that person is breaking through a defensively "magnified" self-image and facing their true state of affairs, thus creating a pathway toward solid self-esteem (marker #5)

2. Came to believe that a Power greater than ourselves could restore us to sanity

This step suggests that trust is necessary to the addiction recovery process and is also the foundation of a secure attachment relationship (Daniel, 2015, p. 115). The person trusts that a Higher Power can help them; they have positive expectations that help will be forthcoming. The reader will also note the similarity between trust in "a Power greater than ourselves" and the description by Bowlby (1988) of an attachment figure as someone who is "stronger and/or wiser" (p. 120). Bill W. is suggesting that this Higher Power at least has the capacity to help the person overcome their suffering and conflict (marker #2).

3. Made a decision to turn our will and our lives over to the care of God as we understood Him [emphasis in original]

This step reflects the deliberate change in attitude the person must make to surrender to and accept the care of a Higher Power (Daniel, 2015, p. 115). The person becomes open to seeking help from God and no longer prefers to handle things themselves (marker #3). The reader will note that Bill W. portrays God as "caring," which reflects one of the hallmarks of a secure attachment relationship.

4. Made a searching and fearless moral inventory of ourselves

This step instructs the person to face their intrapersonal and interpersonal conflicts for the purpose of managing them more effectively or resolving them altogether (Daniel, 2015, p. 115). The securely attached person finds constructive strategies for handling conflicts, and this method of courageously reflecting on these conflicts is one such constructive strategy (marker #8).

5. Admitted to God, to ourselves, and to another human being the exact nature of our wrongs

By opening up to God, oneself, and others, the person can break through the shame of the addiction and live a life connected to God and to others without the barrier of secrets (Daniel, 2015, p. 115). Sharing thoughts and feelings with God and with others strengthens the safe haven facet of the attachment system: without the barrier of shame, the person can now approach God in times of distress (marker #6).

6. Were entirely ready to have God remove all these defects of character

To become ready for a major life change, which often includes pain and loss, the person must entrust themselves to the instrument of this change—in this case, God (Daniel, 2015, p. 115). Preparing for this change requires trust in the other person and a positive expectation that a person's life will be better than it was (marker #2).

7. Humbly asked Him to remove our shortcomings

To ask God for the removal of shortcomings is to ask for help. Bill W. instructs the alcoholic to ask for help from God. This step echoes the interpersonal marker of being open to seeking and receiving help (marker #3) (Daniel, 2015, p. 115). The alcoholic no longer prefers to handle problems themselves. The use of the word "humbly" also suggests deflating one's grandiose self-image, making it more "nuanced," according to Daniel (2015, p. 115). This change in self-image is more aligned with a secure attachment relationship (marker #5).

8. Made a list of all persons we had harmed, and became willing to make amends to them all

This step harkens back to step 4: the alcoholic needs to move from a position of ignoring intrapersonal and interpersonal conflicts to tackling them directly. Bill W. borrowed this idea from the Oxford Groups, whose members "told how their lives had been transformed by the confession of their sins and restitution for harms done" (Anonymous, 2000, p. 156). Conflict management (Daniel, 2015, p. 115) is best served by constructive strategies such as making amends for harms committed against others (marker #8).

9. Made direct amends to such people wherever possible, except when to do so would injure them or others

By making direct amends, the person is practicing disclosing their most vulnerable thoughts and feelings with those they have harmed (Daniel, 2015, p. 115; marker #6) as well as engaging in a constructive strategy of managing conflict (marker #8). In addition, the qualification Bill W. adds—"except when to do so would injure them or others"—also reflects an interest in the other person's welfare; in other words, showing empathy with and care for others (marker #9).

10. Continued to take personal inventory and when we were wrong promptly admitted it

This step follows the same Oxford Group-inspired prescription for conflict management suggested in steps 4 and 8. None would argue that the two-pronged approach of acute self-reflection and prompt acknowledgment of wrongdoing to others is not a constructive strategy for conflict management (Daniel, 2015, p. 115; marker #8).

11. Sought through prayer and meditation to improve our conscious contact with God as we understood Him, praying only for knowledge of His will for us and the power to carry that out [emphasis in original]

As many authors have suggested (e.g., Granqvist, 2020; Kirkpatrick, 2005; Pargament, 2011), prayer is the *sine qua non* of spiritual proximity-seeking (Daniel, 2015, p. 115). In this step, Bill W. suggests improving contact with God through prayer—communicating directly with a person's Higher Power. Ainsworth et al. (1978) indicated that proximity-seeking and contact-maintenance are the hallmarks of attachment security in infancy, and Bill W. underscores their continuing importance for maintaining a secure attachment relationship to God (marker #1). This is the only step that directly urges proximity-seeking of God.

12. Having had a spiritual awakening as the result of these steps, we tried to carry this message to alcoholics, and to practice these principles in all our affairs

This step reflects the expression of care and empathy toward fellow alcoholics who still suffer from the disease (Daniel, 2015, p. 115). Because God has awakened the person to a spiritual awareness that frees them from the bondage of alcoholism, this act of grace also awakens feelings of empathy for fellow sufferers, who need to be told about their encounter with a Higher Power and the 12 steps of addiction recovery. Bill W. encourages the person to share the good news of recovery, which reflects caring for others (marker #9).

The only interpersonal marker not directly represented in the 12 steps is "expression and regulation of emotions" (Daniel, 2015, p. 115). I would suggest, however, that the self-reflective elements of the 12 steps (especially steps 4 and 10) imply emotion regulation. Emotion regulation is sometimes considered a prerequisite for self-reflection, or "mentalization" (Midgley et al., 2017). Thus, even emotion regulation (marker #4) is at least implicitly represented among the 12 steps of AA.

Bill W. had relinquished his use of alcohol as a surrogate attachment figure and instead begun to trust a Higher Power as his attachment figure. Furthermore, the formulation of these 12 steps suggests that Bill W. developed a secure attachment relationship to this Higher Power and treated this Higher Power as both a safe haven (e.g., seeking proximity and contact with God, especially when distressed by one's shortcomings, through prayer and meditation; see steps 5, 7, and 11) and a secure base (e.g., confidently using God to look outside oneself and make amends to others as well as carry the AA message to other alcoholics; see steps 9, 10, and 12). In *Twelve Steps and Twelve Traditions* (Anonymous, 2012), Bill W. writes of step 12: "Here we turn outward toward our fellow alcoholics who are still in distress" (p. 106). This turn outward resembles the infant leaving the secure base—the caregiver's arms—to explore the environment.

Conclusion

In this chapter, I analyzed Bill W.'s (Anonymous, 2000) autobiographical narrative using the nine interpersonal markers of attachment (Daniel, 2015) to determine: (1) the quality of his attachment relationships to his parents and to God, and (2) whether these two sets of attachment relationships (to parents and to God) support the correspondence hypothesis or the compensation hypothesis discussed in Chapter 3 of Goodman (2025). Based on a general reading of the narrative, I conclude that Bill W. developed a secondary strategy of anxious-avoidance in his attachment relationships to his parents and, after his spiritual awakening, a primary strategy of security in his attachment relationship to his Higher Power. Thus, I conclude that Bill W.'s narrative supports the compensation hypothesis.

Examining Bill W.'s (Anonymous, 2000) narrative more closely, I searched for key quotations to support anxious-avoidant attachment relationships to his parents and a secure attachment relationship to God after his spiritual awakening. I used the nine interpersonal markers of attachment (Daniel, 2015) as the primary evidence to support the compensation hypothesis (i.e., anxious-avoidant to secure). A review of the analysis of each of these markers indicates that a compensation of anxious-avoidant attachment relationships to parents with a secure attachment relationship to God was evident on eight of the nine interpersonal markers (there was not sufficient evidence in the narrative to determine Bill W.'s empathy with his parents). This more granular evidence supports my conclusion that Bill W.'s autobiographical narrative supports the compensation hypothesis: Bill W. compensated for his anxious-avoidant attachment relationships to his parents with a secure attachment relationship to God. The narrative does not specify whether his secure attachment relationship to God changed his anxious-avoidant attachment relationships to his parents, but it does seem to have made him less isolated and more connected to others.

Brief Treatment Plan for Bill W.

Based on the preceding narrative analysis, how might I treat Bill W. if he were to schedule a session of psychotherapy with me? The answer to this question would vary, depending on at which point in Bill W.'s life I were treating him. My treatment plan would differ, depending on whether he was active in his addiction or in recovery from his addiction. Using Attachment-Informed Psychotherapy (AIP), I would engage him in a more emotionally expressive manner if he were still active in his addiction and in a more emotionally reserved manner if he were in recovery.

Most therapists would not engage in treatment with a prospective client actively engaged in addiction. An intoxicated client is engaging in behavior specifically designed to protect themselves from any knowledge (delivered through the vehicles of therapeutic experience or interpretation) that might disrupt their sense of security temporarily provided by the alcohol (or any drug of choice). It is important for the therapist to help the client understand that the therapist understands that alcohol is a surrogate attachment figure that provides them with security at any moment of the day or night, whenever the client desires it. In Bill W.'s case, self-consciousness—"that strange barrier that had existed between me and all men and women, even the closest, seemed to instantly go down" (p. 43). In this sense, alcohol becomes more reliable than the unreliable parents from childhood. The goal of treatment of a client addicted to alcohol (or any drug of choice) is to convince the client that, unlike the parents or the God from childhood, people and God can be trustworthy and reliable when relied upon. The first person who needs to demonstrate this quality of reliability is the therapist. It is through the client's relationship to the therapist that the client can experience, perhaps for the first time, the reliability of another person. The client needs to learn how to rely on the therapist for emotional security. Only then might the client develop sufficient trust to rely on significant others in their life to satisfy their attachment need for security.

Thus, the first phase of treatment would consist of demonstrating the therapist's reliability to the client. Illustrations of reliability include being punctual to sessions, providing advance notice of breaks in the treatment (e.g., holidays and vacations), responding to crises outside session times (provided these are not overwhelming to the therapist), and exploring the client's testing of boundaries (e.g., punctuality, prompt fee payment). Because persons classified as anxious-avoidant often seek emotional distance from the therapist, tardiness and skipping sessions are common behaviors. These clients also talk about superficial topics such as the weather, or they recount funny anecdotes designed to entertain the therapist, rather than share deeply personal material that could make them feel vulnerable to rejection. It is unlikely that Bill W. would behave otherwise. I would present myself as reliable, nonjudgmental, and receptive to whatever he would want to talk about, whether it would be making the first boomerang in the Western hemisphere, learning Morse code, or fighting the Germans in France. I would work to help Bill W. develop an initial transference to me resembling his relationship to his maternal grandfather.

Following this induction phase to psychotherapy, I would begin the second phase of treatment by introducing a "gentle challenge" (Dozier, 2003, p. 254) to my interactions with him. In Chapter 6 of Goodman (2025), I discussed that anxious-avoidant attachment represents a deactivating strategy for managing the anxiety stimulated by the threat of rejection and abandonment. Thus, I would behave in a manner that would gently challenge this deactivating strategy by behaving in a more animated, hyperactivating manner. I would ask him specifically about his relationships to his parents and where he might be concealing his angry feelings over his parents' abandonment of him at such a young age. I might even suggest that he might be starting to feel angry with me because I am bringing up these painful events in his life. On the contrary, he is still sitting there, Sphinx-like, rather than expressing these feelings because he fears that I might abandon him just as his parents did if he were to do so. Eventually, I would expect Bill W. to trust in my reliability enough to express his angry feelings toward me for not letting the past go—"Why can't you just let sleeping dogs lie?" Bill W.'s experience of my tolerance of his rage would communicate to him that not even angry feelings can alienate me from him. He would be developing a new, secure attachment relationship with me that, over time, could generalize to other relationships and, eventually, render his relationship to his surrogate attachment figure, alcohol, obsolete.

I would also inquire more deeply into his so-called "spiritual" experiences as an atheist. For example, while in England awaiting deployment to France, Bill W. (Anonymous, 2000) visited Winchester Cathedral, about which he recounts a spiritual experience:

> My mood veered sharply about as the atmosphere of the place began to possess me, and I was lifted up into a sort of ecstasy. And though I was not a conscious believer in God at the time—I had no defined belief—yet I somehow had a mighty assurance that things were and would be all right ... The notion of the supernatural and the notion of God kept crossing my mind, and the sense of some sort of sustaining presence in that place was quite overpowering.
>
> (pp. 50–51)

I would present Bill W. with this paradox of being an atheist yet having had a spiritual experience. How could his intellectual mind be telling him that a Higher Power does not exist, while his perceptual senses were telling him the opposite? Over time, I would draw parallels between his relationships to his unsatisfying, rejecting parents and his unsatisfying, rejecting relationship to a Higher Power. I would point out that his strategy for protecting himself from emotional closeness with a Higher Power temporarily broke down, in that setting and at that time, because of the terror he must have felt preparing himself for impending war and the real possibility of death. Bill W. intuitively sensed that he had crossed a threshold that represented the breakdown of his secondary attachment strategy (see Granqvist & Kirkpatrick, 2018): "[My spiritual experience] had the classic mechanism: collapsed human powerlessness, then God coming to man to lift him up to set him on the high road to his destiny" (p. 51). I would ask him under what conditions he might consider making contact again with this "sustaining presence" (p. 51). I would also invite him to consider whether he needs to fashion his relationship to a Higher Power in the image and likeness of his relationships to his parents (i.e., expectation of mutual abandonment), or whether it can be something different. Would Bill W. be able to explore what a loving, caring relationship to a Higher Power might look like? My task would be to facilitate such an exploration.

Of course, I would also want to refer Bill W. to a support group of other alcoholics committed to living sober lives, embracing their vulnerability and taking emotional risks. Bill W. could then practice establishing secure attachment relationships to a sponsor (i.e., a spiritual mentor) and to other seasoned group members. This group—AA—would, however, still need to be founded!

If Bill W. were coming to me for psychotherapy as a sober person after his spiritual awakening, I would be interested in establishing a therapeutic alliance with him and then helping him to explore the traumatic episodes from his childhood such as his mother's corporal punishment, his father's abandonment and his mother's disclosure of this abandonment, and finally, his mother's abandonment of her son in favor of her daughter. I would also explore whether Bill W. might have any lingering resentments toward God for having allowed these traumatic events to occur in the first place. He might also be prone to self-recrimination for his chronic unreliability toward those he loved, especially his wife Lois: "I was either booze or golf and, you know, she's kind of an also-ran. Poor girl, it's been her lot ever since" (Anonymous, 2000, pp. 76–77). I would want to explore to what extent Bill W.'s feeling of having been forgiven by his Higher Power might liberate him to forgive those who wronged him, such as his parents and school bullies. He might also have experienced war trauma, having almost been killed twice by friendly fire (pp. 47–48, 54). I would pay close attention to the emotional content of his narrative, trying to connect his overwhelming fear to these incidents. He could use his trust in his Higher Power and in me to help him to tolerate this fear, which was isolated from these memories and compartmentalized beneath the surface of consciousness.

During my treatment of Bill W., I would also be aware of my own likely countertransference feelings of sleepiness or tiredness in the therapeutic relationship. My experience working with anxious-avoidant persons is that their superficial storytelling, devoid of genuine emotional connection to what they are describing, can make me feel somnolent. I must interpret this feeling as a signal that Bill W. is avoiding emotional material. I must therefore point out this lack of emotional connection and, in a hyperactivating manner, challenge him to explore the underlying feelings of anxiety and resentment associated with his stories. This work can be painstaking but ultimately rewarding as he gradually develops the capacity to integrate his feelings with his memories, thus circumventing his need to protect himself from his feelings. This process of emotional integration can arouse anger toward the therapist, so I would need to be on hyperalert for any "ruptures" (Safran & Muran, 1996, 2000) that we would need to process together. In so doing, I would be providing him with an "emotionally corrective experience" (Alexander & French, 1946) as a new attachment relationship in which the other person does not run away from conflict but rather works it out by talking about it together. Bill W. would also augment his psychotherapy with the spiritual tools he has so eloquently written about such as routinely taking a personal moral inventory (step 10), prayer and meditation (step 11), and service to other alcoholics (step 12). In fact, Bill W. often recited a motto that reflects his attitude toward service whenever an alcoholic in recovery would express their gratitude to him for helping them to find the spiritual path to recovery through the 12 steps of AA: "Pass it on" (Anonymous, 2013, p. 7).

References

Ainsworth, M. D. S., Blehar, M. C., Waters, E., & Wall, S. (1978). *Patterns of attachment: A psychological study of the strange situation*. Erlbaum.
Alexander, F., & French, T. M. (1946). *Psychoanalytic therapy: Principles and application*. Ronald Press Company.
Anonymous. (2000). *Bill W. my first 40 years: An autobiography of the cofounder of Alcoholics Anonymous*. Hazelden.
Anonymous. (2010). *Alcoholics Anonymous* (4th ed.). Alcoholics Anonymous World Services, Inc.
Anonymous. (2012). *Twelve steps and twelve traditions*. Alcoholics Anonymous World Services, Inc.
Anonymous. (2013). *"Pass it on": The story of Bill Wilson and how the A.A. message reached the world*. Alcoholics Anonymous World Services, Inc.
Bowlby, J. (1982). *Attachment and loss*: Vol. 1. *Attachment* (2nd ed.). Basic Books.
Bowlby, J. (1988). *A secure base: Parent-child attachment and healthy human development*. Basic Books.
Daniel, S. I. F. (2015). *Adult attachment patterns in a treatment context: Relationship and narrative*. Routledge.
Dozier, M. (2003). Attachment-based treatment for vulnerable children. *Attachment and Human Development, 5*, 253–257.
Flora, K., Raftopoulos, A., & Pontikes, T. (2010). A look at the evolution of the self-help movement. *Journal of Groups in Addiction and Recovery, 5*, 214–225.

Fonagy, P., Gergely, G., Jurist, E. L., & Target, M. (2002). *Affect regulation, mentalization, and the development of the self.* Other Press.

Goodman, G. (in press). *Using psychoanalytic techniques to transform the attachment relationship to God: Our refuge and strength.* Routledge.

Granqvist, P. (2020). *Attachment in religion and spirituality: A wider view.* Guilford Press.

Granqvist, P., & Kirkpatrick, L. A. (2018). Attachment and religious representations and behavior. In J. Cassidy & P. R. Shaver (Eds.), *Handbook of attachment: Theory, research, and clinical applications* (pp. 917–940). Guilford Press.

Healy, J. M., Jr., Stewart, A. J., & Copeland, A. P. (1993). The role of self-blame in children's adjustment to parental separation. *Personality and Social Psychology Bulletin, 19,* 279–289.

James, W. (1902). *The varieties of religious experience: A study in human nature.* Longmans, Green, and Co.

Kelly, J. F., Humphreys, K., & Ferri, M. (2020). Alcoholics Anonymous and other 12-step programs for alcohol use disorder. *Cochrane Database of Systematic Reviews, 3,* CD012880.

Kirkpatrick, L. A. (2005). *Attachment, evolution, and the psychology of religion.* Guilford Press.

Lee, J. L. C., Nader, K., & Schiller, D. (2017). An update on memory reconsolidation updating. *Trends in Cognitive Sciences, 21,* 531–545.

Midgley, N., Ensink, K., Lindqvist, K., Malberg, N., & Muller, N. (2017). *Mentalization-based treatment for children: A time-limited approach.* American Psychological Association.

NIV (New International Version). (1978). *The holy Bible.* Zondervan.

Pargament, K. I. (2011). *Spiritually integrated psychotherapy: Understanding and addressing the sacred.* Guilford Press.

Rizzuto, A.-M. (1979). *The birth of the living God: A psychoanalytic study.* University of Chicago Press.

Safran, J. D., & Muran, J. C. (1996). The resolution of ruptures in the therapeutic alliance. *Journal of Consulting and Clinical Psychology, 64,* 447–458.

Safran, J. D., & Muran, J. C. (2000). Resolving therapeutic alliance ruptures: Diversity and integration. *Journal of Clinical Psychology, 56,* 233–243.

Slade, A. (1999). Attachment theory and research: Implications for the theory and practice of individual psychotherapy with adults. In J. Cassidy & P. R. Shaver (Eds.), *Handbook of attachment: Theory, research, and clinical applications* (pp. 575–594). Guilford Press.

The Layman with a Notebook. (1933). *What is the Oxford Group?* Oxford University Press.

Thomsen, R. (1975). *Bill W: The absorbing and deeply moving life story of Bill Wilson, co-founder of Alcoholics Anonymous.* Harper and Row.

Zeifman, D., & Hazan, C. (1997). Attachment: The bond in pair-bonds. In J. A. Simpson & D. T. Kenrick (Eds.), *Evolutionary social psychology* (pp. 237–263). Lawrence Erlbaum Associates.

Zeifman, D. M., & Hazan, C. (2018). Pair bonds as attachments: Mounting evidence in support of Bowlby's hypothesis. In J. Cassidy & P. R. Shaver (Eds.), *Handbook of attachment: Theory, research, and clinical applications* (pp. 416–434). Guilford Press.

Chapter 5

Sigmund Freud

Anxious-Avoidant Attachment—in Denial About the Possibility of a Higher Power

Sigmund Freud was the founder of psychoanalysis, a theory and therapeutic technique of treating patients who manifest emotional problems in their lives. Many of Freud's ideas live on in state-of-the-art, manualized treatments for persons with serious psychopathology such as Mentalization-Based Treatment (MBT; Bateman & Fonagy, 2004) and Transference-Focused Psychotherapy (TFP; Clarkin et al., 2015). These ideas include awareness of unconscious thoughts and feelings, defense mechanisms to keep certain thoughts and feelings outside one's awareness, complex motivational systems that drive human behavior (i.e., sex and aggression), the concept of transference (i.e., attributing thoughts and feelings from the parents of a person's childhood onto the therapist or other emotionally significant persons), the fundamental rule (i.e., in therapy, saying whatever comes into one's mind, trying not to censor), and focusing exclusively on uncovering the meaning of thoughts, feelings, fantasies, and symptoms.

It is well known that Freud was an atheist his entire life. He describes his view of religion and belief in God in some of his most important writings such as "Obsessive Actions and Religious Practices" (Freud, 1907), "Totem and Taboo" (Freud, 1913b), *The Future of an* Illusion (Freud, 1927), Civilization and Its Discontents (Freud, 1930a), and Moses and Monotheism (Freud, 1939). In these writings, Freud (1907) regarded "obsessional neurosis as pathological counterpart to religious formation, neurosis as an individual religion, [and] religion as a universal obsessional neurosis" (Freud, 1907, pp. 126–127). According to Freud, religion and the belief in God are nothing more than manifestations of a particular form of psychopathology. Already at age 17, Freud (1874) described himself in a letter to a friend as a "godless medical man" (p. 70). A year before his death, Freud (1938) reaffirmed his militant atheism in a letter to a historian: "Neither in my private life nor in my writings have I ever made a secret of my being an out-and-out unbeliever" (p. 453). In this same letter, Freud (1938) espoused the idea that "any scientific investigation of religious belief presupposes disbelief" (p. 453). Would he also espouse the idea that any scientific investigation of psychoanalysis presupposes disbelief in psychoanalysis? Thus, Freud reveals his irrational bias against religious belief.

What caused this religious bias to germinate in his mind? And why did he not experience a spiritual awakening as Bill W. did (see Chapter 4)? I suggest that, like Bill W., Freud had developed an anxious-avoidant attachment pattern because of his relationships to his parents and therefore became an atheist. Unlike Bill W., however, Freud never lost faith in his atheism. Thus, despite having developed an anxious-avoidant attachment pattern, Freud's life supports the correspondence hypothesis rather than (as Bill W.'s life did) the compensation hypothesis (see Goodman, 2025, Chapter 3). In other words, Freud's anxious-avoidant attachment relationships to his parents mirror his anxious-avoidant attachment relationship to a God Whose existence he disavows through his militant atheism. The idea that Freud's unbelief might require a psychoanalytic explanation just as urgently as belief does never occurred to Freud because he was too emotionally invested in concealing this divine relationship from himself. In the rock opera *Tommy* by the British rock band The Who, the followers of Tommy, a modern-day Messiah, eventually rebel against him and ultimately disavow him: "We're not gonna take you/ We forsake you/Gonna rape you/Let's forget you better still" (Townshend, 1969). Freud seems to have forgotten that as a young child, he probably had a private belief in God, as most children do (J. L. Barrett, 2012; Rizzuto, 1979). He probably repressed this belief, sealing it over with layers of parental rejection and unsatisfied needs that he displaced onto his relationship to God.

Unlike the other three public figures featured in this book, Freud never wrote a book-length autobiography. Instead, he wrote two career-focused essays. The first essay, "An Autobiographical Study" (Freud, 1925), was written in Freud's twilight years to chart his career trajectory. The second essay, "On the History of the Psycho-Analytic Movement" (Freud, 1914b), was written at the peak of Freud's creative powers and international influence to identify what he believed to be heresies within the psychoanalytic movement and to attack the heretics who espoused them. Despite the shortcomings of these two essays as autobiographical material, I will primarily be using material from these two sources to classify Freud as having had anxious-avoidant attachment relationships to his parents, to God, and to his colleagues. I draw supplemental material from Freud's essays and personal letters as well as the authoritative biographies (Jones, 1953, 1955, 1957; Gay, 1998) and from the trilogy of penetrating biographical papers on Freud's relationships to his mother and nursemaid (Hardin, 1987, 1988a, 1988b) that bear directly on his attachment relationships to these two women. Although Hardin used these papers to argue for the importance to our emotional development of surrogate caregivers, we can underscore the insights gained from his work to develop an understanding of the nature of Freud's attachment relationships to his mother and nursemaid. Then we will be in a better position to draw a connection between these attachment relationships and his likely attachment quality, which in turn likely influenced his theoretical and technical biases.

To summarize my goals for this chapter, I will identify the interpersonal markers of Freud's anxious-avoidant attachment relationships to his parents and to God. I will also explore how Freud's anxious-avoidant attachment pattern potentially influenced his therapeutic technique and, through his profound influence on therapeutic training, the conduct of the psychotherapy sessions of millions of people from the late 1800s to the present day. Finally, I will formulate a treatment plan for Freud as a hypothetical client who prototypically represents anxious-avoidantly attached persons like him who have also renounced any belief in God.

Sigismund Freud (he later changed his first name to "Sigmund" as an adolescent in college) was born in the town of Freiberg in what is now the Czech Republic (Freud, 1925). Perhaps the primary feature of his personhood that he highlights in "An Autobiographical Study" (Freud, 1925) is his Jewish identity: "My parents were Jews, and I have remained a Jew myself" (p. 7). He then immediately discusses the persecution of his Jewish ancestors (p. 8)—one of the few personal details he includes in this essay. Clearly, Freud's Jewish identity was important to him, and his early emphasis on the centuries-long persecution of his Jewish ancestors foreshadows his own persecution complex that emerges repeatedly in both his essays about his career (Freud, 1914b, 1925).

Both a series of changing caregivers and changing surroundings marked Freud's early childhood, which I surmise were, if not traumatic for the little boy, at least disruptive to his sense of attachment security and expectations of emotional availability. Freud (1900) admitted that he manifested the symptom of bedwetting at age 2—just when these traumatic events were unfolding. Research (Joinson et al., 2016) has identified bedwetting as a symptom of stressful events. Thus, we can surmise that Freud's attachment system was producing in him significant anxiety, to which he was responding.

Based on the available evidence, it appears that Freud developed an anxious-avoidant attachment relationship to his mother. Of course, I am speculating because we know so little about Freud's early childhood. We do know, however, that a series of tragedies befell the Freud family during Freud's early childhood. Jones (1953) provides valuable information, and Freud himself provides further clues in a letter to Wilhelm Fliess (Freud, 1897) and in his *The Psychopathology of Everyday Life* (Freud, 1901). Jones (1953) reports that Freud's mother abdicated her role as primary caregiver of her son at the time of the death of Freud's younger brother Julius, when Julius was 8 months old and Sigismund 23 months old. A nursemaid, who had helped Freud's mother with caregiving responsibilities since Freud's birth, became Freud's primary caregiver until the birth of Freud's younger sister Anna, when Sigismund was just over two and a half years old. Simultaneous with this birth, the nursemaid was convicted of stealing from the Freud household and sentenced to prison, at which time Freud's mother presumably resumed primary caregiving duties. Just four months later, the family moved to Leipzig because Freud's father was seeking greater business opportunities; however, due to legal restrictions on Jews, the family again moved to Vienna after only two months (Schröter & Tögel, 2007).

It does not take a psychoanalyst to sense the traumatic quality of these experiences for both the toddler Sigismund and his mother, who had her first child when she was only 20 years of age. When Sigismund was just 15 months old, his mother gave birth to Julius, who no doubt monopolized his mother's attention. The young Sigismund would have felt rejected and excluded from the care that his mother was now showing to this younger brother. We might expect a sense of hopefulness experienced by Freud at the death of his younger brother—a sense of "now, I can get my mother back." Instead, Freud was relegated to the exclusive care of his nursemaid, a woman of questionable character who was stealing from the family. It is not clear why Freud's mother abdicated her role, but one suspects that she was overcome with grief over the loss of her second son. Perhaps to deny the loss, Freud's mother immediately became pregnant again and gave birth to another child nine months later. Sigismund no doubt noticed his mother's pregnancy and likely again felt rejected—another rival for his mother's affection on the way. It seems plausible to assume that, given these circumstances, Freud began to depend on the nursemaid as an attachment figure. In a final series of crushing blows, the new baby was born, and, simultaneously, his attachment figure for the past nine months and caregiver for his entire life of 32 months disappeared from his life. As a toddler, Freud must have experienced the emotional and physical losses of his caregivers—both his mother and nursemaid—as a massive rejection of his own attachment needs. Caregiver rejection has been associated with the anxious-avoidant attachment pattern (Ainsworth, 1979; Ainsworth et al., 1978; Main & Goldwyn, 1994; Main & Stadtman, 1981).

Freud himself confirms some of this speculation in both a letter to Wilhelm Fliess and in his published writing. Freud recalls a memory that occurred at the time of his sister's birth:

> My mother was nowhere to be found: I was screaming my head off. My [half-] brother Philipp, 20 years older than me, was holding open a cupboard for me, and, when I found that my mother was not inside it either, I began crying still more, till, looking slim and beautiful, she came in by the door ... When I missed my mother, I had been afraid she had vanished from me just as the old woman [Freud's nursemaid] had a short time before.
>
> (Freud, 1897, p. 264)

Initially, it seems that Freud is able to empathize with the feelings of his 2-year-old self, yet the fact that he labels the story "amusing" (p. 264) signals his clear devaluation of his feelings of loss. In later years, Freud further dismisses the emotional import of this memory. After retelling the memory in *The Psychopathology of Everyday Life* (Freud, 1901), Freud adds a telling footnote in 1924. The emotion associated with this experience of loss, originally described in 1897 as profound anguish ("screaming" and "crying"), instead becomes "an affect of disappointment" (p. 51) by 1924, "derived ... from the superficial motivation for the child's demand" (p. 51). Using the third person to distance himself emotionally, Freud is characterizing separation anxiety as a superficial motivation for his feelings, which he later characterizes in this footnote as having to do with his sexual desire to have no rivals for his mother's sexual love.

An anxious-avoidant quality pervades the entire memory, from the minimized emotion associated with it to its very interpretation. The sexualization of the memory could reflect a further attempt to avoid the painful feelings of loss and rejection that such a memory elicited. Freud (1899c) labeled this type of memory a "screen memory," and, in his case, the memory also probably contains the traumatic emotions associated with all the other losses of person and place occurring for Freud during this same period.

Freud's childhood seemingly stabilized, and he began attending the University of Vienna at age 19. An atheist, Freud nevertheless maintained his culturally Jewish identity throughout his life (Gay, 1998). After a four-year courtship, at age 30, Freud married his wife. As a trained neurologist, in the 1890s, Freud founded psychoanalysis, both a theory of the mind and a method of treating psychopathology, when he was in his late thirties. Variations of his approach have survived and continue to be popular methods of treatment. He lived modestly with his wife and six children in an apartment in Vienna until just over a year before his death. At age 82, Freud was forced to flee Austria to escape the concentration camps, where four of his five sisters were murdered by the Nazis. He settled in London for his final year of life (Gay, 1998).

Freud's Attachment Relationships to His Parents

We glean considerable information about Freud's attachment relationships to his parents from other sources (e.g., Gay, 1998; Hardin, 1987, 1988a, 1988b). Unfortunately, Freud reveals little of these relationships in "An Autobiographical Study" (Freud, 1925) and "On the History of the Psycho-Analytic Movement" (Freud, 1914b). Based on the available evidence, I suggest that Freud developed an anxious-avoidant attachment relationship to both his parents and that these attachment relationships later influenced his nonrelationship to God that endured throughout his life. Indeed, he professed atheism to be the only stance that an enlightened scientist can take. Later, I will discuss how these parental attachment relationships influenced his theory of the mind and especially his therapeutic technique.

This association between Freud's attachment pattern and the products of his intellectual work demonstrates how a person's "primary mode of relatedness" (Slade, 1999, p. 588) can influence all facets of their life, particularly in areas related to human nature and personal interactions with humans. A pair of sunglasses makes everything seem dark. In the words of the ice queen Elsa from the movie *Frozen*, "It's funny how some distance makes everything seem small" (Anderson-Lopez & Lopez, 2014). Freud made his mother, father, God, and colleagues seem small compared to him.

Against the historical backdrop of Freud's family portrayed earlier, we observe that clues pointing to an anxious-avoidant attachment relationship to his mother exist. Hardin (1988a) argues that Freud suffered profound alienation from his mother that lasted his entire life. From this alienation emerged a peculiar idealization of his mother that even infiltrated his theoretical writing. At age 28, writing to his fiancée, Freud praises his mother: "I do not know one action of hers in which she has followed her own moods or interests against the interests and happiness of one of her children" (E. L. Freud et al., 1978). Freud (1900) also reported a dream in which he saw "my beloved mother" (p. 583), toward whom he uncovered sexual desire. Years earlier, at age 16, Freud had returned to his hometown of Freiberg and developed an admiration for the mother of a friend. Writing to his friend Silberstein, Freud makes a comparison:

> Other mothers—and why hide the fact that ours are among them; we shall not [love] them any the less for it—only look after the physical needs of their sons. Their spiritual development has been taken out of their hands.
> (Clark, 1980, p. 26)

Freud seems to be reproaching his mother for her perfunctory caregiving but quickly interrupts the reproach with an affirmation of love for her. The coding manual of the Adult Attachment Interview (AAI; George et al., 1996; Main & Goldwyn, 1994) describes this form of discourse as "positive wrap-up" in which a negative sentiment about a caregiver is quickly minimized by a positive sentiment. Such discourse is associated with an anxious-avoidant attachment pattern.

Freud (1912b) was aware that his internal dynamics could pose a danger to theory-building through the process of "projecting outwards some of the peculiarities of his own personality, which he has dimly perceived, into the field of science, as a theory having universal validity; he will bring the psychoanalytic method into discredit, and lead the inexperienced astray" (p. 117). Despite this awareness, however, Freud was as vulnerable as any other theoretician to his internal dynamics. Surveying Freud's theoretical work, we notice a pattern of idealizing the mother-son relationship—"the most perfect, the most free from ambivalence of all human relationships," as he described it (Freud, 1933, p. 133). Repeating this theme of maternal idealization, Freud (1921a) underscores "one single exception" to the hostile feelings lurking underneath all emotionally significant relationships: "[The] relation of mother to son which, founded on narcissism, is undisturbed by later rivalry" (p. 101). What happens to the man who is his mother's "undisputed darling"? "He retains throughout life the triumphant feeling, the confidence in success, which not seldom brings actual success along with it" (Freud, 1917, p. 156). These idealistic overgeneralizations are striking because they lack any sense of internal conflict or tension—a trademark of Freud's theory of the mind. Why is the mother-son relationship spared the *Sturm und Drang* characteristic of other emotionally significant relationships? Freud wanted to believe in the security and wholeness of this attachment relationship because he was defensively excluding painful childhood memories that portrayed a different attachment relationship characterized by rejection and loss.

This defensive exclusion (a hallmark of anxious-avoidant attachment; Bowlby, 1980) of psychological knowledge associated with Freud's attachment relationship to his mother can be generalized to his understanding of female psychology. By 1926, Freud (1926) admitted, "The sexual life of adult women is a 'dark continent' for psychology" (p. 212). He could just as easily have substituted the word "me" for "psychology." Jones (1955) quoted Freud as having confided his confusion to his colleague Marie Bonaparte: "The great question that has never been answered and which I have not yet been able to answer, despite my 30 years of research into the feminine soul, is 'What does a woman want?'" (p. 468). We might wonder whether the latent version of this question was, "What does my mother want from me to keep her from rejecting me?"

Further evidence for the anxious-avoidant features of Freud's attachment relationship to his mother comes from a survey of his reactions to his mother's death—a woman he consciously idealized. In a September 15, 1930, letter to his colleague Ernest Jones, Freud (1930b) reveals what he characterizes as a curious reaction to his mother's death: "The increase in personal freedom ... and second, the satisfaction that she obtained at last the deliverance to which she had earned a right after such a long life. Otherwise no mourning ... I was not at the funeral" (p. 677). The following day, Freud (1930d) writes a letter to his colleague Sándor Ferenczi, expressing a similar sentiment: "It has affected me in a peculiar way, this great event. No pain, no grief ... I did not go to the funeral" (p. 400). It is difficult to reconcile Freud's self-described curious reaction to his mother's death with a statement he made earlier in his career about the profound emotional significance of mothers, namely, that "a man['s] ... picture of his mother ... has dominated his mind from his earliest childhood" (Freud, 1905, p. 228). All the evidence points to the conclusion that anxious avoidance characterized Freud's attachment relationship to his mother. The historian Peter Gay (1998) suggests that:

> [Freud] was strenuously defending himself against the recognition that the tie to his mother was in any sense imperfect. He seems to have dealt with the conflicts that his complicated feelings toward his mother generated by refusing to deal with them.
>
> (p. 506)

This is the very definition of defensive exclusion and a classic coping strategy belonging exclusively to the domain of an anxious-avoidant attachment pattern.

Although Freud's memories of his father reflect only subtle devaluation, we can also characterize them as supporting an anxious-avoidant attachment pattern because qualities of both idealization as well as devaluation and dismissal are considered hallmarks of a child whose parents have chronically rejected their attachment needs. Idealization, devaluation, and dismissal are defense mechanisms designed to exclude memories of early rejection. According to the coding manual of the AAI, anxious-avoidant persons "limit the influence of attachment relationships and experiences in thought, in feeling, or in daily life" (Main & Goldwyn,

1994, p. 126). During such interviews as well as therapy sessions, anxious-avoidant persons provide little information about their childhoods and offer schematic memories of idealized caregivers combined with episodic memories of rejection; these persons deactivate attachment needs by "restricting access to attachment memories, idealizing parents, or devaluing attachment relationships" (Kobak et al., 1993, p. 233). Anxious-avoidant persons thus deny distress, limit their emotional engagements with caregivers (Cassidy & Kobak, 1988), and become compulsively self-reliant (Bowlby, 1973). That Freud worked 13½-hour days, six days a week (Freud, 1913a, 1914b), visited his mother only out of obligation (Freud, 1898, p. 306), and analyzed himself (Freud, 1900) further supports the image of a compulsively self-reliant man working in a profession many perceive as lonely (Greenson, 1967) but in no particular need of parental caregiving or help. The concept of attachment as a motivational system distinct and independent from libido remained undiscovered until Bowlby, perhaps because Freud tended to dismiss the emotional significance of attachments in his own life.

Freud indirectly communicates the nature of his attachment relationship to his father in several passages. In one such passage, Freud (1900) recalls urinating in his parents' bedroom at age 7 or 8 and his father's angry reaction, declaring that Freud would never amount to anything. According to Freud, his father's reproach was "a terrible blow to my ambition" (p. 216). We can speculate whether this sort of rejection played out in other situations. An accumulation of such rejections would compel a young child to avoid emotional contact with the rejector. Freud recalls a later memory that by this time in his life casts his father as a cowardly, pathetic object of Freud's devaluation. When Freud (1900) was between 10 and 12 years old, his father told him about an incident that had occurred to his father as a young man in anti-Semitic Freiberg. A Christian had knocked off his cap into the mud and shouted, "Jew! Get off the pavement!" (p. 197). When asked by his son how he had responded, his father replied, "I went into the roadway and picked up my cap" (p. 197). This answer did not impress the younger Freud, referring to his father's behavior as "unheroic conduct" (p. 197), contrasting his father to Hannibal Barca's father, who "made his boy swear before the household altar to take vengeance on the Romans. Ever since that time Hannibal had had a place in my fantasies" (p. 197). At the end of his life, Freud (1939) followed through on his fantasies of vengeance against the Romans: he published a scathing critique of Christianity, comparing it most unfavorably to Judaism (see pp. 85–90, especially p. 88). Even as he was dying of cancer (Gay, 1998), Freud never repeated what he perceived as his father's weak, passive, cowardly behavior in the face of his Nazi persecutors. Freud's derogation of his father as "unheroic" is a hallmark of an anxious-avoidant attachment relationship. On the other hand, remarking on his father's death in 1896, Freud (1900) writes that the death of a man's father is "the most important event, the most poignant loss, of a man's life" (p. xxvi). Thus, despite this anxious-avoidant attachment relationship, Freud is nevertheless able to recognize his father's emotional significance to him.

Freud's Attachment Relationship to God

As previously mentioned, Freud was an atheist his entire life. In *The Future of an Illusion* (Freud, 1927), Freud traces belief in God back to the childhood relationship to the father:

> Religious ideas ... are not precipitates of experience or end-results of thinking: they are illusions, fulfilments of the oldest, strongest and most urgent wishes of mankind. The secret of their strength lies in the strength of those wishes. As we already know, the terrifying impression of helplessness in childhood aroused the need for protection—for protection through love—which was provided by the father; and the recognition that this helplessness lasts throughout life made it necessary to cling to the existence of a father, but this time a more powerful one.
> (p. 30)

In this bold statement, Freud supports the thesis of my book and even uses the language of attachment theory in the process. The utter helplessness of infants and young children and their need for protection are, according to Bowlby (1982), the principal ontological reasons for the existence of the attachment system. Freud reasons that the father fulfills this duty. We now know, however, that because of patriarchy, the mother typically serves the role of primary caregiver in her attachment relationship with the infant, and this relationship, not the father-infant relationship, seems to have the greater influence in the child's later functioning (Main & Weston, 1981). Thus, if we substitute the word "caregiver" for "father" in Freud's description, his understanding of the parallel between caregiver relationships and the relationship to a Higher Power would be contemporary, even though he wrote this passage almost a century ago.

The only problem with Freud's argument, however, is that it does not account for atheism—or the lack of belief in a Higher Power. These "oldest, strongest and most urgent wishes" (Freud, 1927, p. 30) do not simply vanish in adulthood, when a person no longer needs their parents in the way that they did at 12 months of age. In my own experience, I am much more aware of my own powerlessness in the face of the merciless vicissitudes of life—loss, disease, severe weather, economic recessions, the aging process—than I was 15 years ago. Recall the quotation by Voltaire in Chapter 1: "If God did not exist, it would be necessary to invent Him" (Voltaire, 1919, p. 231). According to Freud (1927), quoted in the above passage, "The recognition that this helplessness lasts throughout life made it necessary to cling to the existence of a father, but this time a more powerful one" (p. 30). If we are to take Freud's words seriously—that it is "necessary" to believe in a Higher Power—then how do we understand Freud's atheism, indeed, anyone's atheism?

If, as Freud (1927) suggests, the basis of the relationship to God is founded on the relationship to the father/parents, then perhaps the quality of the relationship with the father/parents influences later belief as well as unbelief in God. Freud is explicit about this point: "[A person's] personal relation to God depends on his relation to his father in the flesh and oscillates and changes along with that relation, and that at the bottom God is nothing other than an exalted father" (p. 147). I mostly agree with Freud's argument; of course, he ignores the potential bidirectionality of this causal relationship: I argue that a person's attachment relationship to God might also influence their attachment relationship to their parents (see Chapter 1). Freud also anticipates the correspondence and compensation pathways (Granqvist, 2020; see also Goodman, 2025, Chapter 3). Yet does the investigation end here?

The need to account for atheism—the absence of belief in God—is missing from all Freud's writings. According to the biographer Gay (1998), "All his life he thought that it was not atheism that needed explaining but religious belief" (p. 526). I agree with Rizzuto (1998) that Freud's atheism requires explanation as surely as does the believer's faith in God. He never questioned his faith in science, however. In the final sentence of *The Future of an Illusion*, Freud (1927) asserts, "Our science is no illusion. But an illusion it would be to suppose that what science cannot give us we can get elsewhere" (p. 56). Why is our knowledge of ourselves, others, and the world limited to only what a scientific worldview can offer? If Freud assumes that only a scientific worldview is valid, but that validity comes from a scientific worldview, then Freud is using circular reasoning to argue against religion.

As a toddler, however, Freud's nursemaid introduced him to God through Roman Catholic church services. According to Freud (1897), his mother remembered that "when you returned home you preached and told us all about God Almighty" (p. 271). At this age, Freud developed a nascent relationship to God. Tragically, Freud experienced an abandonment by this nursemaid, and his mother preoccupied herself with both the loss of a child and the birth of another child, to Sigismund's detriment. Years later, Freud's father rejected him, telling him he would not amount to anything. Rather than turn for comfort to his nascent relationship to God, Freud instead obliterated this relationship. Unable to control his relationships to his parents, he took control of his relationship to God, taking his revenge on God for allowing these abandonments and rejections to accumulate. This control took the form of denial: "If you have turned your back on me, I'm going to turn my back on you." He never revisited his early belief and passion for God.

Mysteriously, Freud (1897) also writes that as a toddler, this nursemaid was "my teacher in sexual matters" (p. 262). He does not provide any interpretation of this statement, but it would not be surprising if Freud sensed, even as a young child, that this sexual teaching was a secretive and perhaps even naughty activity. Ironically, Freud (1921b) experimented with mental telepathy, even involving his daughter Anna in his experimentation (Gay, 1998, p. 445). Despite his own fascination with this most unscientific activity, Freud (1921b) worries about the fate of his own creation, psychoanalysis, if telepathy were to begin to catch on:

> If spiritual beings who are the intimate friends of human enquirers can supply ultimate explanations of everything, no interest can be left over for the laborious approaches to unknown mental forces made by analytic research. So, too, the

methods of analytic technique will be abandoned if there is a hope of getting into direct touch with the operative spirits by means of occult procedures, just as habits of patient humdrum work are abandoned if there is a hope of growing rich at a single blow by means of a successful speculation.

(p. 180)

Clearly, Freud would not be so worried about his scientific legacy, psychoanalysis, if he did not believe that unscientific mental telepathy exists. Thus, Freud disavowed a personal relationship to God on scientific grounds, yet he dabbled in the occult, a nonscientific activity that perhaps harkens back to his early attachment relationship to his nursemaid, who introduced him to both sexuality and God. The well-known aphorism, "Rules for thee but not for me," seems to apply here. Freud could explore his interest in the occult and "spiritual beings," while the believer irrationally expresses "the defense against childish helplessness ... a reaction which is precisely the formation of religion" (Freud, 1927, p. 24).

Interestingly, in Freud's voluminous writings (the *Standard Edition* is 24 volumes), the source material that he most frequently quotes is the Hebrew Bible (Pfrimmer, 1982), citing 21 of its 39 books. Pfrimmer (1982) also identifies a pattern in these quotations: "Their frequency is greater during the moments of crisis in Freud's life" (p. 283)—including the losses of his father and daughter Sophie and near the end of his losing battle with cancer. Thus, although Freud's attachment relationships to his parents and to God seem to characterize the correspondence pathway—a massive disavowal of his parents' influence corresponding to a massive disavowal of God—he nevertheless demonstrates an unconscious pursuit of spiritual comfort through Bible verses when feeling distressed—remnants of the compensation pathway. We know that as a child, Freud (1925) was exposed to the Bible: "My deep engrossment in the Bible story (almost as soon as I had learnt the art of reading) had, as I recognized much later, an enduring effect upon the direction of my interest [in human concerns]" (p. 8). Freud's father Jakob gave Freud a Bible for the occasion of Freud's 35th birthday (Pfrimmer, 1982); thus, one might speculate that Freud's father had exposed his son to Bible stories as a child. In citing the Bible so frequently during crisis moments, perhaps Freud was recalling fond memories of spending time with his otherwise disappointed and disappointing father, teaching him Bible stories.

Freud's psychic economy, however, never permitted this unconscious longing for comfort from a Higher Power to gain conscious awareness or spiritual traction and bring about a spiritual awakening like Bill W.'s psychic economy (see Chapter 4). The severity of the trauma of abandonment in his early childhood, coupled with his relatively stable intrapersonal and interpersonal functioning throughout his life (despite brief moments of distress noted earlier), determined a life path in which an attachment relationship to God might cause more pain of rejection and abandonment than it was worth pursuing for comfort and security. As a toddler, he once believed in God, but the person who introduced him to God—his primary caregiver—abandoned him to a mother who was preoccupied with her own grief and care of siblings younger than Freud. Freud's father also expressed bitter disappointment in Freud, but his father also turned out to be a bitter disappointment. Where was God when Freud really needed God? Investing in spiritual hope is especially dangerous when there is no expectation of deliverance—it makes the outcome only that much more demoralizing.

In summary, Freud (1927) believes that a personal relationship with God is both childish and neurotic: "Religion would thus be the universal obsessional neurosis of humanity; like the obsessional neurosis of children, it arose out of the Oedipus complex, out of the relation to the father" (p. 43). This derogation of those who acknowledge an attachment relationship to a Higher Power, coupled with his own disavowal of the existence of such an attachment relationship to a Higher Power, strongly suggests an anxious-avoidant attachment relationship to his own Higher Power. Thus, his attachment relationship to God corresponds to his attachment relationships to his parents. According to Rizzuto (1998), "As Freud had predicted, his own view of God evolved alongside his relationship with his father: the demoted father called forth a demoted God" (p. 250). Freud (1927) himself first identifies the correspondence pathway between attachment relationships to parents and to God, but he never applies this knowledge to his own denial of an attachment relationship to a Higher Power. Supporting my analysis, Rizzuto (1998) concludes that Freud "accepted no other guide to an understanding of life's mysteries but the 'soft voice' of his self-sufficient intellect" (p. 253). Later, I compare the two life paths that Freud and Bill W. traveled that ultimately diverged. Bill W.'s life path represents the compensation pathway, while Freud's life path represents the correspondence pathway (with some compensatory features). I consider the factors that influenced these divergent life paths.

Markers of an Anxious-Avoidant Attachment Relationship

Because Freud never wrote a book-length autobiography, we are left with the two essays mentioned earlier: "On the History of the Psycho-Analytic Movement" (Freud, 1914b) and "An Autobiographical Study" (Freud, 1925). As mentioned earlier, Freud provides almost no information about his attachment relationships to his parents or to God. I have already summarized what we know about these relationships and concluded that Freud's attachment relationships to his parents and to God can be categorized as anxious-avoidant. Freud, however, does provide plenty of information about his relationships to his colleagues and his attitude about himself, which I use to augment my argument that Freud probably had an anxious-avoidant attachment pattern that served as his "primary mode of relatedness" (Slade, 1999, p. 588) and characterized his attachment relationships to his parents, colleagues, and God. As in previous chapters, I focus only on the interpersonal markers, which Daniel (2015) notes "are systematically and meaningfully connected in treatment providers' assessment of clients" (p. 113). I later use this information to formulate a brief treatment plan for Freud as if he had been referred to me for treatment. This treatment plan would guide me to implement the most effective intervention strategy for Freud.

Freud's Attachment Relationships to His Colleagues

As in previous chapters, I present Table 5.1, which summarizes the findings of my analysis of the nine interpersonal markers of Freud's attachment relationships (Daniel, 2015). In the first column, I list the nine markers. In the second column, I include a key phrase from Daniel (2015) that most closely represents the specific attachment pattern suggested by the quotation. In the third column, I include a key quotation from Freud's writings that supports each of the nine interpersonal markers related to his attachment relationships to his colleagues (Freud, 1914b, 1925).

Proximity/Distance

Because Proximity/Distance relies on visual observation, this interpersonal marker is difficult to assess in text; thus, my analysis is speculative. Based on my earlier general analysis of Freud's attachment relationships to his parents and to God, we are looking for anxious-avoidant dimensions of Freud's attachment relationships to his colleagues. According to Daniel (2015), anxious-avoidant persons "prefer distance and are uncomfortable with proximity. [They c]onsider self 'different'" (p. 115). What follows are select key quotations that address the Proximity/Distance marker.

Although not a colleague per se, Freud's (1925) attitude toward his fiancée exemplifies the need for emotional distance from others, even including his significant other: "While I was in the middle of this work, an opportunity arose for making a journey to visit my fiancée, *from whom I had been parted for two years*" (p. 14; emphasis added). It is difficult to accept the idea that Freud's two-year hiatus from his fiancée was involuntary. Freud often made trips to other European countries and even the United States to give lectures at universities and psychoanalytic conferences. That he could not find time to see his fiancée for two years obviously raises red flags about his attachment pattern. In a 1914 letter to his colleague Ferenczi, Freud brags that he is "working again like a real beast, 8 in the morning–9:30 in the evening!" (Freud, 1914a, p. 560). Freud also kept a six-day-per-week work schedule (Gay, 1998). It seems obvious that Freud later also distanced himself from his wife and his six children. Repeatedly, Freud (1925) reminds the reader that his work takes precedence over his wife and family, indeed, over all other interests: "Scientific research once more became the chief interest of my life" (p. 18). Freud underscores this privileging of his work over emotional connection most definitively in a 1935 postscript: "Psycho-analysis came to be the whole content of my life and rightly assumes that no personal experiences of mine are of any interest in comparison to my relations with that science" (p. 71).

Freud (1925) also viewed himself as "different": "At an early age I was made familiar with the fate of being in the Opposition and of being put under the ban of

Table 5.1 Nine interpersonal markers of attachment for Sigmund Freud

Interpersonal markers	Primary marker with parents	Key quotation/parents	Primary marker with god	Key Quotation/God
Proximity/distance	Prefers distance/ uncomfortable with proximity	"No personal experiences of mine are of any interest in comparison to ... science"	Prefers distance/ uncomfortable with proximity	"Mysticism is just as closed a book as music"
Trust/expectation of others	Ignores feelings of insecurity	"Mothers .... only look after the physical needs of their sons"	Ignores feelings of insecurity	"As a confirmed unbeliever...there is no place where I could lodge a complaint"
Attitude to seeking and receiving help	Prefers to handle things by himself	"I would ... have to devote a part of the already short time to [my mother]"a	Prefers to handle things by himself	"The defense against childish helplessness...a reaction which is...the formation of religion"
Expression and regulation of emotions	Limited expression of emotions, false positivity	"[The mother-son relationship] is ... the most perfect ... of all human relationships"	Limited expression of emotions, false positivity	"Religion would thus be the universal obsessional neurosis of humanity"
Self-image/ self-esteem	Defensively "magnified" self-image to compensate for low self-esteem	"Ever since that time Hannibal had had a place in my fantasies"	Defensively "magnified" self-image to compensate for low self-esteem	"God is now nothing more than an insubstantial shadow"b

Openness and self-disclosure	Reticent about sharing thoughts and feelings	"[In my dream] I was making fun of [my father]; I had to hand him the urinal because he was blind"c	Reticent about sharing thoughts and feelings	"I have one…secret prayer: that I may be spared any…crippling of my ability to work"d
Dependence/ independence	Greatly values independence from others	"Otherwise no mourning … I was not at [my mother's] funeral"	Greatly values independence from others	"Religious ideas…are illusions, fulfilments of the oldest…wishes of mankind"
Conflict management	Uncomfortable with potential conflicts, attempts to ignore these	"[The] relation of mother to son … is undisturbed by later rivalry"	Great attention to conflicts, may be inclined to escalate these	"Analytic technique will be abandoned if there is…direct touch with the operative spirits"
Empathy	Limited empathy and interpersonal "coldness"	"[My mother's death] has affected me in a peculiar way … No pain, no grief"	Limited empathy and interpersonal "coldness"	"Resemblance between the religious ideas… and [thoughts] of primitive[s]"e

Source: Modeled after Daniel (2015, p. 115).

Notes: aNot cited in text (Freud, 1898, p. 306). bNot cited in text (Freud, 1927, p. 32). cNot cited in text (Freud, 1900, p. 217). dNot cited in text (Freud, 1910, p. 35). eNot cited in text (Freud, 1927, p. 38).

the 'compact majority'" (p. 9). Revealingly, Freud (1914b) compares himself to a castaway toiling alone in the field—a pioneer whose achievements would not be discovered for many years:

> I pictured the future as follows: ... science would ignore me entirely during my lifetime ... Meanwhile, like Robinson Crusoe, I settled down as comfortably as possible on my desert island. When I look back to those lonely years, away from the pressures and confusions of today, it seems like a glorious heroic age. My "splendid isolation" was not without its advantages and charms.
>
> (p. 22)

Freud sets himself apart from others, both intellectually and emotionally, and enjoys the distance created by his anxious-avoidant behavior. Freud was not going to seek proximity to anyone, including God: "To me mysticism is just as closed a book as music" (July 20 letter to Romain Rolland; Freud, 1929, p. 389).

Freud's need for spatial and emotional distance even infiltrates his therapeutic technique. Discussing the technique of asking patients to lie down on a couch for their sessions, Freud (1913a) explains that "I cannot put up with being stared at by other people for eight hours a day (or more)" (p. 134). Many psychoanalysts still practice this way—all because of Freud's need for distance from others. Freud also expressed a dim view of his patients, which likewise indicates emotional distance. In a letter to his colleague Ferenczi describing his private practice, Freud (1909b) writes: "The patients are disgusting and are giving me an opportunity for new studies on technique" (p. 85). Feeling disgusted by patients and wanting to keep them from staring at him seem to go hand in hand. Thus, in these quotations referencing the interpersonal marker of Proximity/Distance, we observe extraordinary efforts to achieve distance, which seems to correspond to what we already know about Freud's relationships to his parents and to God.

Trust/Expectations of Others

Based on my earlier general analysis of Freud's attachment relationships to his parents and to God, we are looking for anxious-avoidant dimensions of Freud's attachment relationships to his colleagues. Regarding this interpersonal marker, Daniel (2015) writes that anxious-avoidant persons "fear rejection or ridicule, but try to ignore feelings of insecurity" (p. 115). What are some key quotations that address this marker of Trust/Expectations of Others?

The overall impression of Freud's "autobiographical" writings is that Freud exhibited a degree of wariness and even paranoia regarding his relationships with his colleagues. Some of this wariness is justified; Freud was a Jew living in deeply anti-Semitic Vienna. In the third paragraph, immediately after providing the date and geographical location of his birth, Freud (1925) mentions that he has "remained a Jew myself" (p. 7), and in the following sentence discloses that his ancestors moved out of Germany to what is now the Czech Republic "as a result of a persecution of the Jews" (p. 8). Thus, there is a built-in expectation that others would not treat him fairly. He continues in this vein:

> Above all, I found that I was expected to feel myself inferior and an alien because I was a Jew. I refused absolutely to do the first of these things. I have never been able to see why I should feel ashamed of my descent or, as people were beginning to say, of my "race". I put up, without much regret, with my non-acceptance into the community.
>
> (p. 9)

It is unclear how much of Freud's expectation of mistreatment was warranted and how much was projection onto others around him; however, this attitude of expected mistreatment seems to follow him throughout his life, expressed through antagonistic interactions with previously respected colleagues. In this passage, we observe Freud's attempts to ignore his feelings of insecurity, stating that he has no regrets about his nonacceptance—an extraordinary position to take unless one were anxious-avoidantly attached.

Freud (1925) extended this mental representation of himself as the "outsider" in the context of his ideas about psychopathology. His expectation is that both he and his ideas would be rejected: "The impression that the high authorities had rejected my innovations remained unshaken ... I found myself forced into the Opposition. As I was soon afterwards excluded from the laboratory ... I withdrew from academic life" (pp. 15–16). Feelings of rejection permeate this statement, yet Freud gives the impression that he welcomes this rejection. He expresses no faith in the "high authorities" to give him any recognition and responds by welcoming their rejection. Reflecting on Strümpell's poor review of his first book (*Studies in Hysteria*; Breuer & Freud, 1893–1895), Freud (1925) writes, "I was able to laugh at the lack of comprehension which his criticism showed, but [my co-author] Breuer felt hurt and grew discouraged" (p. 23). Laughing at rejection is a defense mechanism employed to ignore feelings of insecurity. In his co-author's reaction, we observe a more typical response to a poor review—genuine feelings of disappointment. Further, discussing philosophers' general dismissal of his concept of the unconscious, Freud (1925) reacts with seeming indifference: "The philosophers ... could not conceive of such an absurdity as the 'unconscious mental'. There was no help for it, however, and this idiosyncrasy of the philosophers could only be disregarded with a shrug" (p. 31). Once again, Freud is able to dismiss his disappointment and anger at the rejection of these philosophers by shrugging if off, as if to say, "You can't bother me."

Freud (1925) had a falling out with two of his closest colleagues, Alfred Adler and Carl Jung, which deeply affected him. He uses "On the History of the Psycho-Analytic Movement" (Freud, 1914b) to attack these former colleagues and to define the parameters of psychoanalysis, which he felt these two former colleagues were transgressing, turning his innovation into something less scientifically grounded and, well, less Freudian. Looking back to this essay, Freud (1925) writes about the abandonment of his two closest colleagues with feelings of bitterness:

> For the degree of arrogance which they displayed, for their conscienceless contempt of logic, and for the coarseness and bad taste of their attacks there could be no excuse. It may be said that it is childish of me to give free rein to such feelings as these now, after fifteen years have passed; nor would I do so unless I had something more to add. Years later, during the [First] World War, when a chorus of enemies were bringing against the German nation the charge of barbarism, a charge which sums up all that I have written above, it none the less hurt deeply to feel that my own experience would not allow me to contradict it.
>
> (p. 49)

In this passage, Freud is calling these former colleagues arrogant, conscienceless, illogical, and coarse, yet he claims that he cannot contradict these colleagues' attacks on psychoanalysis because the world would accuse him of acting like a barbaric German. Freud acts as though only he can make contributions to the field of psychoanalysis, but those who do make contributions must not dissent from his own views. Though repeatedly calling psychoanalysis a "science" (e.g., "I have always felt it as a gross injustice that people have refused to treat psycho-analysis like any other science" [Freud, 1925, p. 58]), Freud seems to treat psychoanalysis as a religion, with the world divided into devotees and infidels, who must be excommunicated for the heresy of challenging his ideas. Freud admits that he hurts deeply, but not because he has lost two close friends. He hurts deeply because he does not feel permitted to defend himself, which is simply not true. Clearly, Freud fears rejection of his ideas, with which he closely identifies. Whenever Freud refers to "psychoanalysis," one could easily substitute the words "I" or "me," and the sentence would be equally true. Perceived rejection of psychoanalysis is equivalent to a rejection of Freud himself.

Freud (1914b), of course, does vigorously defend himself in the most condescending manner. He compares his former colleagues to psychoanalytic patients who periodically lose their understanding of unconscious motives:

> The disappointment that they caused me might have been averted if I had paid more attention to the reactions of patients under analytic treatment. I knew very well of course that anyone may take to flight at his first approach to the unwelcome truths of analysis; I had always myself maintained that everyone's understanding of it is limited by his own repressions (or rather, by the resistances which sustain them) so that he cannot go beyond a particular point in his relation to analysis. But I had not expected that anyone who had reached a certain depth in his understanding of analysis could renounce that understanding and lose it … I had to learn that the very same thing can happen with psycho-analysts as with patients in analysis.
>
> (pp. 48–49)

Freud is telling his audience of the faithful that these former colleagues disagree with him because they have lost their understanding of psychoanalysis. They no longer have "the truth" and must therefore be banished. Unlike his devotees, all of whom had gone through their own psychoanalytic treatment, Freud is the only psychoanalyst who was never analyzed by another person (Gay, 1998). I believe that he could not sufficiently trust another person with his own vulnerabilities because ultimately, he feared that they would abandon him. Of course, he would never have admitted that to himself.

In fact, Freud (1914b) is the one who seems to have ignored his own unconscious motives in his attacks on his former colleagues. In a stunning passage, Freud tries to justify his attacks against these colleagues—the attacks he feels he is not permitted to make—by disavowing any unseemly personal motives:

> It is no easy or enviable task to write the history of these two secessions [of my former colleagues], partly because I am without any strong personal motive for doing so—I had not expected gratitude nor am I revengeful to any effective degree—and partly because I know that by doing so I shall lay myself open to the invectives of my not too scrupulous opponents and offer the enemies of analysis the spectacle they so heartily desire.
>
> (p. 49)

Thus, Freud demonstrates his uncanny ability to ignore his own feelings of insecurity (Daniel, 2015, p. 115) by interpreting his attacks as having nothing to do with his own personal feelings. The lack of insight is breathtaking, especially in the context of his accusations leveled against his former colleagues for having lost their understanding of unconscious motives.

Freud (1914b) then justifies his attacks by portraying himself as having exercised self-restraint but then feeling compelled to attack: "After exercising so much self-restraint in not coming to blows with opponents outside analysis, I now see myself compelled to take up arms against its former followers or people who still like to call themselves its followers" (p. 49). Freud adopts militaristic imagery, which he employs to protect his brand. Adler and Jung were hurting his brand by renouncing infantile sexuality and the Oedipus complex—in Freud's mind, two essential principles of psychoanalysis. Science works in a Darwinian fashion by testing competing theories of phenomena. The theory supported by the most evidence survives until the next competing theory presents itself (see also Kuhn, 1962). Competition promotes the survival of the fittest theory.

Copernicus's proposed theory that the Earth revolves around the sun and not vice versa upended the current model of the universe and eventually became the dominant theory because it relied on observation. Rather than trusting in science—Freud's *de facto* religion ("our science is no illusion"; Freud, 1927, p. 56)—to figure out which of his ideas would survive the test of time, Freud silenced dissent through excommunication. He tried to protect his preferred theoretical ideas by labeling them "facts I have discovered" (Freud, 1914b, p. 23) and then castigating those who dared to challenge them. This behavior demonstrates a profound mistrust of others and reflects the expectation that his former colleagues would steal his brand and leave him without recognition: "Science would ignore me entirely during my lifetime; some decades later, someone else would ... achieve recognition for them and bring me honour as a forerunner whose failure had been inevitable" (Freud, 1914b, p. 22). Unwittingly, Freud here reveals perhaps his greatest fear—the fear of being forgotten, just as his nursemaid and mother forgot him as a young child. Freud cannot, however, linger on this unpleasant feeling, reflecting that his "'splendid isolation'" was not without its advantages and charms" (p. 22). This undoing of negative attachment-related feelings represents a classic defense mechanism used by anxious-avoidant persons (Daniel, 2015).

Freud's own words strongly support his classification into the anxious-avoidant attachment category. He mistrusted even his closest colleagues and expected betrayal, and he often ignored his feelings of insecurity until they reached a threshold, beyond which he became bellicose. Freud accuses Adler of plagiarism (Freud, 1914b, p. 53) and of having "monstrous notions" (p. 53). Freud also belittles him: "Adler has never from the first shown any understanding of repression [a basic psychoanalytic concept]" (p. 56). In attacking Jung, Freud (1914b) claims to be quoting a former patient of Jung's to reveal the ridiculousness of Jung's modifications of psychoanalytic practice:

> I left [Jung's] analysis as a poor sinner with intense feelings of contrition and the best resolutions, but at the same time in utter discouragement. Any clergyman would have advised what he recommended, but where was I to find the strength?
> (pp. 63–64)

In a final undoing of these defections, Freud (1914b) dismisses these collegial losses in the most condescending fashion:

> Psycho-analysis will survive this loss and gain new adherents in place of these. In conclusion, I can only express a wish that fortune may grant an agreeable upward journey to all those who have found their stay in the underworld of psycho-analysis too uncomfortable for their taste.
> (p. 66)

And so Freud soldiered on without them.

Regarding Freud's attachment relationship to God, there was no trust or expectations: "As a confirmed unbeliever I have no one to accuse and realize that there is no place where I could lodge a complaint" (Freud, 1920a, p. 328). At the loss of his daughter Sophie, who died from Spanish influenza, Freud would like to accuse God but realizes that he cannot because for him, God does not exist.

Attitude to Seeking and Receiving Help

Based on my earlier general analysis of Freud's attachment relationships to his parents and to God, we are looking for anxious-avoidant dimensions of Freud's attachment relationships to his colleagues. Regarding this interpersonal marker, Daniel (2015) writes that anxious-avoidant persons "prefer to handle things themselves" (p. 115). Which parts of Freud's writings address the Attitude to Seeking and Receiving Help marker?

Regarding Freud's attachment relationships to his colleagues (Freud, 1914b, 1925). Freud presents himself as the sole founder of psychoanalysis, toiling in the field alone for many years before others joined him in his labors:

> For psycho-analysis is my creation: for ten years I was the only person who concerned himself with it, and all the dissatisfaction which the new phenomenon aroused in my contemporaries has been poured out in the form of criticisms on my head ... Even today no one can know better than I do what psychoanalysis is.
>
> (Freud, 1914b, p. 7)

This is not a man seeking or receiving help; this is a man who views himself as self-sufficient, preferring to handle things himself.

Perhaps the most telling example of this interpersonal marker comes from his decision to analyze himself rather than make himself vulnerable enough to allow someone else to analyze him, like everyone else in psychoanalysis (Freud, 1914b):

> I soon saw the necessity of carrying out a self-analysis, and this I did with the help of a series of my own dreams which led me back through all the events of my childhood; and I am still of the opinion today that this kind of analysis may suffice for anyone who is a good dreamer and not too abnormal.
>
> (p. 20)

It is not clear how Freud defines "too abnormal," but he clearly did not place himself in that category. There is an old saying in psychoanalytic circles that the problem with self-analysis is the countertransference, and Freud is no exception. Twenty-one years later, Freud (1935) writes of self-analysis, "The danger of incompleteness is particularly great. One is too soon satisfied with a part explanation, behind which resistance may easily be keeping back something that is more important perhaps" (p. 234). Was Freud regretting the incompleteness of his own self-analysis? As far as we know, even with this change in attitude toward self-analysis, Freud never allowed himself to be analyzed, a key piece of evidence documenting his attitude to seeking and receiving help.

Expression and Regulation of Emotions

Based on my earlier general analysis of Freud's attachment relationships to his parents and to God, we are looking for anxious-avoidant dimensions of Freud's attachment relationships to his colleagues. Regarding this interpersonal marker, Daniel (2015) writes that anxious-avoidant persons demonstrate "limited expression of emotions; false positivity; suppression of negative emotions" (p. 115). Which aspects of his autobiography address the Expression and Regulation of Emotions marker?

Regarding Freud's attachment relationships to his colleagues (Freud, 1914b, 1925), he does not seem to fit the prototypical anxious-avoidant interpersonal marker of Expression and Regulation of Emotions of Daniel (2015). On the contrary, Freud's Expression and Regulation of Emotions seem to fit Daniel's description of the anxious-resistant person: "Frequent and dramatic expressions, focus on and intensify negative emotions" (p. 115). As we have already observed, Freud (1914b) engaged in vicious attacks against former colleagues whom he viewed as having betrayed him by forging their own paths of innovation within the psychoanalytic umbrella of ideas. Apparently, Freud (1914b) thought of other choice words not fit to print: "I can be as abusive and enraged as anyone; but I have not the art of expressing the underlying emotions in a form suitable for publication and I therefore prefer to abstain completely" (pp. 38–39). Freud, of course, did not abstain completely or even partially: "Everything that Adler has to say about dreams, the shibboleth of psycho-analysis, is equally empty and unmeaning" (p. 57). Jung does not fare much better, with Freud accusing him of dishonesty: "One is bound to ask oneself how much of [Jung's inconsistencies] is due to lack of clearness and how much to lack of sincerity" (p. 60). In a July 10 letter to his colleague Ferenczi, Freud (1919b) acknowledges that he is "consumed by impotent rage" (p. 363). On this interpersonal marker, therefore, Freud seems to manifest an anxious-resistant attachment relationship to his colleagues.

Self-image/Self-esteem

Based on my earlier general analysis of Freud's attachment relationships to his parents and to God, we are looking for anxious-avoidant dimensions of Freud's attachment relationships to his colleagues. Regarding this interpersonal marker, Daniel (2015) writes that anxious-avoidant persons demonstrate a "tendency to a defensively 'magnified' self-image to compensate for low self-esteem" (p. 115). What aspects of Freud's autobiographical writings address the Self-image/Self-esteem marker?

There are plenty of examples of Freud's inflated self-image (Freud, 1914b, 1925), some of which I have already quoted. After reading these two essays, no one would come away thinking that Freud lacked self-confidence. Describing the feelings that his early use of hypnosis stimulated in him, Freud (1925) writes, "It was highly flattering to enjoy the reputation of being a miracle-worker" (p. 17).

Freud (1925) also believed he had discovered the universal key to all neurosis: "A number of suggestions came to me out of the Oedipus complex, the ubiquity of which gradually dawned on me" (p. 63). In speaking of its presence in Western literature, Freud proudly announces that "a universal law of mental life had here been captured in all its emotional significance" (p. 63). Indeed, his attitude toward psychoanalysis itself is similarly inflated (Freud, 1914b): "Even today no one can know better than I do what psychoanalysis is ... I must be the true originator of all that is particularly characteristic in it" (pp. 7–8). Freud (1914b) even comments on the size of his own self-confidence:

> Since neither my confidence in my own judgement nor my moral courage were precisely small, the outcome of the situation could not be in doubt. I made up my mind to believe that it had been my fortune to discover some particularly important facts and connections.
> (p. 22)

In an April 16 letter to Carl Jung, Freud (1909a), by anointing Jung his "crown prince," alludes to his own kingship: "I formally adopted you as eldest son and anointed you—*in partibus infidelium*—as my successor and crown prince" (p. 218). Again, Freud wants to protect his brand by guaranteeing a worthy successor faithful to his ideas. In the context of this proprietary behavior, his simultaneous insistence that psychoanalysis is a science is hypocritical (Freud, 1925).

Given his self-proclaimed status as a "lonely discoverer," Freud (1914b) dismisses his need to fortify the security of his own sense of conviction challenged by "the lack of sympathy or the aversion" of his contemporaries: "There was no need for me to feel so; for psychoanalytic theory enabled me to understand this attitude in my contemporaries and to see it as a necessary consequence of fundamental analytic premises" (p. 23). In a tone that I can describe only as arrogant, Freud is explaining that unlike other maverick thinkers, he does not need reassurance from others that his ideas are true because he understands the unconscious motives behind his adversaries' opposition to them by virtue of his own psychoanalytic concepts. Thus, for example, anyone who criticizes Freud's Oedipus complex must be doing so because they are acting out their unresolved Oedipal conflicts (e.g., the desire to kill off the father). This circular reasoning protects Freud from criticism and allows him to justify his attacks on his enemies and thereby protect his inflated self-image. On this interpersonal marker, therefore, Freud seems to manifest an anxious-avoidant attachment relationship to his colleagues. He values himself and his accomplishments far more highly than his colleagues, by both inflating his own contributions and diminishing theirs.

Openness and Self-disclosure

Based on my earlier general analysis of Freud's attachment relationships to his parents and to God, we are looking for anxious-avoidant dimensions of Freud's attachment relationships to his colleagues. Regarding this interpersonal marker, Daniel (2015) writes that anxious-avoidant persons "are reticent about sharing thoughts and feelings" (p. 115). What are some key passages in Freud's autobiographical writings that address the Openness and Self-disclosure marker (Freud, 1914b, 1925)?

Freud was certainly reticent about sharing thoughts and feelings about himself, even though he might not have characterized himself as reticent. Freud's *magnum opus*, *The Interpretation of Dreams* (Freud, 1900), includes many examples of dreams, some of which he acknowledges are his own dreams. He interprets the meaning of his own dreams superficially, unlike his patients' dreams. With his own dreams, he stops short of analyzing their latent sexual layers, preferring to interpret only the manifest content. This tendency throughout the book made him vulnerable to criticism, even from his closest colleagues. In a February 17 letter to Carl Jung, just three years before Freud (1914b) publicly denounces him, Freud (1911) explains his reasoning:

> You have very acutely noticed that my incomplete elucidation of my own dreams leaves a gap in the over-all explanation of dreams, but here again you have put your finger on the motivation—which was unavoidable. I simply cannot expose any more of my nakedness to the reader.
>
> (p. 395)

Allegedly, Freud was so reticent to share these thoughts and feelings about himself that he preferred privacy over exhibitionism, forfeiting the opportunity to dazzle his friends and foes alike with his brilliant interpretations to protect his most hidden wishes and motives. Given his inflated self-image and self-esteem (see previous section), the urge to protect his privacy must have been particularly acute.

In his twilight years, Freud (1925) regrets even his superficial self-disclosures. He provides an explanation for not writing a conventional autobiography:

> The public has no claim to learn any more of my personal affairs—of my struggles, my disappointments, and my successes. I have in any case been more open and frank in some of my writings (such as *The Interpretation of Dreams* and *The Psychopathology of Everyday Life*) than people usually are who describe their lives for their contemporaries or for posterity. I have had small thanks for it, and from my experience I cannot recommend anyone to follow my example.
>
> (p. 73)

Freud regrets even the superficial self-disclosures he made in previous writings. On this interpersonal marker, therefore, Freud seems to exemplify an anxious-avoidant attachment relationship to his colleagues.

Dependence/Independence

Based on my earlier general analysis of Freud's attachment relationships to his parents and to God, we are looking for anxious-avoidant dimensions of Freud's attachment relationships to his colleagues. Regarding this interpersonal marker, Daniel (2015) writes that anxious-avoidant persons "greatly value independence from others" (p. 115). What are some key passages in Freud's autobiographical writings that address the Openness and Self-disclosure marker?

Based on the previous quotations of Freud already cited, the reader will already have concluded that Freud greatly valued independence from his colleagues. Freud (1925) places this tendency in the context of his undesirable ethnicity:

> At an early age I was made familiar with the fate of being in the Opposition and of being put under the ban of the "compact majority". The foundations were thus laid for a certain degree of independence of judgement.
>
> (p. 9)

Freud (1925) also takes great pains to remind his reader that the origins of psychoanalysis developed independently of anyone else's ideas. For example,

> psychoanalysis is completely independent of [French psychologist Pierre] Janet's discoveries, just as in its content it diverges from them and goes far beyond them. Janet's works would never have had the implications which have made psycho-analysis of such importance to the mental sciences and have made it attract such universal interest.
>
> (p. 31)

Freud always attempts to demonstrate distinctions between his theories and other theories, not compatibilities.

Perhaps most revealingly, in reminiscing about the early days of his career, Freud (1914b) boldly proclaims his love of independence:

> My "splendid isolation" was not without its advantages and charms. I did not have to read any publications, nor listen to any ill-informed opponents; I was not subject to influence from any quarter; there was nothing to hustle me. I learnt to restrain speculative tendencies.
>
> (p. 22)

Repeatedly, Freud (1914b) reminds the reader that "psycho-analysis is my creation: for ten years I was the only person who concerned himself with it" (p. 7). Freud not only greatly values independence but also flaunts it. On this interpersonal marker, therefore, Freud seems to exemplify an anxious-avoidant attachment relationship to his colleagues.

Conflict Management

Based on my earlier general analysis of Freud's attachment relationships to his parents and to God, we are looking for anxious-avoidant dimensions of Freud's attachment relationships to his colleagues. Regarding this interpersonal marker,

Daniel (2015) writes that anxious-avoidant persons are "uncomfortable with potential conflicts, [and] attempt to ignore these" (p. 115). What are some key texts in Freud's autobiographical writings that address the Conflict Management marker?

Regarding Freud's attachment relationships to his colleagues (Freud, 1914b, 1925), he does not seem to fit the prototypical anxious-avoidant Conflict Management interpersonal marker. of Daniel (2015). On the contrary, Freud's Conflict Management seems to fit Daniel's description of the anxious-resistant person: "Great attention to conflicts; may be inclined to escalate these" (p. 115). As we have already observed, Freud (1914b) seems to accept his fate as the supreme defender of psychoanalysis by first highlighting all the attacks psychoanalysis, and by extension, he himself have endured through the years: "All the dissatisfaction which the new phenomenon aroused in my contemporaries has been poured out in the form of criticisms on my head" (p. 7). Freud then reacts by excommunicating his colleagues from the guild. For example, Freud (1914b) complains that his close colleague Stekel's "behaviour, of which it is not easy to publish an account, had compelled me to resign [Stekel's editorial] direction and hurriedly to establish a new [journal] for psycho-analysis" (p. 47). Freud does not mention talking with Stekel first about his editorship of the journal; he simply acts swiftly to remove the person he perceives to be the problem and then publicly broadcasts this removal in an essay. Writing about this conflict, even after Freud takes action, suggests an intentional escalation of conflict, not a defusing of conflict through negotiation or compromise. Later, history repeats itself when Freud (1914b) similarly removes Adler as journal editor: "After irreconcilable scientific disagreements had come to light, I was obliged to bring about Adler's resignation from the editorship of the *Zentralblatt*" (p. 51). Again, Freud omits from his account any effort to reconcile with Adler.

Freud (1914b) then rationalizes his style of conflict management to his readers: "It is not a desirable thing for people who have ceased to understand one another and have grown incompatible with one another to remain under the same roof" (p. 52). Freud did not tolerate dissension within the ranks of psychoanalysis, and when it did happen, he swiftly made them disappear. He felt justified in his actions because he was simply "repudiating what seems to me a cool act of usurpation" (p. 7). Freud's use of the word "usurpation" suggests that he perceives these men—Stekel, Adler, and Jung—as violently taking away Freud's kingly power. Freud could not tolerate the free exchange of ideas under a big tent. Astonishingly, Freud seems completely unaware that his approach would only escalate these conflicts:

> It has never occurred to me to pour contempt upon the opponents of psychoanalysis merely because they were opponents—apart from the few unworthy individuals, the adventurers and profiteers, who are always to be found on both sides in time of war ... Psycho-analysis brings out the worst in everyone.
> (pp. 38–39)

What does it say about a person's ability to manage conflict when this person openly acknowledges that his own creation—psychoanalysis—makes people behave at their worst? That, of course, would include Freud himself. Therefore, based on a mountain of evidence for this interpersonal marker, Freud seems to exemplify an anxious-resistant attachment relationship to his colleagues.

Empathy

Based on my earlier general analysis of Freud's attachment relationships to his parents and to God, we are looking for anxious-avoidant dimensions of Freud's attachment relationships to his colleagues. Regarding this interpersonal marker, Daniel (2015) writes that anxious-avoidant persons demonstrate "limited empathy and interpersonal 'coldness'" (p. 115). What are some key texts in Freud's autobiographical writings that address the Empathy marker (Freud, 1914b, 1925)?

Despite his gift for understanding humans on a deep unconscious level, Freud often demonstrates a profound lack of empathy for others—even patients and close colleagues. Victor Tausk, one of Freud's closest associates in the early days of his career, committed suicide in 1919. On July 6, 1919, Freud (1919a) writes to his colleague Karl Abraham, "Tausk shot himself a few days ago. You remember his behaviour at the Congress. Despite his outstanding talents, he was of no use to us" (p. 400). In a July 10 letter to Ferenczi four days later, Freud (1919b) also brings up Tausk: "Despite appreciation of his talent, no real sympathy in me" (p. 363). Freud seems to have defensively excluded (Bowlby, 1980) from his conscious awareness any feelings of loss that could trigger the physical and emotional loss of his nursemaid and emotional loss of his mother when he was a toddler. These losses clearly influenced Freud's ability to feel empathy for the tragic loss of Tausk or the loss of those closest to him such as Tausk's fiancée.

After Freud's daughter, Sophie, died, Freud (1920b) writes on February 8 to his colleague Jones that Sophie's death is "a loss not to be forgotten. But let us put it aside for the moment, life and work must go on" (p. 368). And so Freud does what he does best—he immerses himself in 13½-hour days (Freud, 1913a, 1914b). There was simply no time for empathy—even for himself.

Similarly, as mentioned earlier, Freud (1909b) refers to his patients as "disgusting" (p. 85) and shamelessly views at least one of them as a means to an end:

> A patient with whom I have been negotiating, a "goldfish," has just announced herself—I do not know whether to decline or accept. My mood also depends very strongly on my earnings. Money is laughing gas for me ... The goldfish ... has been caught, but will still enjoy half her freedom until the end of October because she is remaining in the country.
>
> (Freud, 1899a, 1899b, pp. 374–376)

Money, not compassion, seems to motivate Freud's treatment of at least some of his patients.

Finally, an analysis of Freud's capacity for empathy would not be complete without discussing his momentous modification of the theory of the neuroses.

Originally, Freud (1925) believed that neurosis originates in child sexual abuse—what he calls "sexual seduction in childhood" (p. 34). Freud discloses that in treatment "with female patients the part of the seducer was almost always assigned to their father. I believed these stories" (p. 34). He then provides confirmation for his observations: "My confidence was strengthened by a few cases in which relations of this kind with a father, uncle, or elder brother had continued up to an age at which memory was to be trusted" (p. 34). In other words, some female patients' memories of their sexual abuse extended into later childhood, when memories are known to endure. Nevertheless, Freud (1925) repudiates this theory of the neuroses by reversing his position: "I was at last obliged to recognize that these scenes of seduction had never taken place, and that they were only phantasies which my patients had made up" (p. 34). This fateful reversal had profound implications for the direction that psychoanalytic theory and treatment were to take. For our purposes, however, this reversal reveals the lack of empathy Freud had for these patients, who were quite possibly suffering from posttraumatic stress disorder (PTSD). Disbelieving a patient's memories of childhood sexual abuse would be considered unethical by today's standards. Perhaps the horror of the stories Freud heard in his practice overwhelmed his desire to view these patients as credible. Nevertheless, treating these memories as *wishes for sexual contact* represents a cruel form of gaslighting perpetrated by a therapist to whom a patient gives her or his trust. It would take a therapist with a profound lack of empathy to ignore this distress and instead reinterpret it as a version of "you wanted it." I therefore conclude that on this interpersonal marker, Freud seems to exemplify an anxious-avoidant attachment relationship to his colleagues.

The Influence of Freud's Anxious-Avoidant Attachment on His Theory and Therapeutic Technique

We have already observed how Freud's profoundly "limited empathy and interpersonal 'coldness'" (Daniel, 2015, p. 115) could have affected his repudiation of the seduction theory. Compared to other pioneers of clinical psychology, however, Freud seems downright warm and fuzzy. Other fathers of clinical psychology would fit the coding guidelines for anxious-avoidant attachment even more closely than Freud. John B. Watson, widely considered the father of behaviorism, displayed a decidedly anxious-avoidant attitude toward parenting:

> Treat [children] as though they were young adults ... Let your behavior always be objective and kindly firm. Never hug and kiss them, never let them sit on your lap. If you must, kiss them once on the forehead when they say good night. Shake hands with them in the morning.
>
> (Watson, 1928, pp. 81–82)

The ideal child, according to Watson (1928), is "a child who never cries unless actually stuck by a pin ... who puts on such habits of politeness and neatness and cleanliness that adults are willing to be around him at least part of the day" (p. 9). Any kind of safe haven behavior exhibited by a mother enraged him: "When I hear a mother say 'Bless its little heart' when it falls down, or stubs its toe, or suffers some other ill, I usually have to walk a block or two to let off steam" (Watson, 1928, p. 82). Outrageous as these words might sound, Watson went further, questioning "whether there should be individual homes for children—or even whether children should know their own parents. There are undoubtedly more scientific ways of bringing up children which probably mean finer and happier children" (Watson, 1928, pp. 5–6). Even though Freud was not known to kiss his own children (Gay, 1998, p. 162), he seems like the paragon of a securely attached person compared to Watson.

Just as there is some truth to the saying "You can tell a lot about a man by the shoes he wears," so too you can tell a lot about a theoretician by the theories they formulate. Watson formulated behaviorism, which postulated that only what is observable exists, and only behavior is observable. Where is the love in this theory? Where was the love in Watson? By contrast, Freud formulated a cure "effected by love" (Freud, 1906, p. 13). In drawing a loose parallel between a mother's sexual activities with her partner and her behavior toward an infant, Freud (1905) writes approvingly that a mother "strokes him, kisses him, rocks him and quite clearly treats him as a substitute for a complete sexual object ... She is only fulfilling her task in teaching the child to love" (p. 223). Even though Freud sexualizes love, love still plays a chief role in healthy human development.

Despite acknowledging the importance of love, Freud's anxious-avoidant attachment infiltrated his technical recommendations and theorizing. After all, Freud (1912b) strongly urges his colleagues to "model themselves during psycho-analytic treatment on the surgeon, who puts aside all his feelings, even his human sympathy, and concentrates his mental forces on the single aim of performing the operation as skillfully as possible" (p. 115). Freud's two technical concepts—neutrality and abstinence—as well as his recommendation to overcome countertransference, the exclusive use of the couch, and his virtual disregard of the importance of the mother-child relationship to development and psychopathology, could reflect "peculiarities of his own personality" that he projected "into the field of science, as a theory having universal validity" (Freud, 1912b, p. 117). Many years later, the field still struggles with Freud's theories and their application to the psychotherapeutic encounter.

It is important to keep in mind that Freud formulated his technical recommendations while working mostly with a population of patients diagnosed with hysteria. Attachment researchers (Bernier & Dozier, 2002; Bernier et al., 2005; Dozier, 2003; Dozier & Bates, 2004; Dozier et al., 1994; Dozier & Tyrrell, 1998; Tyrrell et al., 1999) have begun to demonstrate that the most effective treatments pair a patient with one particular secondary attachment strategy (i.e., anxious-avoidant or anxious-resistant) with a therapist with the other secondary attachment strategy (see Goodman, 2025, Chapter 6). Thus, a treatment is particularly effective if the patient has anxious-resistant features, while the therapist has anxious-avoidant features, and vice versa. This is known as the therapeutic principle of noncomplementarity.

André Brouillet's famous 1887 painting of Jean-Martin Charcot presenting his pet hysteric "Blanche" (Blanche Wittman) to his fellow physicians visually captures the hysteric's signature exaggerated emotional display, perhaps a marker of a hyperactivating attachment strategy. The current label of hysteria—histrionic personality disorder (American Psychiatric Association, 2022)—consists of additional criteria such as demands for reassurance, approval, or praise, sexually seductive behavior, and an excessively impressionistic style of speech—personality traits consistent with a hyperactivating attachment strategy. In fact, this style of speech is one of the hallmarks of an anxious-resistant attachment strategy documented in the AAI coding guidelines (Main & Goldwyn, 1994). If Freud's bread-and-butter patient was the hysteric (e.g., Breuer & Freud, 1893–1895), and hysterics use anxious-resistant attachment strategies to hyperactivate their attachment systems, then it would be reasonable to conclude that many, if not most, of Freud's patients suffered from underregulated emotion associated with an anxious-resistant attachment strategy. If Freud were intuitively aware of the principle of noncomplementarity, then the technical recommendations of neutrality, abstinence, and overcoming the countertransference could be reconceptualized as effective therapeutic tools applied to this particular population. It seems reasonable to suggest that the cure "effected by love" (Freud, 1906, p. 13) requires an overregulated therapeutic technique to contain the underregulated emotion of his hysterical patients. In other words, Freud's apparent dismissing features and overregulated emotion might have served him quite well, given the probable diagnostic and attachment features of some patients in his caseload.

We must also keep in mind that the cultural background at the time of Freud, situated in the sexually repressed and repressive Victorian era (Gay, 1998), could be considered an era in which an anxious-avoidant attachment strategy ruled and, in some regions of Germany, still rules. In a northern German sample, for example, attachment researchers (Grossmann et al., 1985) found a disproportionately high percentage of infants classified as anxious-avoidant. The authors hypothesized that German parents' emphasis on independence and self-reliance contributed to this unexpected outcome. At the time of Freud, nannies often assumed primary caregiving duties in bourgeois society, which no doubt produced feelings of rejection and loss that forced some children to rely on themselves to deactivate attachment needs and overregulate their emotions. Because of their inability to seek help, these children seldom sought psychoanalysis. Freud's childhood history was probably not dramatically different from these particular children growing up during that era. Thus, his technical recommendations and theoretical formulations, however quaint to us, are congruent with his personal childhood history, patient population, and cultural background.

Contemporary psychoanalysis, embodied particularly in relational psychoanalytic theory and attachment theory, recognizes the dialectic of technical recommendations: they must be distinctive enough to be applicable to more than one therapist-patient dyad but flexible enough to be applicable to the unique relationship created between each therapist and patient. Our field has often emphasized one of the poles of the dialectic to the exclusion of the other pole. As I have shown, Freud emphasized the universality of his technical recommendations. Freud's technical recommendations might have been effective with the population with which he was working but ineffective in other therapeutic contexts. One of the champions of universal technical recommendations is Michels (2001), who acknowledges the pitfalls of adhering to "only one right way" (p. 409) of technique; however, he notes, "We do have preferred ways of working, and patients would be foolish to come to us if we did not" (p. 410).

At the other end of the spectrum, champions of the uniqueness of the therapeutic relationship created by the therapist and patient dismiss "preferred ways of working" and, at times, advocate "throwing away the book" (Hoffman, 1994, p. 187). Greenberg (2001a), a proponent of maximum flexibility of technique, argues, "There is no way ... to assert *a priori* the benefit of any technical intervention" (p. 364) because of the uniqueness of the therapeutic dyad and the inherent unpredictability of intervention effects. Other writers (e.g., Kantrowitz, 2001) express similar sentiments:

> An analytic treatment is like a snowflake. Overall, it is easy to identify and distinguish. However, closer scrutiny reveals how different each one is from the others. In fact, no two are alike. Nor are any two patient-analyst pairs. In analytic treatment, the particular aspects of therapeutic action that facilitate psychological change are likely to vary from person to person.
>
> (p. 403)

Therapists within a broad psychodynamic tradition can readily identify with these sentiments because the interaction structures (i.e., patterns of reciprocal interaction; E. E. Jones, 2000) that develop in all our clinical work do feel unique within each therapeutic encounter we have. Yet most of us adhere to a set of technical guidelines that somehow remain constant across patients. Greenberg (2001b) suggests that this technical flexibility—the willingness to vary technique according to the nature of the patient's personality and psychopathology and the ever-changing therapeutic relationship—constitutes an advance in psychoanalytic clinical theory. The parameters of this variation, however, remain largely unspecified in the relational literature.

In an article written during the infancy of relational theory, Greenberg (1986) suggests that technical taboos such as emotional openness, self-disclosure, and even judgment could be used judiciously in certain contexts within the psychotherapeutic encounter to further the treatment aims. For example, expressing surprise and concern at a patient's determined self-destructive behavior could present the patient with a caregiving experience that differs from the indifferent one they knew from childhood. From an object relations perspective, Kernberg and his colleagues (e.g., Clarkin et al., 2015) consider this position as an extension of technical neutrality because any so-called normal person would have the same emotional reaction to this behavior, which is important for the patient to observe and internalize. Under these circumstances, "the traditionally neutral non-judgmental attitude," according to Greenberg (1986), "can be genuinely dangerous" (p. 146). Freud, then, by virtue of his fixed technical recommendations, could have been dangerous because, with certain patients, he was unwittingly repeating their childhood experiences with a neglectful parent.

Greenberg (1986) concluded that an effective treatment requires the patient to experience the therapist as both an old and a new object. In other words, a dialectic exists between the patient's experience of the therapist as an object of the patient's transference and the experience of the therapist as someone who behaves differently from the original parents from childhood. If, like Freud, the therapist adopts a fixed technique vis-à-vis the therapeutic relationship, technical errors in either direction could follow. In the first scenario, the therapist could be behaving too much like the parents of childhood. From an attachment perspective, this technical error comes in two forms: therapists with anxious-avoidant features paired with patients with anxious-avoidant features, and therapists with anxious-resistant features paired with patients with anxious-resistant features (see Goodman, 2025, Chapter 6, Table 6.1). These pairings are less conducive to therapeutic change than noncomplementary pairings in which anxious-avoidant features are paired with anxious-resistant features or vice versa (Bernier & Dozier, 2002; Bernier et al., 2005; Dozier, 2003; Dozier & Bates, 2004; Dozier et al., 1994; Dozier & Tyrrell, 1998; Tyrrell et al., 1999). In the second scenario, the therapist could be behaving so differently from the parents of childhood that the transference is not permitted to emerge, and the therapy thus never gets under way (Greenberg, 1986). Freud (1915) formulated his technical recommendations to maximize the opportunity for the patient to develop the transference. We have seen, however, that the technical concepts of neutrality, abstinence, and overcoming the countertransference fail to promote the perception of the therapist as a mirror because each patient experiences these conditions differently, depending on their expectations of caregiver behavior. These classical technical concepts instead create the conditions for perceiving the therapist as either like the deactivating, dismissing parents of childhood (e.g., abstinent, rejecting, and neglectful), or like a new object who responds differently from the hyperactivating, preoccupied parents of childhood (e.g., calm and reflective). I have argued that, following the principle of noncomplementarity, Freud's technical recommendations are better suited to patients with hyperactivating attachment strategies (like the hysterics he mostly treated) than to patients with deactivating attachment strategies. Relational theory and attachment theory and research suggest, however, that the therapist needs to be flexible (congruent with a secure attachment pattern) and thus be able to adjust his or her technique to accommodate the patient's pattern of emotion regulation and thus create the treatment conditions that optimize the use of the therapeutic relationship. Specifically, the therapist must not only permit the transference to emerge but also must respond to this transference in ways that gently challenge the patient's expectations formed during numerous interactions with the parents during childhood.

Clinical theoreticians and researchers alike have been attempting to enhance our understanding of the patient's mental representations of the therapist and the relationship to the therapist and their roles in therapeutic change. Treurniet (1993) suggested that therapeutic change takes place through the nonverbal interactions between therapist and patient as well as through the classical vehicles of insight and interpretation. Eagle (2003, p. 48) supported this view with a clinical vignette of a female patient who experienced the permanent remission of dyspareunia (i.e., painful intercourse) after an interaction with him that the two of them never discussed following the interaction. According to Eagle, he never made an interpretation of the interaction or the outcome.

Freud never acknowledged a therapeutic role for the nonverbal relationship between the therapist and the patient. Freud (1909c) fed his patient, disparagingly known as the Rat Man, but never considered that behavior therapeutic. In fact, Freud (1919c) considered the uncovering of repressed material through interpretation—"the pure gold of analysis"—superior to "the copper of direct suggestion" (p. 168) and other forms of psychotherapy such as hypnosis, which he had abandoned. He considered the nonverbal aspects of the therapeutic relationship, such as the use of the couch, only as conditions under which the patient's transference could manifest itself. The idea that the therapeutic relationship might have healing properties independent of interpretation received its first hearing with books by Ferenczi and Rank (1924) and Alexander and French (1946), the latter introducing the term "corrective emotional experience." This experience includes not only verbal but also nonverbal interactions between the therapist and patient. Dyadic interactions that do not rely on verbal meanings such as activity level, conversational engagement, prosodic emphasis, and vocal mirroring accounted for 30% of the outcome of the first five minutes of a simulated employment negotiation (Curhan & Pentland, 2007). Both therapist and patient unconsciously monitor these alternative channels of communication to help formulate their mental image of the other person and the interactions between them.

In summary, I have attempted to demonstrate that Freud formulated his technical recommendations consistent with anxious-avoidant features of his attachment organization, hyperactivating patterns of emotion regulation within his patient population, and cultural restrictions (which also reflect anxious-avoidant features of attachment within that culture). I argued that although Freud meant for therapists to apply these technical recommendations universally to all patients, their effectiveness is probably restricted to a subset of patients with anxious-avoidant features of attachment. We will never know how psychoanalytic technique would have evolved had Freud's attachment strategy been less anxious-avoidant. Perhaps the outcome would have been a more relationally oriented clinical technique from the outset.

Relational theory and attachment theory and research have presented credible challenges to classical psychoanalytic technique. Theoreticians working within these perspectives are recommending a more flexible approach to clinical technique, anchored around the pattern of emotion regulation presented by the patient, both within and across sessions. A tentative technical recommendation offered by this school of thought and supported by preliminary evidence is to present a gentle challenge to the patient's preferred pattern of emotion regulation that embodies their attachment strategy. This principle of noncomplementarity provides the broad technical conditions under which a corrective emotional experience can occur.

The target of therapeutic change has also begun to shift away from the verbalization of repressed unconscious material through interpretation and to nonverbal channels of interaction. The study of these nonverbal channels operating between the therapist and patient depends on the metaphor of the caregiver-infant attachment relationship. In Chapter 3 of Goodman (2025), I examined the caregiver-infant attachment relationship as a metaphor for the therapist-patient relationship. As I have demonstrated, Freud did not use this metaphor to guide his thinking about the therapist-patient relationship. For the most part, Freud viewed the patient's relationship to the therapist as a pseudo-relationship in which the patient transfers the childhood relationship to the caregivers onto the therapist. Consistent with this view, the therapist should conduct the treatment in abstinence, analogous to a nongratifying, even rejecting, caregiver. According to Freud (1915), "The patient's need and longing should be allowed to persist in her, in order that they may serve as forces impelling her to do work and to make changes" (p. 165). From this statement, we could surmise that the therapist's conduct resembles anti-caregiving; a caregiver does not permit an infant's need and longing to persist. In Chapter 3 of Goodman (2025), I explored the advantages and disadvantages of using this metaphor for the therapist-patient relationship. Taking Freud's theoretical and therapeutic biases into account, we have observed how the anxious-avoidant attachment pattern can profoundly influence a person's scientific thinking and shape the trajectory of an entire school of thought. History leaves the task of correcting these biases to succeeding generations.

Conclusion

In this chapter, I analyzed Freud's autobiographical writings and some of his letters to colleagues (Freud, 1914b, 1925), using the nine interpersonal markers of attachment (Daniel, 2015), to determine (1) the quality of his attachment relationships to his colleague, and (2) whether these this set of attachment relationships (to colleagues) support the correspondence pathway or the compensation pathway discussed in Chapter 3 of Goodman (2025). Based on a general reading of the narratives, I conclude that Freud developed an anxious-avoidant attachment pattern in relation to his colleagues and probably an anxious-avoidant attachment pattern to his parents and to God. Thus, I conclude that Freud's narratives support the correspondence pathway.

A review of the analysis of Freud's narratives, using the nine interpersonal markers (Daniel, 2015), indicates a correspondence pathway among his anxious-avoidant attachment relationships to his parents, to God, and to his colleagues. The type of attachment insecurity, however, was not evident on two of the nine interpersonal markers—Expression and Regulation of Emotions and Conflict Management. On these two markers, Freud demonstrated anxious-resistant features of attachment. On all nine interpersonal markers, Freud revealed an insecure attachment pattern. This more granular evidence supports my conclusion that Freud's autobiographical writings support the correspondence pathway. Unlike Bill W., Freud did not compensate for his anxious-avoidant attachment relationships to his parents and to colleagues with a secure attachment relationship to God.

In reflecting on the autobiographical accounts of Bill W. and Freud, an obvious question arises: how did one atheist (Bill W.) find a secure attachment to a Higher Power to compensate for his anxious-avoidant attachment relationships to his parents, while the other atheist (Freud) found no such secure attachment to a Higher Power? I suggest that the major difference between these two men lies chiefly in (1) their experiences of distress, and (2) the brittleness of their anxious-avoidant attachment organization. Regarding experiences of distress, Bill W. (Anonymous, 2000) reveals what Dr. Silkworth at Towns Hospital disclosed to his wife Lois shortly before Bill W.'s spiritual awakening:

> His habit of drinking has turned into an obsession, one much too deep to be overcome, and the physical effect of it on him has also been very severe, for he's showing some signs of brain damage … Actually I'm fearful for his sanity if he goes on drinking … You will have to confine him, lock him up somewhere if he would remain sane, or even alive. He can't go on this way another year, possibly.
>
> (pp. 116–117)

Serendipitously meeting a fellow First World War veteran on Armistice Day (on November 11, 1934—just one month before his spiritual awakening), Bill W. and this other man eventually walked into a speakeasy, where Bill W. shared his story of alcoholism. After Bill W. took a drink, however, his companion exclaimed, "'My God, is it possible that you could take a drink after what you just told me? You must be crazy'. And my only reply could be this, 'Yes, I am'" (pp. 119–120). Bill W. was teetering on the edge of insanity.

By contrast, Freud also suffered from an addiction to nicotine delivered through cigar smoking. In an October 16, 1895, letter to his colleague, Wilhelm Fliess, Freud (1895) refers to his nicotine addiction as "the miserable struggle against the craving for the fourth and fifth [cigar] … Abstinence probably is not very conducive to psychic contentment either" (p. 145). Two years after writing this letter, Freud (1897) classifies tobacco as an addiction and a substitute for masturbation: "Masturbation is the one major habit, the 'primal addiction' and that it is only as a substitute and replacement for it that the other addictions—for alcohol, morphine, tobacco, etc.—come into existence" (p. 272). Thus, Freud is aware of his addiction to nicotine, yet he continues to smoke cigars even after he is diagnosed with epithelioma in 1923 (Gay, 1998). In fact, despite this sobering news,

Freud continues to smoke cigars until his death in 1939, even though he declared nine years earlier in a May 8, 1930, letter to his colleague Andreas-Salomé that "I have given up smoking completely, after it has served me for exactly fifty years as sword and buckler in the battle of life" (Freud, 1930c, p. 187). Freud receives "a partial resection of the upper jaw" (Freud, 1923, p. 527), but it does nothing to slow down his addiction.

Both Bill W. and Freud suffered from addiction—one to alcohol, the other to nicotine. Both men were atheists and grew up in essentially secular households. Both men established anxious-avoidant attachment relationships to their parents. So how do we understand their divergent spiritual pathways to establishing an attachment relationship to a Higher Power? Recall the chief determining factor of Granqvist and Kirkpatrick (2018) from Chapter 1: persons insecurely attached to their parents from childhood *compensate* for these insecure relationships when they "cannot bear the high levels of suffering experienced sufficiently well by employing his or her usual [insecure] strategy for managing stress" (p. 934). Let us consider both men's stress management strategies.

Bill W.'s strategy for managing the insanity of his life—drinking large quantities of alcohol as frequently as possible—had made his life unmanageable. He finally encountered the powerlessness of his situation. Freud, on the other hand, was able to continue managing his stress by smoking 20 cigars per day despite his prosthesis and the pain associated with his 34 surgeries for cancer (Adeyemo, 2004). Freud's nicotine addiction seems to have been less debilitating than Bill W.'s alcohol addiction. Bill W. believed that he was losing his mind—there was no way out but to cast his lot with God. It is even possible that Bill W. would have committed suicide before alcohol completed its lethal work: "I had a habit of standing before my father-in-law's medicine cabinet, leaning drunkenly and sizing up the suicide potential that might exist in more forbidden-looking medicine bottles" (Anonymous, 2000, p. 100). As far as we know, Freud never considered suicide (although he consented to euthanasia; see Gay, 1998). There is a moment in his life when he might have considered turning to God for comfort—when his beloved daughter Sophie died. Yet, he declined this option. In a February 4, 1920, letter to his close colleague Ferenczi, Freud (1920a) writes: "As a confirmed unbeliever I have no one to accuse and realize that there is no place where I could lodge a complaint" (p. 328). He instead remains true to his denial of an attachment relationship to God.

A second explanation for the divergent spiritual pathways of these two men is related to the brittleness of the anxious-avoidant childhood attachment relationships to their parents. From the earliest attachment literature, attachment patterns were considered categorical rather than dimensional (see, e.g., Ainsworth et al., 1978). Even within Ainsworth's attachment patterns, however, subcategories exist that reflect the relative presence and brittleness of these patterns' defensive processes. AAI classifications work similarly by rating the person on a series of Likert-type rating scales and then deriving a classification based on the constellation of these ratings (Hesse, 2018). Thus, it is possible for two persons to vary in their level of anxious-avoidance. Considering the anxious-avoidant attachment patterns of these two men, it is possible that not only was Bill W.'s stress more acute, but also his anxious-avoidant attachment pattern was more brittle than Freud's, thus making him more susceptible to a spiritual awakening. According to Kirkpatrick (2005), "Those situations in which human attachment figures are inadequate are, in fact, most likely to be the ones that are *severely* stressful or distressing (p. 154). Bill W.'s addiction to alcohol, and the dire consequences that followed, were so overwhelming that not even his long-suffering wife Lois could protect him.

By contrast, Freud's addiction to nicotine did not produce suicidal thoughts, nor was he ever without the social support of his wife, children, and many close colleagues all over the world to keep him from searching for a surrogate attachment relationship. If Freud's social support system failed him, then perhaps he would have re-engaged in a protesting conversation, and thus a relationship, with a Higher Power. We will never know. We can surmise, however, that a combination of a more brittle insecure attachment pattern, a life-threatening stressor, and inadequate social support to meet the challenges of this stressor provides the sufficient ingredients for a spiritual awakening consistent with the compensation pathway. If one of these ingredients is missing, however, it is possible that the person will continue traveling down the pathway of correspondence.

Brief Treatment Plan for Freud

Based on the preceding narrative analysis, how might I treat Sigmund Freud if he were to schedule a session of psychotherapy with me? It is highly unlikely that Freud would allow me or anyone else to help him. Dozier (1990) reported in her study of persons with serious psychopathological disorders that anxious-avoidant persons were less likely to seek help from therapists, less likely to self-disclose and use therapy productively, and less compliant with therapy than secure or anxious-resistant persons. Thus, Freud would probably never set foot in my office. He is the only psychoanalyst in the history of psychoanalysis never to have been analyzed by someone else. He trusted in his own self-analysis, which did nothing to help him abstain from the cigar-smoking addiction that ultimately killed him. In his discussion of narcissistic personalities, the renowned psychoanalyst Otto Kernberg (1986) notes "the absence of the capacity to depend upon others," demonstrating "a persistent absence of separation anxiety or mourning reactions at weekends, vacation, or illness of the analyst" (p. 255). The overall image is that of an outwardly self-sufficient, fiercely independent individual with an inflated sense of self, disguising feelings of profound rejection, unworthiness, and impoverishment. As a toddler, Freud must have felt rejected, unworthy, and impoverished when his nursemaid suddenly disappeared, and his mother simultaneously had another baby. In a previous book (Goodman, 2014), I argue that anxious-avoidant attachment is often the substrate out of which a narcissistic personality takes root. Based on the foregoing narrative analysis, it is plausible that Freud suffered from narcissistic features of his personality.

Kernberg (1980, pp. 135–153) suggests that narcissistic patients' "pathological grandiose self" does not permit the intrapersonal vulnerability necessary to benefit from psychotherapy. Only in middle age, when their youth, beauty, and health begin to fade and the narcissistic supplies begin to dwindle through the loss of their colleagues, do narcissistic persons seek out and benefit from psychotherapy. Thus, the only time in Freud's life where he might have considered humbling himself to submit to psychotherapy with another mental health professional might have been near the end of his life, when his nicotine addiction was raging, his health was failing as a result, and his jaw pain made working—his constant companion for most of his life—almost unbearable. Could Attachment-Informed Psychotherapy (AIP; see Goodman, 2025, Chapter 4) engage him in a process where he could explore his nicotine addiction without defensiveness as well as his anger toward God and discover a secure attachment relationship that could replace the surrogate attachment relationship to nicotine?

As I mentioned in my brief treatment plan for Bill W. (see Chapter 4), most therapists would not engage in treatment with a prospective client actively engaged in addiction; however, unlike alcohol addiction, nicotine addiction would not make a patient cognitively or emotionally unavailable to the honest, sobering self-reflection required of the psychotherapy process. Thus, Freud could be treated while in active nicotine addiction. The nicotine addiction, however, remains problematic because Freud would have less motivation to transfer his attachment needs to the therapist or to a Higher Power if he were still depending on nicotine to dull and avoid these needs. Of course, I would candidly and straightforwardly discuss these issues with Freud, emphasizing the likelihood that Freud might rationalize his continued attachment to nicotine as his "sword and buckler in the battle of life" (Freud, 1930c, p. 187). I would want Freud to begin to view nicotine as a surrogate attachment figure that provides him with security at any moment of the day or night, whenever he desires it. Freud gradually came to view nicotine as more reliable than his nursemaid, his mother, his father, and his colleagues Adler and Jung. Whenever he was feeling insecure, lonely, helpless, or victimized, he could rely on nicotine to help him ignore these feelings. The goal of treatment would be to convince Freud that, unlike the parents or the God from childhood, people and God can be trustworthy and reliable when called upon. As his therapist, I would need to demonstrate trustworthiness and reliability by showing up to sessions on time, announcing vacations several weeks in advance, demonstrating constant attentiveness and empathy, and showing my concern for his deteriorating health.

As I have written elsewhere (Goodman, 2014), Kernberg (1986) is incorrect to assume that narcissistic personalities demonstrate "a persistent absence of separation anxiety" (p. 255); rather, these persons experience separation anxiety intensely but deny it and therefore lack any awareness of it. For Freud, I believe, nicotine serves the purpose of dulling his awareness of separation anxiety, disappointment, abandonment, and a host of other unpleasant emotions all related to his image of himself as unlovable and unworthy of love and his image of significant others as unloving, unaccepting, untrustworthy, and unreliable. As a therapist, my emotional expressiveness toward Freud would be in the service of showing him that I can be loving, accepting, trustworthy, and reliable toward him. Communicating these sentiments, however, would mean nothing because I could by lying. In this context, the aphorism "actions speak louder than words" is particularly apt.

The first phase of treatment would consist of developing a therapeutic alliance (Wampold, 2001), in which Freud and I would agree on the goals (to quit smoking and become more aware of his underlying attachment needs), tasks (to experience these attachment needs through self-reflection and the therapeutic relationship), and bond (recognizing and experiencing the emotional significance of our therapeutic relationship). Ideally, Freud would develop an initial transference to me resembling his relationship to his nursemaid prior to her abandonment. On the other hand, I might expect Freud to view me as his disappointing father. After all, I did not found psychoanalysis or publish 24 volumes known as the *Standard Edition* or infiltrate the Western cultural landscape. In fact, Freud might easily devalue me and my achievements as an unconscious strategy to neutralize my therapeutic effectiveness and thus derail my attempts to help him to quit smoking. Freud would call this phenomenon "resistance" (Freud, 1912a)—the deployment of a complex network of defense mechanisms to avoid distressing emotions and maintain the psychic status quo.

Freud might even devalue me to the point of ending treatment, as Dozier (1990) found in her study of anxious-avoidant patients. If Freud did leave treatment, I would make every effort to get him back in treatment. I would call him and disclose to him that I am concerned for his health and that psychotherapy represents his best chance of stopping his cigar smoking and extending his life. Note that I would never take this action with an anxious-resistant patient because it could reinforce a dynamic of my chasing a patient who is running away from treatment to test my love, which would hyperactivate their attachment system and thus amplify the drama between us.

Assuming that I could get Freud back into treatment with me, we would discuss his feelings of superiority over me and devaluation of me as strategies for protecting his surrogate attachment relationship to nicotine. I would empathize with his resistance to change and the agony of nicotine withdrawal as well as the surfacing of dormant anxieties and needs that Freud would rather not experience consciously. I would begin to introduce a "gentle challenge" (Dozier, 2003, p. 254) to my interactions with him. In other words, I would gently challenge his deactivating strategy by behaving in a more animated, hyperactivating manner (see Goodman, 2025, Chapter 6). I would inquire about his feelings surrounding his nursemaid and her abandoning him as well as his mother's emotional and physical unavailability. I would empathize with these distressing feelings and emphasize his latent needs for connection and security. I would also hone in on any feelings of anger or resentment that might surface through this exploration and identify these feelings as signals of attachment needs left ungratified. As I work with Freud, I would be particularly on guard for any proneness to intellectualization of these needs. Based on his writings and his vast reservoir of intellect, I would imagine that Freud would try to *think* his way out of his difficulties rather than to *feel* his feelings and mourn the loss of disappointing and rejecting attachment figures from his childhood. I would then gently point out these instances of intellectualization as attempts to avoid unpleasant feelings, while constantly monitoring Freud's reactions to my interventions to determine whether our therapeutic alliance is still intact. My reactions to Freud's anger toward me as a representative of disappointing caregivers from childhood would largely determine the success or failure of this treatment. Will I accept his anger and devaluation without retaliation or condescension, or like his father, will I tell him that he will never amount to anything (Freud, 1900)? That is what Freud unconsciously wants to know. If I can repeatedly defy this expectation, then the treatment has a chance to succeed.

Although I would be aware at the outset of treatment that Freud is an avowed atheist, I would also inquire about his spiritual experiences with the occult. I would want him to tell me about these spiritual experiences and how he feels when he indulges in these interests. Are these clumsy attempts at contacting a Higher Power—a Higher Power Who he believes has rejected him and Whom he has therefore rejected as a grand confluence of "illusions and insusceptible of proof" (Freud, 1927, p. 31)? Freud's dabbling in occult practices might hold clues about his relationship to a Higher Power. If he could keep his intellectualizing to a minimum, talking about a Higher Power might provide an entrée into his disappointing early attachment relationships without directly addressing them. This kind of therapeutic strategy is called "working in the arena of displacements" (D. G. Barrett, 2012, p. 6). By working on his attachment relationship to a Higher Power, I would also be surreptitiously working on his attachment relationships to his caregivers from childhood, an arena that might be too "hot" for him to engage just yet. He might be more receptive to talking about a rejecting Higher Power than he would about his rejecting nursemaid and mother.

Considering Freud's failing health and the reality that he would be near the end of his life, it would be important for me to remember that older adults tend to experience higher rates of death anxiety, particularly if they have physical and psychological problems (Fortner & Neimeyer, 1999). For everyone—but especially for those like Freud who have been avoiding the emotional impact of separations their entire lives—death represents the "final exam" regarding the ultimate acceptance of separation anxiety. For the atheist, the end of life represents a permanent separation from his or her remaining loved ones and from the safe haven of all that is familiar and meaningful. I would ask Freud about his thoughts and feelings about his own death and permanent separation from his children and grandchildren. Such a discussion could stimulate an interest in the possibility of an afterlife, and therefore, a revisitation of his unbelief in a Higher Power. Death anxiety represents a final opportunity to work through his childhood abandonment trauma because he would soon be leaving his remaining loved ones behind, just as his nursemaid and mother left him behind so many years earlier. How we ultimately detach from this world is intertwined with how we initially became attached to this world—through our earliest caregivers. Freud would therefore need to contemplate his own death in the context of these earliest attachment relationships.

I would be remiss in formulating a treatment plan without considering my own likely countertransference feelings evoked in my treatment of Freud. Freud is widely acknowledged as the founder of psychoanalysis (Gay, 1998). Considering my own professional identity as a card-carrying psychoanalyst, Freud has profoundly influenced my scholarship, my technique, and my worldview. Thus, he would be entering treatment with me as an exalted father figure, a genius of a man. I might therefore be susceptible to identifying with his projections of me as devalued and inferior—unable to offer much help. I discuss this familiar role elsewhere in relation to fledgling therapists, who are more likely than more experienced therapists to believe in their own incompetence (Goodman, 2005). I would also be careful not to engage in verbal, intellectual skirmishes with Freud. He might tempt me to gratify my desire to exceed my exalted father's intellect by engaging in clever argumentation and wordplay. These countertransference reactions—incompetence and grandiosity—would only fortify Freud's resistance to change and deprive him of opportunities for connection and growth. We would no longer be cooperating toward a common goal but competing for or capitulating to intellectual supremacy. Given my own faith in a Higher Power, I would also need to guard against a patronizing attitude toward his atheism and give his unbelief as much thoughtful consideration as I would another patient's belief. Adopting a "not-knowing stance" (Volkert et al., 2022, p. 5) might mitigate against conveying a signal of condescension, of which Freud might be wary. If I concluded that my own countertransference reactions might place the treatment outcome in doubt, I might refer Freud to another therapist whose countertransference reactions might be less problematic. Of course, I could be risking a repetition of his childhood trauma of abandonment. Whether I or some other therapist would end up treating Freud, the psychotherapy process would be challenging and possibly futile without a robust external support system to keep Freud accountable to his commitment to sobriety from nicotine. Undoubtedly, the treatment of Sigmund Freud would be my most memorable experience as a therapist.

References

Adeyemo, W. L. (2004). Sigmund Freud: Smoking habit, oral cancer and euthanasia. *Nigerian Journal of Medicine, 13*, 189–195.

Ainsworth, M. D. S. (1979). Infant-mother attachment. *American Psychologist, 34*, 932–937.

Ainsworth, M. D. S., Blehar, M. C., Waters, E., & Wall, S. (1978). *Patterns of attachment: A psychological study of the strange situation*. Erlbaum.

Alexander, F., & French, T. M. (1946). *Psychoanalytic therapy: Principles and application*. Ronald.

American Psychiatric Association. (2022). *Diagnostic and statistical manual of mental disorders* (5th ed., text rev.). America Psychiatric Association.

Anderson-Lopez, K., & Lopez, R. (2014). Let it go. In *Frozen: Original motion picture soundtrack*. Wonderland Music Company/Walt Disney.

Anonymous. (2000). *Bill W. my first 40 years: An autobiography of the cofounder of Alcoholics Anonymous*. Hazelden.

Barrett, D. G. (2012). In and out of the displacement: The roles of interpretation and play in work with children. In K. E. Baker & J. R. Brandell (Eds.), *Child and adolescent psychotherapy and psychoanalysis* (pp. 6–21). Routledge.

Barrett, J. L. (2012). *Born believers: The science of children's religious belief*. Free Press.

Bateman, A. W., & Fonagy, P. (2004). *Psychotherapy for borderline personality disorder: Mentalization-based treatment*. Oxford University Press.

Bernier, A., & Dozier, M. (2002). The client-counselor match and the corrective emotional experience: Evidence from interpersonal and attachment research. *Psychotherapy: Theory/Research/Practice/Training, 39*, 32–43.

Bernier, A., Larose, S., & Soucy, N. (2005). Academic mentoring in college: The interactive role of student's and mentor's interpersonal dispositions. *Research in Higher Education, 46*, 29–51.

Bowlby, J. (1973). *Attachment and loss*: Vol. 2. *Separation: Anxiety and anger*. Basic Books.

Bowlby, J. (1980). *Attachment and loss*: Vol. 3. *Loss, sadness and depression*. Basic Books.

Bowlby, J. (1982). *Attachment and loss*: Vol. 1. *Attachment* (2nd ed.). Basic Books.

Breuer, J., & Freud, S. (1893-1895). Studies on hysteria. In J. Strachey (Ed. and Trans.), *The standard edition of the complete psychological works of Sigmund Freud* (Vol. 2). Hogarth Press.

Brouillet, A. (1887). A clinical lesson at the Salpêtrière. https://en.wikipedia.org/wiki/A_Clinical_Lesson_at_the_Salp%C3%AAtri%C3%A8re

Cassidy, J., & Kobak, R. R. (1988). Avoidance and its relation to other defensive processes. In J. Belsky & T. Nezworski (Eds.), *Clinical implications of attachment* (pp. 300–323). Erlbaum.

Clark, R. W. (1980). *Freud: The man and the cause*. Random House.

Clarkin, J. F., Yeomans, F. E., & Kernberg, O. F. (2015). *Transference-focused psychotherapy for borderline personality disorder: A clinical guide*. American Psychiatric Publishing.

Curhan, J. R., & Pentland, A. (2007). Thin slices of negotiation: Predicting outcomes from conversational dynamics within the first 5 minutes. *Journal of Applied Psychology, 92*, 802–811.

Daniel, S. I. F. (2015). *Adult attachment patterns in a treatment context: Relationship and narrative*. Routledge.

Dozier, M. (1990). Attachment organization and treatment use for adults with serious psychopathological disorders. *Development and Psychopathology, 2*, 47–60.

Dozier, M. (2003). Attachment-based treatment for vulnerable children. *Attachment and Human Development, 5*, 253–257.

Dozier, M., & Bates, B. C. (2004). Attachment state of mind and the treatment relationship. In L. Atkinson & S. Goldberg (Eds.), *Attachment issues in psychopathology and intervention* (pp. 167–180). Erlbaum.

Dozier, M., Cue, K. L., & Barnett, L. (1994). Clinicians as caregivers: Role of attachment organization in treatment. *Journal of Consulting and Clinical Psychology, 62*, 793–800.

Dozier, M., & Tyrrell, C. (1998). The role of attachment in therapeutic relationships. In J. A. Simpson & W. S. Rholes (Eds.), *Attachment theory and close relationships* (pp. 221–248). Guilford Press.

Eagle, M. (2003). Clinical implications of attachment theory. *Psychoanalytic Inquiry*, *23*, 27–53.
Ferenczi, S., & Rank, O. (1924). *The development of psychoanalysis*. International Universities Press.
Fortner, B. V., & Neimeyer, R. A. (1999). Death anxiety in older adults: A quantitative review. *Death Studies*, *23*, 387–411.
Freud, E. L., Freud, L., & Grubrich-Simitis, I. (Eds.). (1978). *Sigmund Freud: His life in pictures and words*. Harcourt Brace Jovanovich.
Freud, S. (1874). Letter from Sigmund Freud to Eduard Silberstein, November 8, 1874. In W. Boehlich (Ed.), *The letters of Sigmund Freud to Eduard Silberstein 1871–1881* (A. Pomerans, Trans.; pp. 70–72). Belknap Press.
Freud, S. (1895). Letter from Freud to Fliess, October 16, 1895. In J. M. Masson (Ed. and Trans.), *The complete letters of Sigmund Freud to Wilhelm Fliess, 1887–1904* (pp. 145–146). Belknap Press.
Freud, S. (1897). Letter 79 extracts from the Fliess papers. In J. Strachey (Ed. and Trans.), *The standard edition of the complete psychological works of Sigmund Freud* (Vol. 1, pp. 270–273). Hogarth Press.
Freud, S. (1898). Letter from Freud to Fliess, April 3, 1898. In J. M. Masson (Ed. and Trans.), *The complete letters of Sigmund Freud to Wilhelm Fliess, 1887–1904* (pp. 306–307). Belknap Press.
Freud, S. (1899a). Letter from Freud to Fliess, September 21, 1899. In J. M. Masson (Ed. and Trans.), *The complete letters of Sigmund Freud to Wilhelm Fliess, 1887–1904* (pp. 373–374). Belknap Press.
Freud, S. (1899b). Letter from Freud to Fliess, September 27, 1899. In J. M. Masson (Ed. and Trans.), *The complete letters of Sigmund Freud to Wilhelm Fliess, 1887–1904* (pp. 375–376). Belknap Press.
Freud, S. (1899c). Screen memories. In J. Strachey (Ed. and Trans.), *The standard edition of the complete psychological works of Sigmund Freud* (Vol. 3, pp. 303–322). Hogarth Press.
Freud, S. (1900). The interpretation of dreams. In J. Strachey (Ed. and Trans.), *The standard edition of the complete psychological works of Sigmund Freud* (Vols. 4–5, pp. 1–625). Hogarth Press.
Freud, S. (1901). The psychopathology of everyday life. In J. Strachey (Ed. and Trans.), *The standard edition of the complete psychological works of Sigmund Freud* (Vol. 6, pp. vii–296). Hogarth Press.
Freud, S. (1905). Three essays on the theory of sexuality. In J. Strachey (Ed. and Trans.), *The standard edition of the complete psychological works of Sigmund Freud* (Vol. 7, pp. 135–243). Hogarth Press.
Freud, S. (1906). Letter from Sigmund Freud to C. G. Jung, December 6, 1906. In W. McGuire (Ed.), *The Freud/Jung letters: The correspondence between Sigmund Freud and C. G. Jung* (R. F. C. Hull & R. Manheim, Trans.; pp. 11–13). Princeton University Press.
Freud, S. (1907). Obsessive actions and religious practices. In J. Strachey (Ed. and Trans.), *The standard edition of the complete psychological works of Sigmund Freud* (Vol. 9, pp. 115–128). Hogarth Press.
Freud, S. (1909a). Letter from Sigmund Freud to C. G. Jung, April 16, 1909. In W. McGuire (Ed.), *The Freud/Jung letters: The correspondence between Sigmund Freud and C. G. Jung* (R. F. C. Hull & R. Manheim, Trans.; pp. 218–220). Princeton University Press.

Freud, S. (1909b). Letter from Sigmund Freud to Sándor Ferenczi, October 22, 1909. In E. Brabant, E. Falzeder, & P. Giampieri-Deutsch (Eds.), *The correspondence of Sigmund Freud and Sándor Ferenczi* (Vol. 1, *1908–1914*; P. T. Hoffer, Trans.; pp. 84–86). Belknap Press.

Freud, S. (1909c). Notes upon a case of obsessional neurosis. In J. Strachey (Ed. and Trans.), *The standard edition of the complete psychological works of Sigmund Freud* (Vol. 10, pp. 151–318). Hogarth Press.

Freud, S. (1910). Letter from Sigmund Freud to Oskar Pfister, March 6, 1910. In H. Meng & E. L. Freud (Eds.), *Psychoanalysis and faith: The letters of Sigmund Freud and Oskar Pfister* (pp. 34–35). Hogarth Press.

Freud, S. (1911). Letter from Sigmund Freud to C. G. Jung, February 17, 1911. In W. McGuire (Ed.), *The Freud/Jung letters: The correspondence between Sigmund Freud and C. G. Jung* (R. F. C. Hull & R. Manheim, Trans.; pp. 393–396). Princeton University Press.

Freud, S. (1912a). The dynamics of transference. In J. Strachey (Ed. and Trans.), *The standard edition of the complete psychological works of Sigmund Freud* (Vol. 12, pp. 97–108). Hogarth Press.

Freud, S. (1912b). Recommendations to physicians practising psycho-analysis. In J. Strachey (Ed. and Trans.), *The standard edition of the complete psychological works of Sigmund Freud* (Vol. 12, pp. 109–120). Hogarth Press.

Freud, S. (1913a). On beginning the treatment (Further recommendations on the technique of psycho-analysis I). In J. Strachey (Ed. and Trans.), *The standard edition of the complete psychological works of Sigmund Freud* (Vol. 12, pp. 123–144). Hogarth Press.

Freud, S. (1913b). Totem and taboo: Some points of agreement between the mental lives of savages and neurotics. In J. Strachey (Ed. and Trans.), *The standard edition of the complete psychological works of Sigmund Freud* (Vol. 13, pp. vii–162). Hogarth Press.

Freud, S. (1914a). Letter from Sigmund Freud to Sándor Ferenczi, June 22, 1914. In E. Brabant, E. Falzeder, & P. Giampieri-Deutsch (Eds.), *The correspondence of Sigmund Freud and Sándor Ferenczi* (Vol. 1, *1908–1914*; P. T. Hoffer, Trans.; pp. 559–560). Belknap Press.

Freud, S. (1914b). On the history of the psycho-analytic movement. In J. Strachey (Ed. and Trans.), *The standard edition of the complete psychological works of Sigmund Freud* (Vol. 14, pp. 1–66). Hogarth Press.

Freud, S. (1915). Observations on transference-love (Further recommendations on the technique of psycho-analysis III). In J. Strachey (Ed. and Trans.), *The standard edition of the complete psychological works of Sigmund Freud* (Vol. 12, pp. 157–171). Hogarth Press.

Freud, S. (1917). A childhood recollection from *Dichtung und Wahrheit*. In J. Strachey (Ed. and Trans.), *The standard edition of the complete psychological works of Sigmund Freud* (Vol. 17, pp. 145–156). Hogarth Press.

Freud, S. (1919a). Letter from Sigmund Freud to Karl Abraham, July 6, 1919. In E. Falzeder (Ed.), *The complete correspondence of Sigmund Freud and Karl Abraham 1907–1925* (pp. 400–401). Routledge.

Freud, S. (1919b). Letter from Sigmund Freud to Sándor Ferenczi, July 10, 1919. In P. Giampieri-Deutsch, E. Falzeder, & E. Brabant (Eds.), *The correspondence of Sigmund Freud and Sándor Ferenczi* (Vol. 2, *1914–1919*; P. T. Hoffer, Trans.; pp. 363–364). Belknap Press.

Freud, S. (1919c). Lines of advance in psycho-analytic therapy. In J. Strachey (Ed. and Trans.), *The standard edition of the complete psychological works of Sigmund Freud* (Vol. 17, pp. 157–168). Hogarth Press.

Freud, S. (1920a). Letter from Sigmund Freud to Sandor Ferenczi, February 4, 1920. In E. L. Freud (Ed.), *Letters of Sigmund Freud 1873–1939* (T. Stern & J. Stern, Trans.; pp. 328–329). Basic Books.

Freud, S. (1920b). Letter from Sigmund Freud to Ernest Jones, February 8, 1920. In R. A. Paskauskas (Ed.), *The complete correspondence of Sigmund Freud and Ernest Jones 1908–1939* (pp. 368–369). Belknap Press.

Freud, S. (1921a). Group psychology and the analysis of the ego. In J. Strachey (Ed. and Trans.), *The standard edition of the complete psychological works of Sigmund Freud* (Vol. 18, pp. 65–144). Hogarth Press.

Freud, S. (1921b). Psycho-analysis and telepathy. In J. Strachey (Ed. and Trans.), *The standard edition of the complete psychological works of Sigmund Freud* (Vol. 18, pp. 173–194). Hogarth Press.

Freud, S. (1923). Letter from Sigmund Freud to Ernest Jones, September 24, 1923. In R. A. Paskauskas (Ed.), *The complete correspondence of Sigmund Freud and Ernest Jones 1908–1939* (pp. 527–528). Belknap Press.

Freud, S. (1925). An autobiographical study. In J. Strachey (Ed. and Trans.), *The standard edition of the complete psychological works of Sigmund Freud* (Vol. 20, pp. 1–74). Hogarth Press.

Freud, S. (1926). The question of lay analysis: Conversations with an impartial person. In J. Strachey (Ed. and Trans.), *The standard edition of the complete psychological works of Sigmund Freud* (Vol. 20, pp. 183–258). Hogarth Press.

Freud, S. (1927). The future of an illusion. In J. Strachey (Ed. and Trans.), *The standard edition of the complete psychological works of Sigmund Freud* (Vol. 21, pp. 1–56). Hogarth Press.

Freud, S. (1929). Letter from Freud to Romain Rolland, July 20, 1929. In E. L. Freud (Ed.), *Letters of Sigmund Freud 1873–1939* (T. Stern & J. Stern, Trans.; p. 389). Basic Books.

Freud, S. (1930a). Civilization and its discontents. In J. Strachey (Ed. and Trans.), *The standard edition of the complete psychological works of Sigmund Freud* (Vol. 21, pp. 57–146). Hogarth Press.

Freud, S. (1930b). Letter from Freud to Ernest Jones, September 15, 1930. In R. A. Paskauskas (Ed.), *The complete correspondence of Sigmund Freud and Ernest Jones 1908–1939* (pp. 677–678). Belknap Press.

Freud, S. (1930c). Letter from Freud to Lou Andreas-Salomé, May 8, 1930. In E. Pfeiffer (Ed.), *Sigmund Freud and Lou Andreas-Salomé letters* (W. Robson-Scott & E. Robson-Scott, Trans.; pp. 187–188). Harcourt Brace Jovanovich, Inc.

Freud, S. (1930d). Letter from Freud to Sandor Ferenczi, September 16, 1930. In E. L. Freud (Ed.), *Letters of Sigmund Freud 1873–1939* (T. Stern & J. Stern, Trans.; pp. 400–401). Basic Books.

Freud, S. (1933). New introductory lectures on psycho-analysis. In J. Strachey (Ed. and Trans.), *The standard edition of the complete psychological works of Sigmund Freud* (Vol. 22, pp. 1–182). Hogarth Press.

Freud, S. (1935). The subtleties of a faulty action. In J. Strachey (Ed. and Trans.), *The standard edition of the complete psychological works of Sigmund Freud* (Vol. 22, pp. 231–236). Hogarth Press.

Freud, S. (1938). Letter from Sigmund Freud to Charles Singer, October 31, 1938. In E. L. Freud (Ed.), *Letters of Sigmund Freud 1873–1939* (T. Stern & J. Stern, Trans.; pp. 453–454). Basic Books.

Freud, S. (1939). Moses and monotheism: Three essays. In J. Strachey (Ed. and Trans.), *The standard edition of the complete psychological works of Sigmund Freud* (Vol. 23, pp. 1–138). Hogarth Press.

Gay, P. (1998). *Freud: A life for our time*. Norton.

George, C., Kaplan, N., & Main, M. (1996). Adult Attachment Interview (3rd ed.). Unpublished manuscript. University of California, Berkeley.

Goodman, G. (2005). "I feel stupid and contagious:" Countertransference reactions of fledgling clinicians to patients who have negative therapeutic reactions. *American Journal of Psychotherapy, 59*, 149–168.

Goodman, G. (2014). *The internal world and attachment*. Routledge.

Goodman, G. (2025). *Using psychoanalytic techniques to transform the attachment relationship to God: Our refuge and strength*. Routledge.

Granqvist, P. (2020). *Attachment in religion and spirituality: A wider view*. Guilford Press.

Granqvist, P., & Kirkpatrick, L. A. (2018). Attachment and religious representations and behavior. In J. Cassidy & P. R. Shaver (Eds.), *Handbook of attachment: Theory, research, and clinical applications* (pp. 917–940). Guilford Press.

Greenberg, J. R. (1986). Theoretical models and the analyst's neutrality. *Contemporary Psychoanalysis, 22*, 89–106.

Greenberg, J. (2001a). The analyst's participation: A new look. *Journal of the American Psychoanalytic Association, 49*, 359–381.

Greenberg, J. (2001b). The analyst's participation: A new look [Response]. *Journal of the American Psychoanalytic Association, 49*, 417–426.

Greenson, R. R. (1967). *The technique and practice of psychoanalysis*. International Universities Press.

Grossmann, K., Grossmann, K. E., Spangler, G., Suess, G., & Unzner, L. (1985). Maternal sensitivity and newborns' orientation responses as related to quality of attachment in northern Germany. In I. Bretherton & E. Waters (Eds.), *Growing points in attachment theory and research: Monographs of the Society for Research in Child Development, 50*(1–2, Serial No. 209, pp. 233–278). Springer.

Hardin, H. (1987). On the vicissitudes of Freud's early mothering. I: Early environment and loss. *Psychoanalytic Quarterly, 56*, 628–644.

Hardin, H. (1988a). On the vicissitudes of Freud's early mothering. II: Alienation from his biological mother. *Psychoanalytic Quarterly, 57*, 72–86.

Hardin, H. (1988b). On the vicissitudes of Freud's early mothering. III: Freiberg, screen memories, and loss. *Psychoanalytic Quarterly, 57*, 209–224.

Hesse, E. (2018). The Adult Attachment Interview: Protocol, method of analysis, and selected empirical studies: 1985–2015. In J. Cassidy & P. R. Shaver (Eds.), *Handbook of attachment: Theory, research, and clinical applications* (pp. 553–597). Guilford Press.

Hoffman, I. Z. (1994). Dialectical thinking and therapeutic action in the psychoanalytic process. *Psychoanalytic Quarterly, 63*, 187–218.

Joinson, C., Sullivan, S., von Gontard, A., & Heron, J. (2016). Stressful events in early childhood and developmental trajectories of bedwetting at school age. *Journal of Pediatric Psychology, 41*, 1002–1010.

Jones, E. (1953). *The life and work of Sigmund Freud*: Vol. 1. *The formative years and the great discoveries 1856–1900*. Basic Books.

Jones, E. (1955). *The life and work of Sigmund Freud*: Vol. 2. *Years of maturity 1901–1919*. Basic Books.

Jones, E. (1957). *The life and work of Sigmund Freud*: Vol. 3. *The last phase 1919–1939*. Basic Books.
Jones, E. E. (2000). *Therapeutic action: A guide to psychoanalytic therapy*. Jason Aronson.
Kantrowitz, J. L. (2001). The analyst's participation: A new look [Commentary]. *Journal of the American Psychoanalytic Association, 49*, 398–406.
Kernberg, O. F. (1980). *Internal world and external reality: Object relations theory applied*. Jason Aronson.
Kernberg, O. F. (1986). Further contributions to the treatment of narcissistic personalities. In A. Morrison (Ed.), *Essential papers on narcissism* (pp. 245–292). New York University Press.
Kirkpatrick, L. A. (2005). *Attachment, evolution, and the psychology of religion*. Guilford Press.
Kobak, R. R., Cole, H. E., Ferenz-Gillies, R., Fleming, W. S., & Gamble, W. (1993). Attachment and emotion regulation during mother-teen problem solving: A control theory analysis. *Child Development, 64*, 231–245.
Kuhn, T. S. (1962). *The structure of scientific revolutions*. University of Chicago Press.
Main, M., & Goldwyn, R. (1994). Adult attachment scoring and classification systems (6th ed.). Unpublished manuscript. University College, London.
Main, M., & Stadtman, J. (1981). Infant response to rejection of physical contact by the mother: Aggression, avoidance and conflict. *Journal of the American Academy of Child Psychiatry, 20*, 292–307.
Main, M., & Weston, D. R. (1981). The quality of the toddler's relationship to mother and to father: Related to conflict behavior and the readiness to establish new relationships. *Child Development, 52*, 932–940.
Michels, R. (2001). The analyst's participation: A new look [Commentary]. *Journal of the American Psychoanalytic Association, 49*, 406–410.
Pfrimmer, T. (1982). *Freud, lecteur de la Bible*. Presses Universitaires de France.
Rizzuto, A.-M. (1979). *The birth of the living God: A psychoanalytic study*. University of Chicago Press.
Rizzuto, A.-M. (1998). *Why did Freud reject God? A psychodynamic interpretation*. Yale University Press.
Schröter, M., & Tögel, C. (2007). The Leipzig episode in Freud's life (1859): A new narrative on the basis of recently discovered documents. *The Psychoanalytic Quarterly, 76*, 193–215.
Slade, A. (1999). Attachment theory and research: Implications for the theory and practice of individual psychotherapy with adults. In J. Cassidy & P. R. Shaver (Eds.), *Handbook of attachment: Theory, research, and clinical applications* (pp. 575–594). Guilford Press.
Townshend, P. (1969). We're not gonna take it. In *Tommy*. Decca/MCA.
Treurniet, N. (1993). What is psychoanalysis now? *International Journal of Psycho-Analysis, 74*, 873–891.
Tyrrell, C. L., Dozier, M., Teague, G. B., & Fallot, R. D. (1999). Effective treatment relationships for persons with serious psychiatric disorders: The importance of attachment states of mind. *Journal of Consulting and Clinical Psychology, 67*, 725–733.
Volkert, J., Taubner, S., Byrne, G., Rossouw, T., & Midgley, N. (2022). Introduction to mentalization-based approaches for parents, children, youths, and families. *American Journal of Psychotherapy, 75*, 4–11.

Voltaire. (1919). *Voltaire in his letters, being a selection from his correspondence* (S. G. Tallentyre, Trans.). Putnam. (Original work published 1769).

Wampold, B. E. (2001). *The great psychotherapy debate: Models, methods, and findings.* Erlbaum.

Watson, J. B. (1928). *Psychological care of infant and child.* Norton.

Part II

A Clinical Application of Attachment-Informed Psychotherapy

Chapter 6

A Yogi in Attachment-Informed Psychotherapy

A Spiritually Informed Case Conceptualization

In this chapter, I discuss a psychotherapy treatment from my own practice of a 41-year-old Caucasian man who grew up in the Presbyterian Church but abandoned the church by the time he reached adulthood (he provided written consent to the publication of his narrative). He entered treatment for a somatic symptom that he characterized as an "energy" migrating upward from his groin to his upper chest, neck, and jaw that formulates the words, "I'm gay." This patient has been exploring Eastern spirituality, including Hinduism, yogic philosophies, and psychedelic trips, which have helped him to gain insight into his relationships to members of his family of origin as well as clarify a sense that someone—perhaps a priest—sexually abused him at the age of 8 or 9. I discuss the similarities and differences between this patient's attachment relationships to his parents and to God. I then use the Adult Attachment Interview (AAI) to assess the quality of his attachment relationships to his parents, and use my own modified version of this interview—the Adult Attachment to God Interview (AAGI)—to assess the quality of his attachment relationship to his conceptualization of a Higher Power. I also discuss the attachment-informed interventions I used in Attachment-Informed Psychotherapy (AIP) that have propelled the treatment forward, and I end the chapter by posing spiritual and emotional questions that linger in my ongoing treatment of this man.

Before I begin, however, I must declare my own spiritual subjectivity, which inevitably plays a role in how this treatment has unfolded. According to Griffith (2010), "When the otherness of a strangely different religious patient can be personally sensed, then interest and intrigue build, and even emotions of wonder and exuberance may be experienced" (p. 79). In this chapter, I endeavor to sense both the otherness and the commonality of this man in my treatment of him. As you journey through this treatment with me, may I generate in you, the reader, the wonder and exuberance that I felt in caring for him.

My Spiritual Perspective

I believe that out of infinite love, God created human beings to love God and to love each other. At some point in human history, people stopped loving God and each other and instead loved themselves exclusively—the origin of evil. God is the embodiment not only of love but also of justice, which demands punishment for evil. Rather than condemn human beings to this punishment of eternal separation from God, God, through infinite love, intervened in human history and space to satisfy this requirement of punishment of eternal separation from God for the evil of human beings—rebelling against God and loving themselves exclusively rather than loving God and loving each other. Because God, in the temporal and spatial form of Jesus of Nazareth, bore this punishment of eternal separation from God through dying on human beings' behalf, this relationship between God and human beings is now restored. Human beings can now love God and love each other imperfectly and still know that God loves them in return with no conditions attached. Loving perfectly, Jesus conquered death and lives in spirit form in all human beings. When human beings surrender their own will and turn themselves over to the love of God, they can know the love of God for themselves as well as others (Matthew 16:25; NIV, 1978). The purpose of human life is to express gratitude for God's sacrifice by loving God and loving each other. I want to live my life in loving service to God and others—to love God and be loved by God.

For me, psychotherapy consists of offering patience, understanding, insight, acceptance, compassion, relationship, and a secure base and safe haven to persons suffering from burdens too heavy to carry alone (Galatians 6:2; NIV, 1978). I compare myself to a container into which my patients pour their unbearable feelings. My task is to detoxify these feelings and make them easier to understand and tolerate. I help my patients to use healthy relationships with others to meet their emotional needs and the emotional needs of others. I aspire to treat my patients as if they were Jesus (Matthew 25:35–40; NIV, 1978), and equally, I want to be the face of Jesus to my patients.

Case Conceptualization Introduction

The following treatment presents me with an ideal opportunity to demonstrate how to use Attachment-Informed Psychotherapy (AIP) to work with a patient who manifests a distressing somatic symptom with a clearly discernible spiritual component. I trace the layers of this man's spirituality from early childhood through adolescence to middle adulthood and demonstrate how each layer might play a role in this symptom. Because this treatment is ongoing, not all the perplexities posed by this symptom, nor the other symptoms experienced by this patient, have been resolved. Perhaps they never will be resolved. With these perplexities firmly in mind, how does a spiritually informed therapist leverage this dimension of experience to facilitate the spiritual journey of a man whose complex spirituality is literally screaming to be understood? I attempt to answer this question in this brief case conceptualization.

At the beginning of treatment during the pandemic, Séamus (a pseudonym) was a 38-year-old college graduate of Irish American descent. Séamus was raised in an intact, two-parent household in a middle-income suburb of New York City. He has a brother born two years earlier. Séamus identifies as cisgender and heterosexual. Currently, he works as a finance executive at an upscale clothing company in Manhattan and in his spare time as a bartender in his Brooklyn neighborhood. He used to have his own yoga studio but gave that up at the beginning of the pandemic. He still practices yoga, however.

Séamus was referred to me by the *Psychology Today* website, where I maintain a therapist profile. He noticed that my office was located in Lynbrook on Long Island, which is where his father grew up, and viewed the location as a sign that he should contact me. Séamus has been in and out of therapy since 2009. He started therapy with me on September 17, 2021. He requested and received 90-minute sessions rather than the standard 45-minute sessions. For the first two months of treatment, we met for weekly sessions, then, for cost reasons, he asked to change the frequency to biweekly sessions. In April, 2022, seven months after treatment began, Séamus ended treatment because he felt he had achieved his goal of learning who is sexual abuser was (see below). On August 25, 2023, however, Séamus returned to treatment to complete additional work on his conflicts with his father. Once again, for four months, we met for weekly sessions. That December, four months after resuming treatment, Séamus mentioned that he would like to take a break from therapy, and I interpreted that this desire for a break from therapy was a pattern, signifying that he wanted to avoid feeling close to me. He agreed with this interpretation and has stayed in therapy, meeting biweekly, since December 29, 2023. As of this writing (March 17, 2024), I have met with Séamus for a total of 41 sessions. Throughout the treatment, Séamus has supplemented our work, approximately five times per year, with periodic lysergic acid diethylamide (LSD) and psilocybin trips.

Presenting Issues and Diagnosis

Séamus's chief complaint was that there was an energy located in his pelvis that shouts, "I'm gay!" He first experienced this sensation in early 2020 as a yoga instructor during a session. Séamus had asked the students, "What is your deepest desire?" and at that moment, he experienced a sensation in his "Sacral Chakra" (pelvic region) accompanied by the words, "To be gay." Séamus reported that he experiences this sensation nearly every day, which causes him both anxiety and depression. Previous therapy was not effective in treating this symptom. On one of his psychedelic trips prior to beginning treatment with me, he developed the belief that a male authority figure from his childhood had sexually abused him. Based on his reading of psychological literature and previous therapy experience, he formulated a tentative hypothesis that his symptom, "I'm gay!" had something to do with this alleged childhood sexual abuse. Séamus has always maintained that this somatic experience, coupled with the thought, "I'm gay!" is intensely uncomfortable. I quickly determined that Séamus had not had a psychotic break. He was oriented to time, person, and place, and seemed to have good judgment and was a reliable reporter of his experience. He denied suicidal and homicidal ideas or intentions as well as delusions and hallucinations. He seemed highly motivated for treatment because he wanted to "release this energy inside me" (session notes, 12/1/23).

On February 9, 2024, a graduate student certified to administer the Adult Attachment Interview (AAI; George et al., 1996) conducted this interview with Séamus to assess the quality of his attachment pattern. Two other graduate students certified to code the AAI coded his AAI transcript independently of each other. Both students classified him as "angrily preoccupied" (E2; i.e., anxious-resistant; Hesse, 2018). Both students certified as reflective-functioning coders also independently coded him as having "Definite or Ordinary Reflective Function" (rating of 5) on the 11-point Reflective-Functioning Scale (RFS; Fonagy et al., 1998, p. 41). These ratings are thoroughly consistent with my experience of Séamus in treatment. Based on the persistence of his somatic symptom that causes him significant pain, I believe he warrants a diagnosis of Somatic Symptom Disorder, Moderate (SSD; 300.82; American Psychiatric Association, 2022). Interestingly, risk factors associated with SSD include "a reported history of sexual abuse or other childhood adversity" (American Psychiatric Association, 2022, p. 313; see below).

Biopsychosocial History

As already mentioned, Séamus was raised in an intact, two-parent household in a middle-income suburb of New York City. He achieved all his developmental milestones on time. His father was a loan officer at a commercial bank, his mother an elementary school science teacher. During his early and middle childhood, Séamus described himself as joyful, flamboyant, sensitive, and full of zest for life. He excelled in school and had many friends. Regarding his emotional response to separations from his parents as a child, Séamus reports, "I was definitely the kid that was crying, like before I got on the [school] bus" (AAI, p. 10). Somewhere between the ages of 8 and 10, however, Séamus remembers "shutting down": he became withdrawn and made few self-disclosures to his parents. On one of his psychedelic trips, Séamus recalled that a male authority figure had allegedly sexually abused him. He remembered that he had performed fellatio on a man but could not recognize the man's face. On a recent psilocybin trip, this person's head and face seem to be an amalgamation of the head and face of his father and a defrocked priest, his father's close friend from childhood who often came to their house and who was later convicted of sexual abuse of children in his position as a priest. Séamus made a connection between his memory of shutting down between the ages of 8 and 10 and this alleged incident, which he believes also probably took place during the same timeframe. Séamus reported in one of our first sessions that his father, noticing his adolescent son's withdrawn, sullen behavior, asked him whether he was gay, in a misguided attempt to get Séamus to open up about what was bothering him (session notes, 10/15/21).

Despite continuing to withdraw from his family, Séamus rebounded in high school, getting straight As, becoming the captain of the basketball team, earning the love and admiration of his classmates (especially girls), maintaining a months-long heterosexual romantic relationship, and then attending an elite midwestern university on a partial academic scholarship. After graduation, Séamus moved back to New York, where he enjoyed success on Wall Street as a financial analyst. As an adult, Séamus has had two heterosexual romantic relationships lasting one and three-and-a-half years each. When not in a romantic relationship, however, Séamus's sexual encounters consist mostly of "friends with benefits"—female friends with whom he has occasional sexual encounters but no romantic commitments.

Séamus has always had a highly conflictual relationship to his father. On the AAI, when asked to select five adjectives to describe his relationship to his father between the ages of 5 and 12, he selected the words "fear," "shame," "resentment," "anger," and "withdrawn" (AAI, p. 6). Séamus summarized his experience of his attachment relationship to his father as "Running to my father to share some excitement or to, like, ask for something very specific and being shut down or rejected about it" (AAI, p. 11). Séamus blames his father for not protecting him from the alleged sexual abuse. Séamus also blames him for creating a household atmosphere in which Séamus felt restricted from exhibiting his true personality.

Séamus's relationship to his mother was always more loving. On the AAI, when asked to select five adjectives to describe his relationship to his mother between the ages of 5 and 12, he selected the words "caring," "loving," "helpful," "encouraging," and "warm" (AAI, p. 4). Séamus captured his experience of this relationship to his mother as the following: "She was just a mom; she she took care of me and, you know, um, you know, just was a mom" (AAI, p. 4). Despite the positive affective valence of these adjectives to describe his mother, Séamus nevertheless did not feel close to either parent as a child: "I think the sad reality is, I probably wasn't that close with either of them" (AAI, p. 8).

Séamus's Goals for Treatment

Séamus wanted: (1) to release the thought-energy from his body that was telling him, "I'm gay!," (2) to discover the perpetrator of the alleged sexual abuse that he uncovered during an LSD trip, and (3) to get his father to take responsibility for not protecting him from the alleged abuse and for not allowing him to be his true self as a child.

Spiritual History

Séamus reports that he attended a Presbyterian (Protestant denomination) church in a suburb of New York City, where he was raised. His family attended this church weekly on Sundays, which included Sunday School. Séamus's father was raised in a nominally Catholic household on Long Island and served his parish as an altar boy, while Séamus's mother was raised as a Protestant in Canada (less is known about her spiritual upbringing).

On March 8, 2024, a graduate student certified to administer the Adult Attachment Interview (AAI; George et al., 1996) conducted the Adult Attachment to God Interview (AAGI) with Séamus. The AAGI is my modification of the AAI to access narrative memories of the attachment relationship to God (see Goodman, 2025, Chapter 2). Two other graduate students certified to code the AAI coded his AAGI transcript independently of each other. Both students classified him as "angrily preoccupied" (E2; i.e., anxious-resistant; Hesse, 2018). Both students certified as reflective-functioning coders also independently coded him as having "Questionable or Low Reflective Function" (rating of 3) on the Reflective-Functioning Scale (RFS; Fonagy et al., 1998, p. 40). Séamus emphatically states that he had no connection to God as a child: "For most of my childhood, I did not feel close to God at all. I feel like I rejected the connection with God or the idea of God, or the existence of God" (AAGI, p. 5). On the AAGI, when asked to select five adjectives to describe his relationship to God between the ages of 5 and 12, he selected the words "controlling," "powerful," "masculine," "anthropomorphic," and "omnipresent" (AAGI, pp. 2–3). Séamus summarized his experience of his relationship to God: "A masculine figure and kind of like, you know, an older, an older man with white hair and in that vibe" (AAGI, p. 4).

In 2014, a college friend recommended yoga to help Séamus rehabilitate a back injury. He became enamored with yoga and its underlying Hindu philosophy, studying yogic philosophies in yoga instructor training and eventually becoming a certified yoga instructor himself. In early 2020, just before the pandemic, Séamus was finishing up teaching a yoga class at his studio when he asked the class a question while the students were lying down in the Savasana pose: "What is your deepest desire?" In that moment, Séamus recounts, "I had this energetic release in my body and the words 'to be gay'—three words kind of like arose out from my Sacral Chakra—and that set off this, this spiritual journey over the last four years" (AAGI, p. 12). Séamus refers to this energy as kundalini energy—a feminine energy in Hinduism—that is being blocked from "bursting forth" by anger and sadness (session notes, 2/29/24). According to Séamus, release of this energy would restore his connection to God.

Treatment Plan and Brief Overview of Therapy

I currently meet with Séamus biweekly for 90 minutes. We now meet online, as I now live in Atlanta, while he remains in New York. Until his first departure from therapy on April 9, 2022, we usually met in person; occasionally, we met online if he was feeling ill or was having car trouble. In the early spring of 2022, I announced that I would be moving to Atlanta in June and invited him to continue working with me remotely. Initially, he agreed to this plan; however, after an LSD trip in which he supposedly learned the identity of his childhood abuser, he announced in our April 9 session that he had accomplished his treatment goal. He denied that his symptom "I'm gay!" had abated, but he also noted a lack of funds as a reason for leaving treatment at this juncture. I did not bring up with him the possibility that he did not want to continue therapy with someone who would be leaving him, at least geographically, and that he was exerting control over the situation—to be in charge of the leaving. I regretted not raising this possibility with him.

Upon returning to therapy on August 25, 2023, Séamus accepted the fact that we would be having all our sessions online. He suggested "taking a break" from therapy on December 29 of that year, but I was able to explain to him that his leaving was part of a pattern that protects him from getting too close to me—a pattern that we have also observed in his romantic relationships. Getting too close would raise the possibility of abandonment by me and produce emotional pain that he would much rather avoid. This interpretation helped him to understand his motivation for leaving and enabled him to stay in treatment to continue our work and learn how to tolerate emotional closeness to me.

After first establishing a therapeutic alliance in the understanding phase of treatment (Kohut, 1984), I sought to provide emotion regulation and identify the underlying emotional landscape that might be producing Séamus's somatic symptom. Early in the treatment, I surmised that Séamus's secondary attachment strategy of hyperactivating/preoccupied (i.e., overdramatizing his attachment needs to maximize their fulfillment by others; see Goodman, 2025, Chapter 3) would require a complementary attachment strategy on the deactivating/dismissing end of the spectrum to provide the "gentle challenge" (Dozier, 2003, p. 254) needed to regulate his emotional material with a more cognitive understanding of his conflicts with his father, his alleged sexual abuse, and his somatic symptom, "I'm gay!" I also use mentalizing (see Goodman, 2025, Chapters 4–6), a form of interpretation that explains others' and one's own behaviors as products of their underlying mental states (i.e., intentions, wishes, beliefs). Why is mentalizing an important therapeutic technique to use with Séamus? According to Wallin (2007):

> Mentalizing has the potential to free us from embeddedness in the internal world and external reality by fostering awareness of the interpretive depth and representational nature of subjective experience in ourselves and others ... Because it opens a mental space—and often an interval of time—between our experience and our responses to experience, mentalizing is "disembedding" (Safran & Muran, 2000).
>
> (p. 309)

Mentalizing would help Séamus to facilitate his capacity to reflect on his somatic symptom and his anxious-resistant relationship to his father. Séamus might eventually be able to adopt an observer stance rather than a participant stance. This observer stance might help Séamus to experience a feeling of greater control over his somatic symptom and relationship to his father and facilitate the integration of both with the rest of his personality. Mentalizing might also provide the distance needed to help Séamus understand how his somatic symptom and relationship to his father might be related to his representation of God as a duality of energies flowing through him (session notes, 2/29/24).

In addition, I use the idea of "story-making" of Holmes (1998)—to restory Séamus's overwhelming unstoried experience—to give him the language to describe the emotions connected to his fragmented memories of sexual abuse, conflicts with his father, and experience of his somatic symptom, "I'm gay!" Holmes (1998) identifies "story-making" as a therapeutic strategy uniquely suited to patients who have a preoccupied (i.e., anxious-resistant) attachment pattern (see also Goodman, 2025, Chapter 6). I believe that co-constructing a coherent narrative for Séamus's experiences could be enormously helpful in helping him to feel as though his life makes sense as a person with a stable identity and definable goals who can also form a stable romantic relationship without a debilitating fear of abandonment. Mentalizing is one therapeutic technique I use to enable the process of story-making. I have yet to use this mentalizing technique to invite Séamus to explore God's motives for allowing Séamus to experience this somatic symptom and conflictual relationship to his father. He has alluded to God's motives, however, when he mentions that he could share his trauma journey to help others who have been abused. Séamus has suggested to me that God might be leading him through this struggle to help usher others out of the darkness and into the light (session notes, 12/3/21).

During my 41 double sessions with Séamus, I have identified three recurring themes in our work: (1) the movement of the so-called "kundalini energy" from his pelvic region to his upper chest, neck, and jaw; (2) his belief that he was sexually abused by a male authority figure when he was age 8 or 9; and (3) his conflictual relationship to his father. Throughout the course of therapy, Séamus has experienced the gradual upward movement of his kundalini energy, which started in his pelvic region and has steadily moved up to his lower jaw. He views this movement as progress toward the goal of releasing this energy either out of his mouth or through the top of his head. He believes that when this goal is completed, the words "I'm gay!" will stop, and he will be free from this symptom.

Regarding the feeling that he was sexually abused, Séamus has been frustrated that this feeling has not progressed beyond an intuition to an actual face and name. Séamus has repeatedly stated that he wants to name his abuser, which he views as a satisfactory resolution because it will remove the uncertainty that he feels around this imagined incident. I have shared my openness to believing that Séamus was sexually abused as well as my openness to believing that Séamus was not sexually abused. If sexual abuse were a verified piece of Séamus's autobiographical history, his somatic symptom would make more sense to him (and to me). Through our work together, Séamus has developed a more coherent narrative of his childhood experiences and his current symptom. At other times, however, Séamus has questioned this narrative, wondering aloud in therapy whether he created the sexual abuse incident to explain his somatic symptom, "I'm gay!" (session notes, 2/2/24).

Regarding his conflictual relationship to his father, Séamus blames him for both sins of commission and sins of omission. First, Séamus views his father as partly responsible for changing Séamus's personality—initially joyful, flamboyant, and sensitive, and later, withdrawn, emotionally constricted, and unhappy. He marks this change as having occurred at 8 or 9 years of age, when he began to notice that his father would often reprimand him by yelling at him and sometimes using corporal punishment. Séamus has complained that his father used coercion to control all Séamus's choices and, as Séamus approached puberty, forbade him from being the joyful, flamboyant, sensitive boy of his earlier childhood. Perhaps threatened by these qualities, his father seemed to want Séamus to become a "man's man," which did not align with Séamus's authentic self. In Séamus's early teen years, his withdrawn behavior eventually attracted his father's attention, who asked him if he were gay. His father was apparently struggling to understand his son's chronic sullenness and reasoned that, considering his son's less masculine personality traits, Séamus might be struggling with homosexuality. Séamus denied it, but the incident showed him what his father thought of his masculinity, further alienating him from his father.

Second, assuming that he was sexually abused by a male authority figure—perhaps even his father's pedophilic friend—Séamus has expressed rage that his father did not protect him from the abuse. A father's prime directive is to protect his children, and in Séamus's mind, his father failed to do that. Recently, Séamus has begun to wonder whether perhaps his father sexually abused him—alone or in collaboration with the defrocked priest—or at least was aware of the alleged sexual abuse but did nothing to stop it (session notes, 12/15/23). Séamus's father offered to send a long e-mail message to his old friend (who now lives in a neighboring state), asking this man whether he had sexually abused Séamus. The man tersely replied that he had searched his conscience and had no memory of sexually abusing Séamus. In our most recent session (session notes, 3/15/24), Séamus expressed rage toward his father for not having traveled to this man's home and looked him in the eye while asking him about his son's abuse. In Séamus's mind, "my father supported his friend over his son." At other times, Séamus has wondered whether, as an altar boy in the Catholic church, his father also experienced sexual abuse and repressed it (session notes, 11/3/23).

Since we started working together, Séamus has adopted his father as his pet reclamation project, trying to convince him to enter psychotherapy to become less stoic, less emotionally constricted. His father, however, has repeatedly refused, further frustrating Séamus because he has reasoned that if his father truly loved him and his family, he would want to get help for himself and confront the damage he has caused. Séamus believes that if he can repair his relationship to his father, the kundalini energy currently residing in his upper chest, neck, and jaw will be released. I have wondered with Séamus whether he is looking for his father's acceptance of the feminine aspects of his personality. Séamus has reflected that as a child, he never wanted to "outshine" his father, who emphasized humility and austerity (session notes, 12/29/23). In recent years, Séamus has deliberately defied his father's ethos, purchasing a flashy jeep and renting a beautiful (and expensive) apartment space in a trendy area of Brooklyn. I interpreted this reluctance to outshine his father as suggesting that as a child, Séamus perhaps felt guilty about being the object of his father's envy and therefore tried to blend in to remain loyal to his father. Séamus agreed that perhaps due to his father's own upbringing, his father never felt permitted to indulge in flamboyant behavior and therefore looks upon his son's flamboyant behavior with scorn. Séamus's paternal grandmother suffered from depression, which affected his father's own emotional expression. Thus, Séamus exhibits some degree of empathy for his father's austere personality.

Interventions

Rather than forcing a discussion about spirituality, I have looked for opportunities that Séamus himself offered to explore his spirituality as it arises organically in our work together. The therapist's practice of listening rather than imposing a discussion of spirituality onto the patient is key:

> Dialogue about spirituality mostly consists of listening for and inquiring about referents to religion and spirituality as they appear naturally in conversations. Religious experience can be presented as idioms, metaphors, narratives (stories), beliefs, prayers (or other intrapersonal dialogues with nonmaterial beings), spiritual practices, rituals and ceremonies, religious or spiritual communities, and daily practices of ethical living (Griffith & Griffith, 2002). It is important to listen broadly for any of these, because some forms are emphasized in particular religious traditions more so than others ... Well-practiced, disciplined listening for any of these symbolic forms prepares a clinician to attend to a person's unique spirituality and experiential world (Griffith & Griffith, 2002).
>
> (Griffith, 2010, p. 64)

Thus, any clinical material that alludes to any of these categories of religious experience is pregnant with spiritual meaning that the therapist can explore with the patient. In other words, if the patient brings it up, it is fair game for exploration.

When the patient does bring spirituality into my field of vision, I sometimes ask how the material relates to their connection to a Higher Power. Where is Séamus's Higher Power in his symptom? How does what he is talking about make him feel closer to or further away from a Higher Power? In Séamus's treatment, I look for ways in which his relationship to God compensates for his inadequate relationships to his parents, especially his father. How does Séamus's cultivation of a spiritual life help him to cope with his disappointing parental relationships? According to Séamus, "In the last couple of years, reconnecting with God, um, has given me more purpose and meaning and comfort and joy, and I'm still in the thick of the craziness of it all" (AAGI, p. 9).

On the AAI, Séamus was classified as "angrily preoccupied" (E2; Hesse, 2018). In treatments with angrily preoccupied patients, I apply a "gentle challenge" (Dozier, 2003, p. 254) to the secondary attachment strategy of hyperactivation by behaving in a complementary, moderately deactivating manner. Thus, I use mentalization and other more cognitively based intervention strategies on the deactivating end of the emotion regulation spectrum to help him modulate his emotional expression. I also use "story-making" (Holmes, 1998) to help Séamus articulate what he is feeling in his body and to create a narrative around that sensation. How is this narrative related to his connection to a Higher Power? Aware of the influence of Hindu philosophy on Séamus's spiritual worldview, which includes the practice of acceptance, I also wonder with Séamus how he can use his connection to God to provide him with the vulnerability of acceptance of his father's shortcomings and stoicism. Certainly, an acceptance of these shortcomings would relieve him of much of the suffering he has expressed over the past two-and-a-half years. Even though acceptance for Séamus is difficult, his relationship to a Higher Power seems to be growing: "I'm feeling that I can access that connection [to God] much more frequently, um, in the last couple of months, even though it may be only a day or two at a time" (AAGI, p. 12).

I also reflect on my countertransference reactions such as feelings of helplessness and subsequent desire to make suggestions to force myself out of these feelings. Anxious-resistant patients often display helplessness to elicit help from others (Daniel, 2015), but if I offered direct help, this intervention would only delay the development of his own self-reliance. I need to be constantly aware of my feelings of helplessness and then wonder with him whether he might be feeling helpless at that moment and wanting me to rescue him. I would also ask him directly whether he feels that I am doing enough to help him find relief for his somatic symptom.

Spiritual Countertransference

My spirituality consists of relating to a Higher Power Who exists inside me but Who also simultaneously exists separately from me. God is the Creator; I am the creation. This distinction is important to me because it provides a basis for my own humility, imperfection, and need to surrender my pride. On the other hand, Séamus's spirituality consists of a unity between himself and God:

> I'm approaching this idea of unity, of connection where, like, the energy of God is the energy that is me, in my essence, and I'm an expression of that, as opposed to a duality, um, of like a separate entity.
>
> (AAGI, pp. 14–15)

Does Séamus depersonify God, turning God into an impersonal energy that exists within himself and all living things to avoid the possibility of divine separation and abandonment, or am I imposing my own spiritual values onto him? To what extent do my spiritual values interfere with Séamus's expression and development of his own spirituality? One might argue that the entire project of applying attachment theory to our understanding of patients' spirituality is culturally biased because it does not apply to pantheistic religions such as Hinduism. In his discussion of "noncorporeal attachments in nontheistic religions," Granqvist (2020) writes that many adherents of these Eastern religious traditions actually focus their spiritual attachment on a person, pointing out that "one of the most common Buddhist prayers is 'I take refuge in the Buddha, the Dharma [his teachings], and the Sangha [the Buddhist community]'" (p. 67). Granqvist (2020) concludes that "the attachment system finds noncorporeal targets even when the mind is trained and 'socialized' *not* to do so" (p. 68; emphasis in original).

Séamus describes his spiritual awakening as having occurred in early 2020, but much earlier in life, he was exposed to the Presbyterian God in the church he attended with his parents. According to Rizzuto (1979), "No child arrives at 'the house of God' without his pet God under his arm" (p. 8). Thus, as a young child, Séamus initially constructed an idiosyncratic God untouched by theology or doctrine, then was introduced to the Presbyterian God of his parents, and finally, only four years ago, discovered the God-as-energy metaphor of Hinduism. Like an archeological expedition, we observe successive layers of spirituality haphazardly built on top of each other, held together by an incoherent spiritual narrative. He has not integrated these various layers of spirituality into a coherent narrative yet: "I'm still in the thick of the craziness of it all" (AAGI, p. 9). By drawing connections between Séamus's spirituality and his relationship to his father, I might be subtly privileging exploration of the layer of spirituality identified by the Western Presbyterian God. If Granqvist (2020) is correct, however, then there must be "noncorporeal targets" (p. 68) from these earliest layers of spirituality that require exploration. When Séamus characterizes the God of his childhood as "a masculine figure and kind of like, you know, an older, an older man with white hair and in that vibe" (AAGI, p. 4), is he referencing his father? Is he referencing me? It appears that these earliest layers of spirituality are thus also fair game for exploration, even though his current spirituality derives from a completely distinct religious tradition.

Ultimately, I want Séamus to discover his authentic spirituality, whether it aligns with a monotheistic tradition, a nontheistic tradition, or a coherently constructed integration of the two. Séamus and I share a deep longing for connection to a Higher Power; thus, I have profound respect for his spiritual journey. I did not find my own authentic spiritual connection until I was in my forties, so Séamus's developmental timetable parallels my own. Thus, I have positive as well as negative spiritual countertransference feelings. I want to use this awareness to facilitate Séamus's own spiritual journey, not hinder it.

With that in mind, I now present a microcosm of my work with Séamus on his spiritual journey in a recent psychotherapy session with me. The following transcript is a reconstruction of a session excerpt based on my session notes (sentences in **bold** indicate possible transference references).

Session Excerpt (February 29, 2024)

Séamus: I planned to travel to Florida for a shuffleboard tournament, but I changed my mind when I learned that some of my friends had backed out of the tournament. I feel like I'm losing interest in this activity and maybe also in this group of friends.

Me: Mm hm.

Séamus: I talked to my dad recently. I feel like I'm beginning to understand him better. **I really think he's doing his best.** I didn't tell you—I went on a psilocybin trip last month, and all this anger and sadness came up. It's blocking my kundalini energy from bursting forth. My dad restricted my expression of kundalini energy—I couldn't be joyful, flamboyant, and free.

Me: It would be really challenging for you to forgive your father because that would make you feel vulnerable to more rejection and shame from him.

Séamus: That's right. I'm remembering an incident a couple of years ago with him. I had a great conversation with him about all the pain I was going through and specifically how his lack of emotional connectivity as a parent, and the way he yelled at me sometimes as a kid, is part of the healing process I'm going through now. We had a pretty good conversation, and it felt like he was actually starting to accept the fact and show some remorse. Then as I left to drive home, he made a joke about me being a couple of pounds overweight. Like, "So are you gonna hit the gym when you get back and shed a few pounds?" And then I think he even said, "Just kidding." I think it was his unconscious way of trying to dig at me a little bit after I had yelled at him and called him out for a couple of hours in our conversation that day. And also weirdly his way of trying to connect in some way to show he cares about me and my health, but he doesn't know how to do that in an emotionally mature way. What enraged me when he made his comment was like, "You're part of the reason I'm going through this pain, and you don't even get it, and then you have the nerve to say something like that to me after I've come up here and bared my soul to you." So that's what pissed me off.

Me: And forgiving him might make you vulnerable to another attack.

Séamus: Right.

Me: On the one hand, you want to understand your dad, but, on the other hand, you still feel enraged and needing to protect yourself from being hurt by your dad again.

Séamus: I do feel like I understand my dad better, but the pain of his controlling behavior is still with me. **It isn't going away.**

Me: You needed to hide your feminine, flamboyant self from your father to earn his love.

Séamus: I look at it a bit differently. I wasn't trying to earn my father's love so much as trying to avoid his shaming and yelling.

Me: You had to hide that part of yourself—your true self—and now, it's leaking out in this thought-energy that "I'm gay!"

Séamus: Yes, and not only the feminine energy. The masculine energy is also coming to the surface—I've noticed that I'm being more assertive at work now.

Me: Your father restricted both masculine and feminine energy—two important parts of yourself—that you're now trying to release and assimilate into a broader sense of yourself.
Séamus: Right.
Me: I wonder how all this ties in to your connection to God.
Séamus: I grew up learning about a male God that I never believed in. Growing up, my understanding was that God was this omnipotent white male figure that had a bunch of rules, and we were kinda in trouble if we didn't follow them. Since starting yoga in 2014, though, I've come to believe in a God that can be feminine and even gender-neutral.
Me: I can imagine it might feel difficult to have a relationship with a masculine God, given that all you know about male authority figures is through your relationship to your father.
Séamus: Yeah, it's hard to conceptualize an all-loving God when my own father has been so controlling and shaming. **I want to continue working toward releasing this energy, which feels stuck in my chest, neck, and jaw area.**
Me: You're in pain. Let's keep working on it.
Séamus: Okay.

Session Excerpt Commentary of Psychotherapy Process

I want to comment on Séamus's possible references to his transference to me. Near the beginning of this session excerpt, Séamus tells me about a recent conversation with his father, after which he provides an assessment of his father: "I really think he's doing his best." At that moment, I had not considered this comment as transference material, but while writing my session notes, I recognized this possible reference. Does he think that I am a well-meaning, fatherly psychologist who is doing his best but who nevertheless is not helping him? Later in this excerpt, there is tentative evidence for the conjecture that he does not feel helped by me. First, he lets me know that the pain of his father's controlling behavior "isn't going away." He could be saying, "Aren't you supposed to be relieving me of this suffering at the hands of my father, or are you just another ineffectual 'older man with white hair and in that vibe'?" Later, Séamus returns to his chief complaint—his somatic symptom: "I want to continue working toward releasing this energy, which feels stuck in my chest, neck, and jaw area." He reminds me of his somatic suffering in nearly every session. Again, he could be saying, "Aren't you supposed to be relieving me of this suffering in my own body?" Unconsciously, Séamus might be viewing father = therapist = God: an unholy symbolic equation of ineffectual older men who cannot or will not help him to stop suffering. I have not yet made these potential connections with him in our work together.

I do not sense a strong influence of my countertransference feelings in this session, but I want to comment on what might be faint traces of them in a couple of my interventions. First, early in this excerpt, I point out that "it would be really challenging for you to forgive your father." The idea of forgiveness is coming from me, not him. He might not be considering forgiveness; moreover, he might never want to forgive his father. My motives for bringing it up are twofold: (1) I know that forgiveness will most likely lead him to let go of his anger toward his father and thus bring him relief; and (2) I feel helpless and want to accelerate the process to alleviate this feeling in myself as quickly as possible. The latter motive directly relates to my countertransference feeling, which might have stimulated this intervention. Second, near the end of this session excerpt, I interpret his difficulty in having a relationship with a masculine God as having to do with his difficult relationship with his father. One possible implication of this interpretation is that a resolution of Séamus's difficult relationship with his father might occasion a restoration of Séamus's nonexistent relationship with a masculine God. I need to be aware of my own belief in a personified God and not allow this belief to influence my interventions with Séamus.

Despite a possible transference-countertransference matrix of helpless boy-ineffectual father figure observed in the psychotherapy process, I believe that I have successfully contained his anxiety and rage and have at times deactivated his attachment system when it was hyperactivated. I also believe that he is aware of my role in this deactivating process. In a future session, I could ask him how he feels about the effectiveness of our work together and his perceptions of me as his therapist. I could interpret the potential parallels among his relationships to his father, to God, and to me, and see where that interpretation might lead us. The therapeutic goal would be to make Séamus aware of the possibility that remaining in a helpless (angrily preoccupied) state of mind protects him from becoming an intentional agent whose actions on his own behalf—including the action of forgiveness—might make him "vulnerable to another attack" or at least expose him to "more rejection and shame." Reviewing this chapter, Séamus highlighted his fear of rejection and shame, "and because of that I've been wearing all these masks to fit it. And the 'true self' ... is screaming to be heard and seen" (Séamus, personal communication, April 10, 2024).

I am gradually helping Séamus to develop a new, secure attachment relationship by remaining committed to this process and by allowing him to share any anger that he might feel toward me for not helping him yet in the ways that he wants to be helped. This permission that I am giving him to express himself without restrictions sharply contrasts with his father's attitude of toxic masculinity, which has often been to deflect and deny Séamus's feelings, especially his negative feelings, when confronted. Having also had a father who sometimes yelled at me and a mother who mostly observed and seldom intervened, I believe that I understand his resentment and tendency not to trust the effectuality of others. I have faith that he will work through his feelings and develop a deeper connection to God, however he understands God. Wallin (2007) writes that enactments—transference-countertransference matrices—are inevitable. How can I use my awareness of our enactment to bring spiritual and emotional healing to this man?

What about This Kundalini Energy?

One of the most fascinating aspects of this treatment has been Séamus's somatic symptom of kundalini energy slowly making its way from its place of origin—his pelvic region (Sacral Chakra)—upward to his upper chest, neck, and jaw accompanied by the words, "I'm gay!" After 41 sessions, mystery still shrouds this symptom. Séamus and I have taken turns interpreting the underlying meaning of this symptom, but it persists. The following is a series of interpretations in chronological order that have plausibly explained its presence in Séamus's life. None of these interpretations, however, has produced any significant change in the presence or severity of this symptom.

- "I'm gay" signifies an act of defiance against his father's rigid Catholic sexual attitudes (session notes, 10/15/21).
- "Gay" might mean "joyful," "flamboyant," and "sensitive" (session notes, 10/29/21).
- Pronouncing "I'm gay" might diminish the guilt and shame over his alleged sexual abuse (i.e., if I'm gay, then it wasn't abuse) (session notes, 12/3/21).
- Believing "I'm gay" protects Séamus from intimacy with women, which arouses fears of abandonment (session notes, 1/5/24).
- Believing "I'm gay" reassures Séamus that he will not get a woman pregnant, echoing his father's stern warning delivered during Séamus's adolescence (session notes, 1/5/24).
- Pronouncing "I'm gay" might represent a primitive attempt to seduce Séamus's father for the purpose of extracting some display of love from him (session notes, 2/16/24).

Séamus denied the plausibility of only the final interpretation. Of course, the content of these various interpretations might be less important to the treatment than the collaboration that we experience together in working on this symptom. Séamus observes me inviting him to work with me on figuring out this puzzle, which his father will not do. I have not yet explored with Séamus the possibility that he is not releasing this energy because he is unconsciously identifying with his father's prohibitions against the femininity that this energy symbolizes. Instead of striving to get rid of this energy through a cathartic release, perhaps Séamus needs to embrace this feminine energy and mobilize its power to live his authentic self, free from the prohibitions of toxic masculinity embodied in his father's attitude.

What about Séamus's Shutting Down During Middle Childhood?

Because the information gleaned from Séamus's LSD and psilocybin trips is unreliable, I remain agnostic about Séamus's reports of sexual abuse during middle childhood. I do believe, however, that some event or series of events caused

Séamus to shut down during middle childhood. Séamus's father's chronic yelling and gross misattunement to Séamus's needs to be joyful, flamboyant, and sensitive might have produced a sufficiently severe distress to force Séamus to muffle these personality traits to "avoid his [father's] shaming and yelling" (here, I am applying the concept of the false self and the role that parental impingements play in its development; Winnicott 1965). During middle childhood, Séamus constructed a façade to accommodate his father's yelling and shaming to protect his personality characteristics typically associated with femininity—joy, flamboyance, and sensitivity—which comprised his true self. Séamus perceived his father's behavior as an impingement on this true self; thus, the false self of a stoically masculine, withdrawn boy was born to mask these unacceptable qualities. According to Séamus, the goal was not to earn his father's love but to avoid the screaming and shaming. Unfortunately, even this withdrawn, false self attracted his father's attention, who asked him during middle school whether he had become so reserved because he was struggling with being gay. In high school, however, Séamus was able to allow himself to exhibit his true self and become sociable—and not allowing his father's criticism to control him.

Mysteries that Remain in My Treatment of Séamus

Through the process of writing this case conceptualization of Séamus, I have become more explicitly aware of the transference-countertransference matrix that appears to dominate our work together. Séamus seems to regard me as a well-meaning older man who has tried but ultimately failed to cure him of his somatic symptom, while I feel at times helpless and incompetent, actualizing the ineffectual therapist that Séamus seems to have projected onto me. I have resolved to introduce this dynamic with Séamus in our next session to hear his point of view. Rather than providing Séamus exclusively with a secure attachment relationship, I have allowed him to turn me into a more benevolent version of his ineffectual father, who seems willing to help (e.g., writing a letter to the defrocked priest about the potential sexual abuse of his son) but who nevertheless makes no tangible effort to solve the problem (e.g., not going to the priest's house to demand answers). What efforts can I make to facilitate Séamus's new, secure attachment relationship to me rather than recapitulate the old, anxious-resistant attachment relationship to his father, with which Séamus is already so familiar? One advantage of being spiritual myself is that I know that I am not helpless. A Higher Power is ultimately in control; I always have help available to me. My secure attachment relationship to a Higher Power can help me navigate my helpless countertransference feelings by realizing that Séamus is also not helpless because a Higher Power is also always available to him.

We still have not resolved the issue of whether Séamus was sexually abused by a male authority figure, whether that person was a babysitter's brother, a priest, or even his father. One of the therapeutic goals in Attachment-Informed Psychotherapy (AIP) is to become the patient's assistant autobiographer (Holmes,

1998) by helping them to create a coherent narrative of their childhood and uncover the meaning that they derive from that childhood. In this view, narrative truth supersedes factual truth (Green, 1996; Schafer, 1996); thus, whether someone *actually* sexually abused Séamus is not as important to Séamus's personal development as how he might construct a coherent narrative around this childhood myth and what meanings he might derive from it to construct his current and future life narrative. No LSD or psilocybin trip is going to give him the definitive proof of abuse he is currently seeking. Helping Séamus to reject the importance of historical truth and embrace his narrative truth would be the next step in the treatment.

Finally, Séamus's perception of thought-energy stuck in his upper chest, neck, and jaw accompanied by the pronouncement, "I'm gay!" is also an unresolved feature of the treatment. As his therapist, I need to be content to sit quietly and just be a witness to his suffering. No intellectualized interpretation of its meaning is going to make this somatic symptom magically disappear. His observation of my own suffering along with him—without my necessarily trying to fix him—risks his categorizing me as just another ineffectual father figure, but with one significant difference: I am allowing myself to feel his pain without looking away. That is the one gift I can give him that he never received before from his father. Séamus chose to work with an older male therapist. He must have entered treatment with the expectation that I could help him with his conflictual relationship to his father. Perhaps he also wanted to test me (Weiss & Sampson, 1986) to determine whether I would behave in the same ways he had come to expect his father to behave. Can I defy his father's familiar behavior (i.e., lack of empathy, avoidance, stoicism) and come alongside him amid his pain? That is the underlying question that he seems to be asking me.

Conclusion

I have sketched out my treatment of a man who presented to me with a somatic symptom—a perception of thought-energy trapped inside his body accompanied by the pronouncement, "I'm gay!" as well as unresolved conflicts with his father and with serious questions about childhood memories of alleged sexual abuse by an unknown male authority figure. I argued that Séamus is using his understanding of the Hindu God-as-energy metaphor to compensate for his anxious-resistant attachment relationship to his father and to compensate for his rejecting relationship to the God of his childhood. I also argued that his growing awareness of his kundalini energy (feminine energy in yoga practice) corresponds to his acknowledgment of the divinity of the feminine, perhaps drawing power from the somewhat secure attachment to his mother. Thus, both the compensation and correspondence pathways to Séamus's current understanding of a Higher Power serve explanatory functions in analyzing his attachment relationships to both his parents. I also outlined a transference-countertransference matrix of a well-meaning but ultimately ineffectual male authority figure trying to help a helpless, disappointed boy. Can I use my awareness of this enactment to move the treatment forward and bring healing to

Séamus? Can Séamus harness this feminine God-energy to live in synchrony with his joyful, flamboyant, sensitive true self that he had to hide from his father? Must Séamus work through the trauma of sexual abuse, or is it a distraction from more emotionally salient issues? As my treatment of Séamus is ongoing, our spiritual journey continues.

References

American Psychiatric Association. (2022). *Diagnostic and statistical manual of mental disorders* (5th ed., text rev.). .American Psychiatric Association.
Daniel, S. I. F. (2015). *Adult attachment patterns in a treatment context: Relationship and narrative*. Routledge.
Dozier, M. (2003). Attachment-based treatment for vulnerable children. *Attachment and Human Development, 5*, 253–257.
Fonagy, P., Target, M., Steele, H., & Steele, M. (1998). *Reflective–functioning manual, version 5: For application to adult attachment interviews*. University College, London.
George, C., Kaplan, N., & Main, M. (1996). Adult Attachment Interview (3rd ed.). Unpublished manuscript. University of California, Berkeley.
Goodman, G. (2025). *Using psychoanalytic techniques to transform the attachment relationship to God: Our refuge and strength*. Routledge.
Granqvist, P. (2020). *Attachment in religion and spirituality: A wider view*. Guilford Press.
Green, A. (1996). What kind of research for psychoanalysis? *International Psychoanalysis: The Newsletter of the IPA, 5*, 10–14.
Griffith, J. L. (2010). *Religion that heals, religion that harms: A guide for clinical practice*. Guilford Press.
Griffith, J. L., & Griffith, M. E. (2002). *Encountering the sacred in psychotherapy: How to talk with people about their spiritual lives*. Guilford Press.
Hesse, E. (2018). The adult attachment interview: Protocol, method of analysis, and selected empirical studies: 1985–2015. In J. Cassidy & P. R. Shaver (Eds.), *Handbook of attachment: Theory, research, and clinical applications* (pp. 553–597). Guilford Press.
Holmes, J. (1998). Defensive and creative uses of narrative in psychotherapy: An attachment perspective. In G. Roberts & J. Holmes (Eds.), *Healing stories: Narrative in psychiatry and psychotherapy* (pp. 49–66). Oxford University Press.
Kohut, H. (1984). *How does analysis cure?* University of Chicago Press.
NIV (New International Version). (1978). *The holy Bible*. Zondervan.
Rizzuto, A.-M. (1979). *The birth of the living God: A psychoanalytic study*. University of Chicago Press.
Safran, J. D., & Muran, J. C. (2000). *Negotiating the therapeutic alliance: A relational treatment guide*. Guilford Press.
Schafer, R. (1996). Authority, evidence, and knowledge in the psychoanalytic relationship. *Psychoanalytic Quarterly, 65*, 236–253.
Wallin, D. J. (2007). *Attachment in psychotherapy*. Guilford Press.
Weiss, J., & Sampson, H. (1986). *Psychoanalytic process: Theory, clinical observation and empirical research*. Guilford Press.
Winnicott, D. W. (1965). *The maturational processes and the facilitating environment: Studies in the theory of emotional development*. International Universities Press.

Chapter 7

What I Have Personally Learned from Writing this Book

What Have I Personally Learned?

While writing this book, I opened myself to be surprised by gaining new insights into the application of attachment theory to humans' relationship to a Higher Power. First, based on Anne Frank's narrative (see Chapter 3), I learned that the correspondence and compensation pathways can be caregiver-specific. Internal working models of attachment relationships are not always integrated into a unitary mental structure but instead can exist in multiple forms, depending on the attachment quality of each attachment relationship. For example, Anne Frank was securely attached to her father and anxious-resistantly attached to her mother; thus, she developed two different internal working models of emotionally significant relationships. During her two years in hiding, Frank experienced a spiritual awakening, becoming securely attached to a Higher Power. Did Frank's secure attachment relationship to a Higher Power correspond to her secure attachment relationship to her father, or did it compensate for her anxious-resistant attachment relationship to her mother? Or can both pathways contribute to the development of an attachment relationship to God, traversing a hybrid pathway?

From one point of view, Frank's attachment relationship to a Higher Power corresponded to one caregiver relationship, but from another point of view, her attachment relationship to a Higher Power compensated for the other caregiver relationship. In persons who develop multiple internal working models to the caregivers during childhood (see Daniel, 2015, pp. 123–125), identifying whether they follow a correspondence or compensation pathway to a Higher Power is a challenging and complex task. We need research to understand these complexities more clearly. Is the patient's mental representation of God a facsimile of one parent or a reaction against the other parent? In treatment, the therapist can explore these dynamics with the patient.

Second, based on Bill W.'s narrative (see Chapter 4), I learned that both external and internal forces predispose a person to turn to God as a surrogate attachment figure to compensate for insecure attachment relationships to the caregivers during childhood. These forces must be overwhelming—perhaps even life-threatening—to break down the secondary (defensive) attachment strategy learned during childhood, thus allowing the primary attachment strategy of proximity-seeking to emerge. According to Granqvist and Kirkpatrick (2018), insecurely attached persons compensate for their attachment insecurity when they "cannot bear the high levels of suffering experienced sufficiently well by employing his or her usual [insecure] strategy for managing stress" (p. 934). Of course, Granqvist's idea of "socialized correspondence" (Granqvist, 2020, p. 127; see also Goodman, 2025, Chapter 3) also applies here because a person would have to have been exposed to the concept of God before that person could place their trust in God and establish a secure attachment relationship to God. Thus, overwhelming stressors represent the external forces needed to rely on God as a compensatory attachment figure for insecure attachment relationships to the caregivers during childhood.

The internal forces that also contribute to the compensation pathway include the brittleness of the person's insecure attachment subclassification (see discussion in Chapter 5). The four attachment classifications (i.e., secure, anxious-avoidant, anxious-resistant, disorganized/disoriented) have 12 subclassifications that further distinguish persons from each other with respect to the mental representations of their attachment relationships. For example, the Ds1 attachment subclassification of the dismissing (anxious-avoidant) category represents a person who idealizes one or both caregivers during childhood, while the Ds2 attachment subclassification represents a person who contemptuously derogates one or both caregivers (Hesse, 2018, pp. 565, 567). Both persons are avoidant of attachment relationships; however, this avoidance manifests in different ways. I argued that some of these 12 attachment subclassifications might be more brittle or unstable than others, thus making the compensation pathway a more likely outcome when severe stress precipitates a crisis (colloquially referred to as a "come-to-Jesus moment").

Bill W. had a conversion experience in his hospital room, while Sigmund Freud never did (see Chapters 4 and 5). Bill W. believed that his addiction to alcohol was threatening his life (severe stress), whereas Freud never believed that his life was in imminent danger (his chronic mouth cancer notwithstanding). Bill W. and Freud also developed qualitatively different attachment relationships to their parents, even though both sets of attachment relationships were likely anxious-avoidant. Furthermore, Bill W.'s anxious-avoidant attachment subclassification was likely more brittle than Freud's; thus, Bill W.'s higher external stress, coupled with his more brittle internal working model of attachment relationships, could account for his conversion experience and subsequent journey down the compensation pathway. Therapists need to consider all these factors in determining their patients' likelihood of developing a secure attachment relationship to a Higher Power at any given time in their lives.

Third, I learned that regardless of religious or spiritual belief or nonbelief, every person has a spiritual essence, of which the therapist must maintain an acute awareness. Barrett's extensive research on the spiritual beliefs of children (Barrett, 2012)—raised in both religious and nonreligious families—strongly suggests that children are practically born to believe in a Higher Power, regardless of cultural milieu or historical epoch. Rizzuto (1979) observed that "no child arrives at the 'house of God' without his pet God under his arm" (p. 8). According to Lanzetta (2019):

> The deepest river of feeling is the speaking of the spiritual heart, and the innate desire and affective drive longing within us. It is the true self, the ground of being, or the source of knowing that seeks to express itself through the complexity of mind-body-spirit. It is often the still, small voice that is the least noticed of our inner life.
>
> (p. 80)

Lanzetta is writing about the universality of this spiritual essence in all humanity. She suggests that the most meaningful layer of the human personality is the spiritual layer. Similarly, Rohr (2016) suggests that "we're all united to God, but only some of us know it" (p. 109). If a therapeutic goal of Attachment-Informed Psychotherapy (AIP) is enhanced awareness of the patient's mental life, then surely, a growing awareness of their connection to a Higher Power needs to be part of the therapeutic process for patients who are seeking spiritual meaning.

Throughout this book, I have suggested that therapists need to help their patients to listen to this "gentle whisper" (I Kings 19:12; NIV, 1978) that resides within us all. The therapist might first need to help the patient remove the wax from their ears to hear this voice. That might mean providing a "gentle challenge" (Dozier, 2003, p. 254) to the prevailing secondary (defensive) attachment strategy interfering with the primary attachment strategy of seeking closeness to God. Through using a noncomplementary secondary attachment strategy, the therapist gradually breaks down the patient's secondary attachment strategy that blocks their use of the primary attachment strategy to seek proximity to a Higher Power, to Whom they can experience a secure attachment relationship. This therapeutic process facilitates the patient's spiritual listening skill so that they can tune into this gentle whisper. The psalmist sings, "I praise you because I am fearfully and wonderfully made" (Psalm 139:14; NIV, 1978). One of the therapist's goals in AIP is to restore the person to their factory settings so that they have the opportunity to (re-)experience a secure attachment relationship to a Higher Power.

Finally, during the process of writing this book, I wondered whether I had mislabeled humans' primary attachment relationship. Throughout this book, I have written as if the attachment relationships to the caregivers during childhood are primary, while the attachment relationship to a Higher Power is secondary. Is this assumption valid? Could it be the other way around? Are the caregivers during childhood the secondary attachment figures, while God is the primary attachment figure? Perhaps infants are seeking proximity to their Higher Power at birth but instead attach to the second-best option available to them—their parents. Earlier, I quoted Lanzetta (2019), who characterized "the deepest river of feeling" as "the speaking of the spiritual heart, and the innate desire and affective drive longing within us" (p. 80). She identifies this speaking as "the still, small voice that is the least noticed of our inner life" (p. 80). How do we listen to this still, small voice, which rises out of "the deepest river of feeling"? Rohr (2016) suggests that "all you can do is to recognize [the river], enjoy it, and ever more fully allow it to carry you" (p. 58). Perhaps we are all born with a rudimentary awareness of this deepest river of feeling, but through blemishing childhood experiences, this awareness gradually fades away, along with our ability to hear the gentle whisper speaking from our spiritual heart. We must therefore return to our primordial innocence to hear this voice. Perhaps this is what Jesus meant when He said, "Anyone who will not receive the kingdom of God like a little child will never enter it" (Mark 10:15; NIV, 1978; see also Matthew 18:3; Luke 18:17, NIV, 1978).

Viktor Frankl (1946) believed that the deepest longing of the human heart was the search for meaning. Why have I been placed on this Earth? What is the purpose of my life? Therapists often hear these questions percolating under the surface of our patients' complaints. But can we always hear them? Listening to the gentle whisper, we might hear the answers to these existential questions. The psychoanalyst Erik Erikson (1981) suggested that

> human childhood, besides being an evolutionary phenomenon, may well have been created so as to plant in the child at the proper time the potentiality for a comprehension of the Creator's existence, and a readiness for his revelations. And, indeed, the way the father can be experienced in childhood can make it almost impossible *not* to believe deep down in (and indeed to fear as well as to hope for) a fatherly spirit in the universe.
>
> (p. 337)

One way of perceiving the human family—with parental figures in relationship to a child—is to consider it a facsimile of God's relationship to humans. Of course, this metaphor anthropomorphizes the Higher Power, but that does not exclude the possibility that the Higher Power created humans to live in relationship to Them as a stronger and wiser (Bowlby, 1988) Caregiver. The Higher Power is always waiting for us to (re-)establish an attachment relationship to Them.

Burtchaell (1985) provides a thought-provoking interpretation of Jesus's parable of the Prodigal Son, one of the most famous passages in the New Testament from the gospel of Luke 15:11–32 (NIV, 1978). A man has two sons, one faithfully working for his father, the other wanting his inheritance now so that he can travel the world. After squandering his inheritance on debauchery, the prodigal son returns to his father's house, prepared to work as a servant in exchange for food and shelter. Instead of castigating this son, the father prepares a banquet to celebrate his return. The faithful son, however, expresses bitter resentment at the forgiveness that his father extends to the no-good son. Burtchaell (1985) suggests that neither son "can grasp that the father loves him not for what he has done, but for what he has always been: his own child" (p. 15). Each son could think that the father loves him because he has always been a faithful worker or because he has eventually returned to his father. But their father does not set any conditions on his love for both sons. In applying the parable to humans' relationship to a Higher Power-Caregiver, Burtchaell writes, "The Lord demands no satisfaction, because it is not in him to turn away from us in the first place" (p. 15). Elsewhere, Burtchaell (1985) uses the metaphor of God as light to demonstrate God's constant love for us: "The sun is always there and shining; whenever the shade is raised, the light streams in" (p. 21). Will we raise the shade to receive the sunlight? The songwriter Leonard Cohen (1992) expresses this sentiment differently: "There is a crack, a crack in everything. That's how the light gets in." The therapist must gently crack open the patient's secondary (defensive) attachment strategy to help the patient recognize their need for the Primary Attachment Figure, Who has always been there, waiting for them.

The Higher Power is always within us, waiting for us to return, just like the prodigal son. The therapist must be prepared to help the patient realize that "while he was still a long way off, his father saw him and was filled with compassion for him" (Luke 15:20; NIV, 1978). The Higher Power wants humans to recognize this ongoing loving attachment relationship, even when we are still a long way off from recognizing the reality of this attachment relationship. The therapist must be prepared to help the patient "ever more fully allow [the river] to carry [them]" (Rohr, 2016, p. 58).

Some patients are content to work on restoring attachment relationships only to human caregivers and other emotionally significant persons. Others (re-)find their Primary Attachment Figure, Who has been waiting for them the whole time. AIP can help restore interpersonal and intrapersonal harmony for both kinds of patients. The therapist must be prepared, however, to work on all attachment relationships—including supernatural ones—with all patients. No one knows just who is ready to (re-)connect to the spiritual within. Jesus said, "The kingdom of God is within you" (Luke 17:21; NIV, 1978). The therapist must treat every patient as a spiritual being, regardless of whether they recognize it for themselves. Only then can the therapist and patient together transform attachment to the living God.

References

Barrett, J. L. (2012). *Born believers: The science of children's religious belief*. Free Press.
Bowlby, J. (1988). *A secure base: Parent-child attachment and healthy human development*. Basic Books.
Burtchaell, J. T. (1985). An ancient gift, a thing of joy. *Notre Dame Magazine*, Winter 1985–1986, 14–22.
Cohen, L. (1992). Anthem [Song]. On *The future*. Columbia Records.
Daniel, S. I. F. (2015). *Adult attachment patterns in a treatment context: Relationship and narrative*. Routledge.
Dozier, M. (2003). Attachment-based treatment for vulnerable children. *Attachment and Human Development, 5*, 253–257.
Erikson, E. H. (1981). The Galilean sayings and the sense of "I." *Yale Review, 70*, 321–362.
Frankl, V. (1946). *Man's search for meaning: An introduction to logotherapy*. Beacon Press.

Goodman, G. (2025). *Using psychoanalytic techniques to transform the attachment relationship to God: Our refuge and strength.* Routledge.

Granqvist, P. (2020). *Attachment in religion and spirituality: A wider view.* Guilford Press.

Granqvist, P., & Kirkpatrick, L. A. (2018). Attachment and religious representations and behavior. In J. Cassidy & P. R. Shaver (Eds.), *Handbook of attachment: Theory, research, and clinical applications* (pp. 917–940). Guilford Press.

Hesse, E. (2018). The adult attachment interview: Protocol, method of analysis, and selected empirical studies: 1985–2015. In J. Cassidy & P. R. Shaver (Eds.), *Handbook of attachment: Theory, research, and clinical applications* (pp. 553–597). Guilford Press.

Lanzetta, B. (2019). *Foundations in spiritual direction: Sharing the sacred across traditions.* Blue Sapphire Books.

NIV (New International Version). (1978). *The holy Bible.* Zondervan.

Rizzuto, A.-M. (1979). *The birth of the living God: A psychoanalytic study.* University of Chicago Press.

Rohr, R. (2016). *The divine dance: The trinity and your transformation.* Whitaker House.

Author Index

Note: Tables are indicated by **bold**.

Adeyemo, W. L. 162
Ainsworth, M. D. S. 130, 162
Alexander, F. 125, 159
Allen, J. G. 77, 89
Anderson-Lopez, K. 131

Barnett, L. 155, 158
Barrett, D. G. 128, 166
Barrett, J. L. 197
Bateman, A. W. 127
Bates, B. C. 155, 158
Bernier, A. 155, 158
Blehar, M. C. 130, 162
Bowlby, J. 50, 118, 133–5, 153, 199
Bradley, R. 26
Breuer, J. 143, 156
Brouillet, A. 156
Burtchaell, J. T. 199–200
Byrne, G. 167

Cassidy, J. 11, 134
Clark, R. W. 132
Clarkin, J. F. 127, 157
Cohen, L. 200
Cohen, S. 67
Cole, H. E. 134
Conrad, R. 49, 55
Cue, K. L. 155, 158
Curhan, J. R. 159

Daniel, S. I. F. 11, 14, 15, 25–7, **28**, 29–36, 38, 40, 42–4, 48, 55–7, **58**, 59, 61, 63, 65, 66, 69, 72, 74, 76–7, 79, 80, 82, 83, 85, 86, 101, **102**, 104–7, 110, 111, 113, 114, 116, 118–22, 138, 139, 140, **141**, 142, 145–8, 150–4, 160, 187, 196

Dozier, M. 45, 87, 123, 155, 158, 163, 165, 183, 186, 198

Eagle, M. N. 159
Emerson, R. W. 54
Ensink, K. 121
Erikson, E. H. 199
Evers-Williams, Myrlie 37

Fallot, R. D. 155, 158
Ferenczi, S. 159
Ferenz-Gillies, R. 134
Ferri, M. 92
Fleming, W. S. 134
Flora, K. 92
Fonagy, P. 116–17, 127, 180, 182
Fortner, B. V. 166
Frank, A. 15, 47–56, 59–91
Frankl, V. E. 199
French, T. M. 125, 159
Freud, E. L. 132
Freud, L. 132
Freud, S. 15, 33, 51, 127–39, 142–66

Gamble, W. 134
Gay, P. 128, 131, 133, 134, 136, 139, 145, 155, 156, 161, 162, 167
George, C. 26, 55, 132, 180
Gergely, G. 116–17
Gilmore, K. J. 35
Goldwyn, R. 130, 132–4, 156
Goodman, G. 9–14, 23, 26, 32, 35, 39, 44, 45, 48, 55, 59, 86, 87, 92, 95–9, 104, 121, 123, 128, 136, 155, 158, 160, 163–5, 167, 182–4, 197

Granqvist, P. 9, 10, 21, 52, 92, 98, 120, 124, 136, 162, 187–8, 197
Green, A. 194, 195
Greenberg, J. R. 157, 158
Greenson, R. R. 134
Griffith, J. L. 177, 186
Griffith, M. E. 186
Grossmann, K. 156
Grossmann, K. E. 156
Grubrich-Simitis, I. 132

Hardin, H. 128, 131, 132
Hazan, C. 98
Heron, J. 129
Hesse, E. 162, 182, 186, 197
Hoffman, I. Z. 157
Holmes, J. 184, 187, 193–4
Humphreys, K. 92

James, W. 10, 15, 92
Joinson, C. 129
Jones, E. 128, 133
Jones, E. E. 157
Jurist, E. L. 116–17

Kantrowitz, J. L. 157
Kaplan, N. 11, 26, 55, 132, 180
Kelly, J. F. 92
Kernberg, O. F. 127, 157, 163, 164
King, M. L. Jr. 44
Kirkpatrick, L. A. 9, 10, 15, 21, 52, 55, 92, 120, 124, 162, 163, 197
Kobak, R. R. 134
Kohut, H. 183
Kübler-Ross, E. 45
Kuhn, T. S. 145

La Roche, M. J. 45
Lanzetta, B. 198–9
Larose, S. 155, 158
Lee, J. L. C. 116
Lindqvist, K. 121
Liu, L. 67
Lopez, F. G. 66
Lopez, R. 131

Main, M. 11, 26, 55, 130, 132–5, 156, 180
Malberg, N. 121
May, R. 13
Meersand, P. 35
Michels, R. 157
Midgley, N. 121, 167

Muller, N. 121
Muran, J. C. 45, 125, 183

Nader, K. 116
Nakash, O. 26
Neimeyer, R. A. 166

Orwell, G. 50

Pargament, K. I. 8, 13, 45, 120
Pentland, A. 159
Pfrimmer, T. 137
Pontikes, T. 92
Popper, K. 10

Raftopoulos, A. 92
Rank, O. 159
Rizzuto, A.-M. 8, 98, 128, 136, 138, 188, 198
Rogers, C. R. 45
Rohr, R. 198, 199
Rossouw, T. 167

Safran, J. D. 45, 125, 183
Sampson, H. 194
Schafer, R. 194
Schiller, D. 116
Schröter, M. 129
Schulz, M. S. 67
Scott King, C. 14, 21–6, 29–45
Shaver, P. R. 9
Slade, A. 45, 95, 131, 138
Soucy, N. 155, 158
Spangler, G. 156
Stadtman, J. 130
Steele, H. 180, 182
Steele, M. 180, 182
Suess, G. 156
Sullivan, S. 129

Tan, J. S. 77, 89
Target, M. 116–17, 180, 182
Taubner, S. 167
Teague, G. B. 155, 158
Thomas, C. 26
Thomsen, R. 94
Thoreau, H. D. 54
Tillich, P. 13
Tögel, C. 129
Townshend, P. 128
Treurniet, N. 159
Tyrrell, C. L. 155, 158

Unzner, L. 156

Volkert, J. 167
Voltaire 7, 135
von Gontard, A. 129

Waldinger, R. J. 67
Wall, S. 130, 162
Wallin, D. J. 66, 80, 88, 183, 191
Wampold, B. E. 45, 165

Waters, E. 130, 162
Watson, J. B. 154–5
Weiss, J. 194
Westen, D. 26
Weston, D. R. 135
Winnicott, D. W. 87, 193

Yeomans, F. E. 127, 157

Zeifman, D. 98

Subject Index

Note: Figures are indicated by *italics*. Tables are indicated by **bold**.

abstinence 155, 156, 160, 161
addiction 122, 197; as a false god 13; Goodman's 2–8, 13; Goodman's mother's 6–9; nicotine 162–4; sex 13; *see also* alcoholism; 12 steps
Adler, Alfred 143–6, 148, 152
Adult Attachment Interview (AAI) 25–6, 180–2
Adult Attachment to God Interview (AAGI) 182, 186–8
alcohol, attachment relationship to 98–9
Alcoholics Anonymous (AA) *see* Bill W.; 12 steps
alcoholism 98–9; *see also* Bill W.: alcoholism
amends, making 120
anger 88
anxiety 60, 87–8
anxious-avoidant attachment *see under* Bill W.; Freud, Sigmund
anxious-resistant attachment: helpless *vs.* angry types of 88; *see also* helplessness; *see also under* Frank, Anne
atheism 166; Bill W.'s 92, 95, 99, 104, 114, 123, 124, 161, 162; Freud's 127, 128, 131, 135, 136, 161, 162
Attachment-Informed Psychotherapy (AIP) 178; goals 193; *see also specific topics*

behaviorism 154, 155
Bible 198–200; Freud and the 137; Goodman and the 3, 4, 11; *see also specific topics*
Bill W. (Bill Wilson) 92–4; addiction (alcoholism) 114, 162–4, 197; atheism 92, 95, 99, 104, 114, 123, 124, 161, 162; attachment relationship to parents and God 94–9, 101, 104–18; compensation hypothesis, compensation pathway, and 92, 99, 105–7, 109–12, 114, 116–18, 121–2, 138, 161, 196, 197; depression 93, 95, 115; Ebby (friend) and 99, 106, 117; interpersonal markers of attachment 101, 102, **103**, 104–18; life history 93–4; Lois Burnham (wife) and 93–5, 98, 112, 124; markers of anxious-avoidant attachment relationship 101; Oxford Group and 99, 106, 112, 115, 120; spiritual awakening/conversion 48, 92–3, 99–101, 104–7, 109, 112, 114–16, 137, 161, 163, 197; treatment plan for 122–5; 12 steps and 93, 94, 112, 115, 117–21; *see also* 12 steps
Bill W.: My First 40 Years (autobiography) 92, 94–7, 101, 107–16
Buddhism 187–8
Burnham, Lois (Bill W.'s wife) 93–5, 98, 112, 124

Cady's Life (Frank) 53–4, 59–60, 73, 85, 89
character defects 119; readiness to have God remove one's 119
Christianity: Coretta Scott King and 25, 41, 43; Freud on 134; God of 13–14, 188; Goodman and 3–5, 8; *see also* Jesus; Oxford Group
Christians and Jews 90
compensation hypothesis (and compensation pathway) 9–11, *12*, 148, 162, 163, 196–7; Anne Frank and 48, 52, *52*, 54, 64, 66, 68–9, 73, 76, 79, 82, 86, 196; Bill W. and 92, 99, 105–7,

206 Subject Index

109–12, 114, 116–18, 121–2, 138, 161, 196, 197; Coretta Scott King and 38, 39, 44; defined 10; falsifiability problem 10; Freud and 136, 137; Goodman and 11; Séamus and 186, 194
confession of sins (12 steps) 120
conflict management (interpersonal marker) 39–41; Anne Frank and 79–82; Bill W. and 114–16; Freud and 151–3
corrective emotional experience 45, 125, 158–60
correspondence hypothesis (and correspondence pathway) 9–11, *12*, 196; Anne Frank and 44, 48, 52, 86; Coretta Scott King and 21, 44; defined 9–10; Freud and 128, 136–8, 160, 161
counter transference 167, 187, 190–1, 193; Freud and 147, 155; spiritual 187–188

death anxiety 166
dependence/independence (interpersonal marker) 38–9; Anne Frank and 76–9; Bill W. and 113–14; Freud and 150–1
Diary of a Young Girl (Frank) 47, 49–50, 55, 69–72; *see also* Frank, Anne
distasnce *see* proximity/distance
Dussel, Albert (Fritz Pfeffer) 47, 49, 51, 59, 75, 83

emotion regulation and expression (interpersonal marker) 121, 156, 158–60; Anne Frank's *57*, 66–9, 80; Bill W.'s 102t, 107–9; clinical material 183, 186; Coretta Scott King's **27**, 33; Freud's 140, 148; Freud's patients' 156; 12 steps and 121
empathy (interpersonal marker) 41–3; Anne Frank and 82–5; Bill W. and 116–18; Freud and 153–4
enmeshment 61–2; *see also* fusion
existential questions 199
expectations of others *see* trust/expectations of others
expression *see* emotion regulation and expression

faith: Anne Frank's 64, 66, 69; Bill W. and 100, 105; Coretta Scott King's 25, 30, 31, 39; Freud and 136; nature of 13
false gods 8; the problem of 13–14
false positivity 109
false self 193

father, death of 134
Frank, Anne 47–9, 85–6; anxiety 87; attachment relationship to God 56, 59–85; attachment relationship to parents 50–2, 56, 59–85; *Cady's Life* 53–4, 59–60, 73, 85, 89; Christians and 90; compensation hypothesis, compensation pathway, and 48, 52, 86; correspondence hypothesis, correspondence pathway, and 44, 48, 52, 86; *Diary of a Young Girl* 47, 49–50, 55, 69–72; faith 64, 66, 69; on God 90; guardian angels and 39, 55, 60; interpersonal markers of attachment 56, 57–**58**, 59–85; Jews and 49, 64, 66, 83, 84, 90; life history 47; markers of an anxious-resistant attachment relationship 55; oedipal conflicts 51; overview 47–50; prayer and 52–4, 56, 60, 66, 69, 80–2, 84–6; secure attachment relationship to God 52–5; short stories 79, 84; short stories, "The Fairy" 60; short stories, "Fear" 60; short stories, "The Guardian Angel" 60; short stories, "Happiness" 61, 68; short stories, "Katrien" 61, 70–4, 79; treatment plan for 87–90; *see also* van Pels, Peter
Frank, Margot (sister) 47–9, 71; Anne's relations with 50, 51, 63, 75, 80
Frank, Otto "Pim" (father) 47–52; and Anna's relationship with Peter van Pels 65, 71, 78, 81, 83; Anne's secure attachment relationship to 48, 50–1, 86
Freud, Amalia (mother): birth of her children 129, 130, 136; Freud on 130, 132; Freud's alienation from 132; Freud's anxious-avoidant attachment relationship to 129, 131–3; Freud's defenses against his feelings toward 133; Freud's loss of and abandonment/rejection by 129, 130, 133, 153, 163; Freud's reaction to the death of 133; Freud's sexual feelings regarding 131–3; Freud's sibling rivalry for the attention/affection of 129–31, 136, 163; and Freud's theoretical work 132, 133; Freud's visits to 134; on God 136; nursemaid (Monika) and 129, 137
Freud, Anna (sister) 129, 130
Freud, Jakob (father): death 134; Freud's relationship with 133, 134, 136–8; Freud's relationship with, attachment relationship 133, 134

Freud, Sigmund: anxious-avoidant attachment 128; anxious-avoidant attachment, influence on his theory and technique 154–60; atheism 127, 128, 131, 135, 136, 161, 162; attachment relationship: attachment relationship, to colleagues 139, 142–54; attachment relationship, to God 135–8; attachment relationship, to parents 131–4; *see also under* Freud, Amalia; Freud, Jakob; on belief in God 127, 137, 138 (*see also* atheism); bias against religion 127–8; Bible and 137; childhood 130–1; *see also* (Monika (Freud's nursemaid)); childhood, bedwetting 129; childhood, introduced to sexuality by nursemaid 136, 137; childhood, oedipal conflicts *see under* Freud, Amalia; correspondence hypothesis, correspondence pathway, and 128, 136–8, 160, 161; fear of being forgotten 146; intellectualization and 165–7; interpersonal markers of attachment 139–**141**; Jewish identity 129, 131, 134, 142–3; John Watson contrasted with 154–5; life history 131; on love 155, 156; markers of anxious-avoidant attachment relationship 138–9; narcissism 163, 164; nicotine/cigar addiction 161–4; and the occult 136–7, 166; overview 127, 131; personality 154; and relationship with father 135–7; on religion 127–8; self-analysis 147, 163; self-description 127; self-image 139–40, 148–9; technical recommendations 155–7; treatment plan for 163–7; writings of 127, 128; writings of, autobiographical 128, 129, 131, 138, 142, 148–53, 161
Freud, Sophie (daughter) 146, 153, 162
fusion, interpersonal 56, 59–60; *see also* enmeshment

"gentle challenge" 45, 87, 123, 160, 165, 183, 186, 198
"gentle whisper" 198, 199
God/Higher Power 200; asking him to remove one's shortcomings 119–20; children as born to believe in 197–8; conceptions of 188; Goodman and 3–5, 7–14; improving one's contact with God (12 steps) 120; turning will and life over to the care of 119; twelve steps and belief in 119; will of 120; *see also specific topics*
Goodman, Geoff: attachment relationships to parents and God 1–12; attachment relationships to parents and God, reflections on his autobiographical narrative 9–12; attachment relationships to parents and God, timeline of events *12*; education 1–5; father 1–7, 9, 11, 13; marriage 6, 7; mother 1–3, 5–9, 11, 12; personal analysis 5; spiritual perspective 177–8; things learned from writing this book 196–200; *see also specific topics*
Goslar, Hanneli (Anne Frank's friend) 60, 66, 84
guardian angels 39, 55, 60

help, attitude to seeking and receiving 31–2, 64–6; Bill W. and 106–7; Freud and 147
helplessness 80–1, 88, 89, 135, 187, 191, 193
Higher Power *see* God/Higher Power
homosexuality *see* Séamus
hysteria 155, 156

independence *see* dependence/independence
intellectualization, Freud and 165–7

Janet, Pierre 151
Jesus 100, 178, 199–200; Coretta Scott King and 25, 43; Goodman and 2, 178
Jewish identity, Freud's 129, 131, 134, 142–3
Jews: Anne Frank and 49, 64, 66, 83, 84, 90; Christians and 90
Judaism 64
Jung, Carl G. 143–6, 148–50

King, Coretta Scott *see* Scott King, Coretta
King, Martin Luther, Jr. 22, 24, 25, 43, 44; arrests and incarceration 37, 42–3; assassination 25, 32, 33, 41, 43, 45; stabbing 31
kingdom of God 199, 200
kundalini energy 182, 184, 185, 189, 192

listening and spirituality 186
love 155; Freud on 155, 156

meaning, search for 199
meditation 120

mentalization 121, 183, 184, 186
Monika (Freud's nursemaid): Amalia Freud and 129, 137; Freud's abandonment by and loss of 129, 130, 136, 146; Freud's relationship with 129, 130, 136, 137; God and 136, 137
moral inventory, making a 119; and admitting the nature of one's wrongs 119; *see also* personal inventory

narcissism 163; Kernberg on 163, 164
neutrality 155–8
nicotine/cigar addiction 161–4
noncomplementarity, therapeutic principle of 155, 156, 158, 160
nonverbal interactions between therapist and patient 159, 160

openness and self-disclosure (interpersonal marker) 36–8; Anne Frank and 73–6; Bill W. and 111–12; Freud and 149–50; Oxford Group 99, 106, 112, 115, 120

Paul the Apostle 13–14
personal inventory, taking 120; *see also* moral inventory
Pfeffer, Fritz *see* Dussel, Albert
powerlessness over alcohol (12 steps) 118
prayer 120; Anne Frank and 52–4, 56, 60, 66, 69, 80–2, 84–6; Coretta Scott King and 29, 35–6, 38, 39, 43
Presbyterian God 188
primary mode of relatedness 45, 95, 131, 138
Prodigal Son, parable of the 199–200
proximity/distance (interpersonal marker) 26, 29–30; Anne Frank and 56, 59–61; Bill W. and 101, 104–5; Freud and 139, 142
psychoanalytic technique 156–7; flexibility in 156–7; Freud's anxious-avoidant attachment and 154–60; Freud's technical recommendations 155–9

relational psychoanalysis 156–60
reparation *see* amends
resistance, Freud and 165

Scott King, Coretta 21, 43–4; attachment relationships to parents and God 22–5; attachment relationships to parents and God, interpersonal markers of 26, 27, **28**, 29–44; background and early life 21–4; Christianity and 25, 41, 43; faith 25, 30, 31, 39; father 23, 42; mother 22–3; *My Life, My Love, My Legacy* 21, 37; overview and life history 21–2; prayer and 29, 35–6, 38, 39, 43; treatment plan for 44–5
Séamus, case of 194–5; as angrily preoccupied 180, 182, 186, 191; biopsychosocial history 180–1; case conceptualization introduction 178–9; homosexuality 179–85, 189, 192–4; interventions 186–7; kundalini energy 182, 184, 185, 189, 192; mysteries that remain in his treatment 193–4; overview of therapy 182–6; presenting issues and diagnosis 179–80; session excerpt 188–90; session excerpt, commentary of therapy process 190–1; sexual abuse 179–81, 183–5, 192; shutting down during middle childhood 192–3; spiritual countertransference 187–8; spiritual history 181–2; transference 190, 191, 193; treatment goals 181; treatment plan 182–4
secondary revision 33
secure attachment relationship: markers of 25–6; *see also* Scott King, Coretta
seduction theory 154
self-disclosure *see* openness and self-disclosure
self-image/self-esteem (interpersonal marker) 34–6; Anne Frank and 69–73; Bill W. and 109–11; Freud and 148–9
separation anxiety 163, 164, 166
sex addiction 13
sexual abuse: Séamus's 179–81, 183–5, 192; seduction theory and 154
"sick souls" 92
small gods, the problem of 13–14
Smith, Bob ("Dr. Bob") 94, 99
smoking *see* nicotine/cigar addiction
socialized correspondence 197
spiritual awakening 163; Anne Frank's 48, 54, 196; and attachment relationship to God 101, 104–7, 109, 112, 114; Bill W.'s 48, 92–3, 99–101, 104–7, 109, 112, 114–16, 137, 161, 163, 197; Freud and 128, 137, 163; Séamus's 188; 12 steps and 121
Stekel, W. 152
story-making 184, 187

Tausk, Vicor 153
telepathy, Freud and 136, 137

therapeutic alliance 45, 87
tobacco: Freud on 161; *see also* nicotine/cigar addiction
transference 127, 158; Freud and 158, 159 (*see also* love); Séamus's 190, 191, 193
transference-counter transference matrix 191, 193
transference love *see* love
trust/expectations of others (interpersonal marker) 30–1, 61–4; Bill W. and 105–6; Freud and 142–6
12 steps 92, 109; analysis of 118–21; Bill W. and 93, 94, 112, 115, 117–21 (*see also* Bill W.); Goodman and 7–9, 12; and secure attachment to God 118

van Pels, Peter (Anne Frank's romantic interest): affection between Anne Frank and 59, 71, 78, 81, 83; Anne Frank's feelings toward 51, 59, 60, 65, 84, 89, 90; Anne Frank's relationship with 59, 65, 66, 84, 88–9; Anne Frank's spirituality and 66, 69, 89, 90; Otto Frank and 65, 71, 78, 81, 83

Wilson, Bill *see* Bill W.

For Product Safety Concerns and Information please contact our EU
representative GPSR@taylorandfrancis.com
Taylor & Francis Verlag GmbH, Kaufingerstraße 24, 80331 München, Germany

www.ingramcontent.com/pod-product-compliance
Lightning Source LLC
Chambersburg PA
CBHW050534300426
44113CB00012B/2099